CRICKET

CRICKET LEXICON

by the same authors
Football Lexicon
Racing Lexicon

CRICKET LEXICON

LEIGH & WOODHOUSE

ff

faber and faber

First published in 2006 by
Faber and Faber Limited
3 Queen Square, London WC1N 3AU

Typeset by Faber and Faber Ltd
Printed in England by Mackays of Chatham plc, Chatham, Kent

All rights reserved

© John Leigh and David Woodhouse, 2006

The right of John Leigh and David Woodhouse to be identified as
authors of this work has been asserted in accordance with Section 77
of the Copyright, Designs and Patents Act 1988

A CIP catalogue record for this book is available
from the British Library.

ISBN 978–0–571–22990–1
ISBN 0–571–22990–5

2 4 6 8 10 9 7 5 3 1

Acknowledgements

Thanks to: Bill Appleby, Ian Bahrami, Richard Clayton (stingy bowler and generous reader), Will Clayton, Angus Crowther, Phil Danbury, James Donaldson, Shomit Dutta, Gardeners Cricket Club, Vivian Greene, Sam Hayward, Dan Higgins, Ludo Hunter-Tilney, Hugh Johnstone ('I always room with Smithy'), Noel Lebon, John Lloyd, Julian Loose, Guy Lowton, Shailen Modi, John O'Keeffe, Mariya Petkova, Andrew Peaple, Jean Price and the team of tea-making volunteers in the New Road Ladies Pavilion, Jon Pritchard, Mike Richards, Kevin Robson, Shaftesbury Cricket Club, Rob Smith, Peter Straus, Will Sutton, Ian Thomas, Henry Volans, Duncan Weir, Henry Wells, Frank Woodhouse, Jonty Woodhouse, Jim Wynn.

This lexicon is dedicated to the memory of John Sterry and Samuel Woodhouse, Worcestershire men and gentlemen.

Preface

More books have been written in English about cricket than about any other sport. Some recount tales of traditional battles, like *Ashes* Tests or *Roses* matches; some give technical instruction on how to develop an imperturbable *straight bat* or an indecipherable *googly*; some faithfully record for posterity the statistics, like *five-fors* and *red-inkers*, about which cricketers can become obsessed; some wax lyrical about the sound of *leather on willow* or the *spirit of the game*. There is even the odd book devoted specifically to the language of cricket, so distinctive and idiomatic is its terminology.

Cricket's biggest characters are not necessarily bookish, even if they may take their duties seriously when producing the books their public expects. Arthur Porritt, who put together W. G. Grace's *Cricketing Reminiscences*, reported that the great man sprang to life only when 'unaccustomed vocabulary', like the word 'inimical', was suggested for inclusion: 'Why, if that went into the book I should have the fellows at Lord's coming to me in the pavilion and saying, "Look here, W. G., where did you get that word from?"' Frank Keating tells the story of Ian Botham looking particularly downcast on a West Indies tour because he thought his ghost-writer was 'sending back absolute crap'. Andrew Flintoff, in his autobiography *Being Freddie*, pays tribute to the 'patience and perseverance' of his collaborator Myles Hodgson, whose role was to act as a kind of Bernie Taupin to Flintoff's Elton John.

Yet story-telling is such a strong force in the culture of cricket that vivid examples of the language used by its protagonists play themselves effortlessly into the literature. One of the many anecdotes about Grace's constant 'nattering' on and off the pitch (which sometimes involved 'unparliamentary language') has him triumphantly reworking a bit of jargon after he had been warned that a certain bowler 'mixed up' his deliveries: 'Run up, run up, we'll mix 'em up for him, we'll mix 'em up for him.' Whether Botham, when encouraging Graham Dilley to 'give it some humpty' at Headingley in 1981, came up with a new word for slogging or was using a term already common in the trade, his extraordinary innings ensured the phrase a place in the game's folklore. Similarly, Flintoff may have encouraged Tino Best to 'mind the windows' of the Lord's pavilion in 2004 on the spur of the moment, or he may have learnt the expression from the bitter experience of being tempted into indiscretion himself (the houses adjacent to the ground at St Anne's Cricket Club in Preston, where he played as a teenager, are within easy reach for a big-hitter). That the language of cricket evolves through its oral traditions as well as its written records should not be surprising, since no other sport allows so much time and opportunity for its players to talk to each other. Many of the game's most memorable anecdotes involve an exchange of pleasantries – now known as 'sledging' – between opponents on the pitch. Cricket also has intervals allowing for more reflective interaction between the two teams. The lunch and tea breaks

built into the game, as well as the time spent before
and after a day's play in the pavilion and pub, amount
to a raconteur's charter.

Neville Cardus, the game's greatest raconteur, was
thinking precisely of its 'leisurely' cadences when he
asserted in an essay on Grace that 'cricket is without
rival amongst open-air pastimes for the exhibition of
native characteristics in Englishmen'. His point was
proved by the fact that the anecdotal tradition allowed
him to construct a living portrait a generation after the
great man's death. Grace, as famous as any Victorian
in his lifetime, is recognised even today both by his initials and his image: W. G. beards were a popular acces-
sory for those who attended the 2005 Ashes series in
fancy dress. A colossus of cricket in every sense, his
first-class career spanned from 1865 (the year after
over-arm bowling was legalised) to 1908 (the year in
which the next giant of the game, Don Bradman, was
born). The cliché has it that Grace found cricket a
country pastime and left it a national institution. The
way his celebrity was curated also suggests that it
suited 'the fellows at Lord's' very well, as they institu-
tionalised the sport, to play down his reputation for
living life to the full and for stretching the Laws of the
game to their limits. Grace's decision to accept MCC
membership and play as an amateur (whilst receiving
extremely generous 'expenses') may have been the
most significant factor in prolonging the distinction
between 'gentlemen' and 'players' around which so
many of English cricket's antinomies organised themselves. When two stalwarts of cricket's officer class,
Lord Harris and Lord Hawke, helped edit a memorial
biography immediately after the First World War, their
emphasis was on the Corinthian spirit of the game
more than W. G.'s high spirits. Cricket, as Cardus puts
it in his less straitlaced tribute, 'acquired a cant of its
own, and you might well have asked why two umpires
were necessary at all'.

Today's game could not be more professional, yet
its 'native characteristics' remain. Like Botham before
him ('the first rock and roll cricketer'), Flintoff
('Beard of the Year 2005') has a physical presence
about him which endorses Cardus's judgement on
Grace: 'There is a lot in "appearance" if the crowd is
to give full respect and worship.' And although
Freddie seems too good-natured to indulge in the
darkest arts of sledging, an exchange of on-pitch ban-
ter recorded by Ed Smith in his diary of the 2003 season glances back to the many historical encounters
between a northern pro and a southern gent:

> AF: Come on, let's get Ed out and let him go
> beagling on the downs!
> ES: Beagling? That's a good word, Andrew. Are
> you sure you know what it means?
> AF: All right, let's get Ed out and let him go punt-
> ing on the Cam!

Flintoff continued the tease later that season by pre-
senting Smith with a congratulatory gin and tonic
when they shared a Test dressing room. His own celebrations after the Ashes victory, mostly lager-fuelled,
have become legendary. But while his determination
to be one of the lads helps make Freddie a much-loved
hero of the Barmy Army, he is also looked upon as a
role model in the members' enclosures and corporate
boxes. If this partly reflects changes in the physiog-
nomy of English society, it also says something about
the character-forming and character-reflecting qualities of cricket. However sanctimoniously its apolo-
gists can harp on about cricket being 'a moral lesson
in itself', it is a game where selflessness and sportsmanship are still prize exhibits. The 'abiding image'
of the Ashes series was that of Flintoff stooping to
console a dejected Brett Lee after England's two-run
victory at Edgbaston. This chivalrous gesture was
cited by one BBC correspondent to support the view

that cricket was suddenly being perceived not only as 'sexy' but also as 'brimming with good values'.

Of course, cricket did not become sexy overnight. Symbolically, perhaps, it was in 1963 – the year when 'sexual intercourse began', according to Philip Larkin, and the English establishment was rocked by the Profumo affair – that the game began to shed some of its reputation for encouraging fustiness and deference. Already an *annus mirabilis* for cricket by virtue of being the centenary year of its Bible, *Wisden*, 1963 was also the first season when there was no Gentlemen v. Players fixture at Lord's, the distinction between amateur and professional having finally been abolished. The West Indian tourists, led by their first black captain, Frank Worrell, won the inaugural *Wisden Trophy* with, to use the jargon of the period, an exhibition of 'brighter cricket'. The climate was therefore perfect for the publication of *Beyond a Boundary* by the Trinidadian Marxist C. L. R. James, an influential book which sought to debunk many of the game's myths without being able entirely to resist them (in a brilliant portrait James concludes that W. G. had a 'heart of gold'). The year of the first Beatles album also saw the introduction of the first limited-overs competition, the Gillette Cup, to the English county circuit. For traditionalists one-day cricket seemed like disposable pop music compared to the classical compositions allowed by the longer forms of the game. Their distaste for this 'perverted' version of cricket only increased after Kerry Packer introduced American-style razzmatazz to the format as part of his circus (or revolution, depending on your point of view) at the end of the 1970s.

In the twenty-first century we find that the current focus is not so much on the new forms of the game that have arrived but rather on the impact that they are now having upon the old. Tim de Lisle begins his Notes to the 2003 *Wisden* by commenting on how

Test cricket has sharpened up its act: 'One-day
cricket, often regarded as a little trollop lowering her
older sister's standards, has actually enabled her to let
her hair down.' And the reporting style of the distinguished *Almanack* is definitely following suit. Rob
Smyth's account of the second Test between the West
Indies and England, played in March 2004, reads
almost like a working manifesto for the cause. This
encounter, up to the point when it defined itself as
'Harmison's match' on the fourth morning, was
'closely fought' or 'fiercely contested' in the best tradition. But in contemporary language this comes out
as 'a gritty arm-wrestle of a match'. The opening
action finds the reporter in Twenty20 mood, with 'a
pack of virile young bowlers pummelling a bouncy
castle of a pitch'. When the West Indies' turn comes to
bowl, he pushes the recognised idiom of 'scorching
pace' into something more distinctly abrasive – 'the
sheer, paint-stripping pace of Edwards'. For a moment
we are in the world of blue overalls rather than white
flannels. As for the various dismissals, we might pick
out the snappy sporting cross-reference in 'Chanderpaul nutmegged himself'. After which, when we are
told that 'Hoggard clutched a scorching return chance
from Smith that threatened to rearrange his face', it is
difficult not to admire the way in which a euphemism
usually reserved in cricket for 'shattering the stumps'
has been taken back to its origins in underworld
slang. In short, this mode of writing is freed up, street-
wise, matey and not, on the face of it, intended pre-
scriptively for the MCC membership.

The one-day game has, of course, refused to lie
down. In March 2006 the highest score achieved in a
limited-overs international surpassed the biggest total
ever made in the fourth innings of a Test. But the key
factor in recent years is, as Simon Barnes has observed,
'that the thought processes of one-day cricket have
been adapted to the Test context'. Barnes's essay on

Steve Waugh, again in 2003's *Wisden*, noted that 'the Australian batsmen seek to frighten opponents every bit as much as the fast-bowling quartet of the 1980s West Indians'. Nor is it necessary to look too hard in the same volume to find the phenomenon of fast batting being faithfully recorded by Gideon Haigh:

> When Henderson came on, Langer hefted him into the crowd at mid-on. When he resumed after lunch, Langer hop-scotched into a cover drive to the boundary. Pollock gave himself one more over: Hayden walloped a long-hop over the mid-wicket fence. Donald was recalled: Langer slashed through gully for four. Kallis returned: Hayden flailed three consecutive boundaries.

Two centuries duly followed, but the quality of the verbs in this passage is already enough to show the reporter going head-to-head with the two centurions in the business of self-expression. The extract also demonstrates cricket's capacity as a first-class vehicle for narrative. But the more immediate point to observe is that the climate change brought about by the Packer era, of which Haigh is himself a notable historian, can be registered also in the language of the game.

Clearly, with cricket reporting, the medium will influence the kind of messaging that goes on. While Richie Benaud, the doyen of TV commentators, believed in being unobtrusive, it was readily understood that such reticence was actually an expression of expertise. On radio, with its obscured view of the discontinuities in the action, there is a greater need for what in BBC terminology used to be known as 'associative material', which is allowed by convention to include pigeons and passing traffic. The new medium of the internet allows either for immediacy, as in *Cricinfo*'s breathless ball-by-ball commentary, or colour, as in the over-by-over summaries Rob Smyth now provides as part of the *Guardian*'s team. Writing a newspaper report is more distinctly akin to going out to bat and building an innings that combines substance with style. Not that everything will come as effortlessly as it did for Frank Woolley, who was, according to Ian Peebles, 'the most graceful of the efficient, and the most efficient of the graceful'. But every correspondent has to set out his stall.

Christopher Martin-Jenkins has attested, looking back to his apprenticeship days, that 'Jim' Swanton trained him to avoid clichés: 'I remember him writing C.L.I.S.H. on anything of which he didn't approve.' Here the very form of the interdict – presumably an acronym for something like 'Can't Let It Stand Here' – would seem to exemplify the process of receiving a well-drilled education. But the more instructive inference could be that Swanton, through being defensive-minded, actually missed out on the full range of scoring opportunities. Admittedly, some of the stock locutions can become vexatious through repetition, like the all-too-mechanical 'red cherry' to stand in for 'new ball'. All the same, given that the basic activities of cricket are naturally repetitive, working some of the clichés around may be a good method of keeping things moving.

We might contrast the older attitude with that of the Indian journalist Dileep Premachandran, who regularly goes for his shots on the assumption that knowing what they are technically called does not rule out improvisation. Or perhaps the better analogy is with the spin bowler systematically exploring his repertoire. So, for example, Premachandran is familiar with the topos of the batsman who 'shines in the gloom'. Here is his standard delivery of the theme: 'Virender Sehwag lit up a gloomy day with a sparkling innings.' And here comes the flighted variation: 'Virender Sehwag lit up the Mohali gloaming with luminous batsmanship.' As a poet himself, this reporter is programmed to know that the moment for intimating elegy is that of parting day. Jack Fingleton had the same intuition when he entitled his book on Bradman *Brightly Fades the Don*.

Another writer who represents the vibrancy of the new India is Rahul Bhattacharya, especially in the way he has caught the tempo of the modern one-day game in his coverage from Pakistan. Bhattacharya might almost be seen as the Gary Sobers of modern cricket reporting because of his quickfire ability to enter into all the roles. Some of his improvised touches are meant to be as exhilarating as the strokes that prompted them, as with the four no-balls 'smashed to itty bits' by Sehwag, or, as an explicit *pièce de résistance*, Inzamam at the moment he 'disdained it to behind square'. At the same time, Bhattacharya is content to rely on some of the older tricks as well, like tne mix of adjectives called up to record 'the continuous undulating vivid gasps of a packed house under lights' and the rhetorical question provoked by Inzamam's dismissal at a crucial point – 'What is the sound of 33,000 hearts wilting?' In fact, the crowd scenes are surely the finest in the genre since Cardus. What this newbie shares with the old master is the knowledge that, as they like to say in French cricket, *le style c'est l'homme*.

One of the longest-serving clichés regarding cricket was formulated by the eponymous hero of *Tom Brown's Schooldays*, published in 1857: 'It's more than a game. It's an institution.' The gloss which follows from Tom's friend Arthur is hardly less memorable, to the effect that cricket 'is as British as *habeas corpus* and trial by jury'. As twenty-first-century Britain, for one reason and another, is reviewing the merits of trial by jury and has looked again at the lapse of time allowable under *habeas corpus*, the moral fervour of the aphorism becomes all the more susceptible to deconstruction. For the other great claim with respect to cricket's higher institutional purpose we can turn to the words of Lord Harris, who became President of the

MCC in 1896, just after a five-year term as Governor of Bombay: 'Cricket has done more to consolidate the Empire than any other influence.' Again, in a post-colonial age, this pronouncement comes across as impossibly smug about both the importance of cricket and the sanctity of the British Empire. But the game can still claim to be the leading 'Commonwealth' sport. When informed that 'Alex Loudon bowls an Anglo-Indian doosra of Australian origins', readers are more likely to be intrigued by the mechanics of the delivery than surprised by its mixed provenance. Furthermore, however ambivalent attitudes may be in Caribbean and Asian societies to a game originally introduced by an imperial master, cricket has been consolidated deeply into their cultures. Although prepared to die and to kill for his jihadist beliefs, Shahzad Tanweer spent the last evening of his life, on 6 July 2005, playing cricket in a park in Leeds.

Ramachandra Guha, in his history of the game's development in India, notes that 'cricket has been successfully indiginized, made part of the fabric of everyday life and language'. India now has the largest English-speaking population in the world, and the zing in the writing of Premachandran and Bhattacharya may tempt us to add that the Test-playing nations of the old Empire strike back, not just through square leg and cover point, but by the way they add to the fabric of the game's everyday vocabulary. Sometimes this can be a consciously political process, as when Dr Winford James argues that indigenous words like 'voop' should receive positive discrimination in Trinidad over Anglo-Saxon words like 'swipe'. More often usage evolves gradually and by chance – witness the journey of the word 'yakka' from Aboriginal language through Australian slang into the particular vernacular of the English county cricketer. Cricket, like language, may sometimes be threatened by change, but change is what renews the game and its lexicon.

A

Abandoned: This word makes most impact in the sombre but sonorous phrase *abandoned without a ball being bowled*. And yet, if play does proceed, it may be that one of the sides will be *praying for rain* or even *doing a **rain dance*** by the final day.

Accept the light: 'The first day ended with the batsmen *accepting the light* and losing nine overs.' A paradoxical effect is produced by this reporting shorthand. The batsmen have in fact rejected the light but accepted the umpires' *offer*.

Accumulator: 'Crawley forsook *fluency* in favour of slow *accumulation*.' This term frequently describes the main characteristic of a batsman's style, which may of course evolve through a combination of experience and age: 'Gooch nowadays is more a remorseless *accumulator* than a *destroyer*'; 'No longer the thrilling counter-attacker of old, Thorpe has become an utterly dependable, no frills *accumulator*.' The seasoned player will have his own method for keeping the scoreboard *ticking along*: 'Martyn made a career-best 161, *accumulating* as assiduously as a squirrel in autumn.'

Across the line: According to the *classical* precepts, playing *straight*, or *down the line*, is *orthodox* and playing *across the line* is heretical. But batsmen need in any case to judge the prevailing **conditions** and the context of the game: 'The odd *jagging* ball demanded a **straight bat**; instead, three of the top four fell playing *across the line*.' Scoring shots are usually exempt, or exempted, from such criticism, and the terminology of the modern game (see **heave**, **smear**, **work**) allows considerably for *productive* improvisation. **Flat-batted** clearly denotes horizontality but it also clearly outplays *cross-batted*.

Action: It would be possible to construct a whole typology of bowling *actions* on the basis of the various adjectives in use to describe them. Our own sample includes such terms as *bustling*, *chest-on*, *loose-limbed*, *slinging* and *whippy* – not to mention, of course, *suspect*. We would select *whirling*, however, as the type of *action* that offers the greatest descriptive potential for any cricketing scribe. Sometimes the attempt at evocation stays more or less within the natural limits of anatomy, as in the case of Bill O'Reilly, 'with an *action* that was all elbows and *whirring* arms'. But often the lure of some machine-minded analogy is hard to resist, so that we find Matt Mason bowling 'with a delivery that looks like a windmill crossed with a helicopter'. The classic instance, in this particular area of the typology, remains the description of Paul Adams, the **Chinaman** bowler, as a 'frog in a blender'.

Adhesive: 'Richardson was at his *adhesive* best until his considerable patience ran out just before **lunch**.' When the team needs a defensive-minded batsman to *occupy the crease* for long periods, he will be praised for his *adhesive powers* or *qualities*. Indeed, when it comes to **stickability**, there may be a franchise on offer: 'Darren Bicknell began one of his familiar

Bostik innings, venturing little but concentrating fiercely.' When, on the other hand, a batsman becomes ***bogged down***, especially if his footwork is poor, any descriptions of him as *stuck* to the crease will be less complimentary. See also ***limpet***.

Adjacent: 'Next ball, Nehra struck again, Alec Stewart looking *fairly adjacent* as the ball ***darted*** into his pads.' In practice, the word means 'as close as you can get to lbw without necessarily being given out.' Here is an illustrative example from Richie Benaud, remembering an inswinger from Lindwall which beat Colin McDonald *all ends up*: 'I have scarcely ever seen a *more adjacent* lbw turned down.' In the age of television the word will emerge, most typically, from an examination of the replay when a batsman has been allowed the ***benefit of the doubt***: 'I have to say that one looked *very adjacent*.' But in Justin Langer's usage the answer is, quite unequivocally, *out*: 'An inswinger from Richard Johnson trapped the West Indian maestro *adjacently **in front*** of all three stumps.' In short, the word admits of degrees but wants to mean only one thing in cricket.

Agricultural: 'Damien Fleming could not resist an *agricultural **heave***.' This kind of effort is the very antithesis of the *cultured* stroke or the *cultivated* innings. The distinction seems to hark back to the games gentlemen landowners used to arrange on their grounds, where the farm-workers would be lucky to get a bat – and probably ***hoicked*** it to ***cow corner*** if they did. Or perhaps it is encouraged as much as reflected by the genre of village-cricket-match fiction. In L. P. Hartley's evocation of an Edwardian game, the farmer Ted Burgess (Alan Bates in the film of *The Go-Between*) ***thrashes*** Lord Trimingham's team to ***all parts*** in rustic fashion. For the young narrator, who had earlier seen a much more *correct* innings from the

City banker Mr Maudsley, farmer Ted becomes a symbol of some menace: 'Dimly, I felt the contrast represented something more than the conflict between Hall and village. It was that, but it was also the struggle between order and lawlessness, between obedience to tradition and defiance of it, between social stability and revolution, between one attitude to life and another.' But then many of us would have thrown away the *MCC Coaching Manual* if it ensured a *knock-up* with Julie Christie.

Air hostess: 'That ball went so high it could have got an *air hostess* down with it.' A flight of fancy from Navjot Singh Sidhu to convey the elevation on an especially *steepling* catch. Given ever more sophisticated television coverage of the game, an interactive *drinks interval* along these lines cannot be ruled out in the future.

Airy: Used when a batsman essays his stroke – almost always a drive in these contexts – with too much of a flourish, so that he may be playing *away from his body* or not getting to the *pitch* of the ball: 'Harmison then bowled Ottis Gibson through an *airy* drive'; 'James Hildreth drove *airily* at Breese and was bowled.' A spinner would not be said to bowl 'airily' but he might well *give it more air* in the hope of deceiving the batsman in the *flight*.

All parts: 'Trescothick set off cutting, carving and driving the ball *to all parts* of the ground.' This expression is so well understood that often *of the ground* can be taken as read: 'Worcestershire lost all **semblance of control** after tea as David Sales **flayed** their attack *to all parts*.' In practice, a batsman will probably *favour* certain **areas**, but *to all parts* is a formula which indicates that the bowlers are being well and truly **carted** and that the fielding captain seems powerless to staunch the flow of runs. If the intention really is to report that the batsman is playing *every shot in the book*, the phrasing modulates slightly: 'The England left-hander relished the pace and the bounce of the Wankhede Stadium and unleashed attractive strokes *all around the wicket.*'

Analyst: *Analysis* used to mean just a bowler's *figures*, especially if the overs and maidens were listed as well as the runs and wickets. Simon Hughes changed all that when Channel 4 agreed to his proposal to become a kind of 'Peter Snow of cricket'. Hughes playfully suggests that the seeds of his role as *the Analyst* were planted towards the end of his Middlesex career when he tried to chat up female acquaintances by elucidating the finer points of the game. Then, continuing fieldwork on the prettier spectators in the 'gloom' of BBC video-tape trucks, he had the idea 'to use the various gizmos to explain the more baffling aspects of cricket'. Hughes also acknowledges the encouragement of Richie Benaud, and it is a tribute to his own dispatches from the car park that they will be missed almost as much as the great man's wisdom in the commentary box.

Anchor: 'I don't know why they pick McMorris in place of Carew. You can't have two *sheet-anchors* as opening batsmen.' But it is normally advisable to have one *anchor* or *anchorman* to lend stability to an innings while the more flamboyant shot-makers *play around* him: 'In perfect one-day style Atherton *dropped anchor* while Lloyd *injected* the mid-innings impetus.'

Angle: Bowlers looking to make something happen will often *change* the *angle* by *using all of the crease* or by going around the wicket, especially to left-handers. Batsmen play with an *angled* (as opposed to *crooked*) bat when they are consciously trying to keep the ball down; when the *angle* of the bat to the ground becomes obtuse, rather than acute, the terminology changes and the strokes are *lofted*. A sense of practical geometry is also helpful when constructing a one-day innings: 'Collingwood *worked* the *angles* in his usual efficient manner.'

Apiece: This word is a linguistic relic from the pre-marketing age: 'In 1991 DeFreitas claimed 22 Test wickets at 20.8 *apiece*.' Cricketers speak of *economy rates* but not yet of 'unit cost'.

Application: A more aloof way of saying that the batsmen need to get their heads down but, with all the demands of the modern game, it may not be for long enough: 'England batted with minimum *application* under sustained *pressure*.'

Approach: A bowler's *approach* to the wicket comes under particular scrutiny from technicians when he is overstepping the mark or struggling for rhythm: 'Giles has just lost it for the moment, and his new, straighter *approach* to the stumps appears to have robbed him of the pivot and brace that came with his *angled* run-up.' But, in the case of Doug Wright, the technical discussion begins to give way to comic description: 'From the start he needed a team of surveyors with theodolites to help him mark out his *approach run*.' Given that the duration of a bowler's *approach* is longer than that of his *action*, there is more time for the observer to work up an imaginative picture of the bowler running in. Here is Frank Keating on Bob Willis: 'A 1914 biplane tied up with elastic bands trying vainly to take off.' Followed by Martin Johnson on Merv Hughes: 'The mincing *run-up* resembles someone in high heels and a panty girdle chasing after a bus.' But for purity of concept we are inclined to give pride of place here to the anonymous correspondent of the 1890s who described William Hillyer as *'shuffling* to the crease as if carrying hot plates he wanted to set down'. See **sightscreen**, however, for a second Johnson nomination.

Areas: As in football, one of the modern mantras is to find *good areas* consistently and let the ball do the work: 'We didn't bowl well. The guys knew the plan, but the harder they tried, the less they seemed to *land* it in the *right areas.*' It is accepted that in normal circumstances the best *area* of all is the one which circumscribes the **corridor of uncertainty** and **two-man's-land**: 'Gul, by relentlessly *peppering* what they call "the *business area*", had drawn the error.' A batsman will also have *areas* in which he likes to score and will often find, by his *second season*, that the opposition captain knows where they are: 'Lancashire employed intelligent fields to *cut off* the runs in Montgomerie's *favourite areas* on the leg side.'

Arm ball: The delivery in a spinner's **repertoire** that goes *straight on*, not to be confused with the **doosra**. In this age of *covered wickets*, some English finger-spinners appear to bowl the *arm ball* as their **stock** delivery. The *arm ball* can be called an *armer*, especially in India, or commentators may refer to the *one* that *goes on with the arm*. However, an *arm bowler* is less likely to be a slow bowler who never tries to give it a real **tweak** but rather a pace *merchant* who fails to put his torso into his **action**. According to *Wisden*, before Frank Tyson was sent for coaching at Alf Gover's indoor school, 'he was almost solely an *arm bowler*'.

Armour: The players' collective term for all their protective equipment, in spite of which Jonathan Agnew was still able to find himself discomfited in all senses: 'I was wearing more *armour* than a jousting knight,

and then got *pinned* on the one bit that was not covered by foam or something similar.'

Arse: 'His *arse* has *gone*, boys' – **sledging** to be used
when the batsman is apparently not *relishing* the pace
of the attack. There may be an implication of a skid-
marked jockstrap, but the main idea is that the player
concerned is not quite *getting into line* and hence his
posterior is moving towards square leg, to the point
where he may end up on the umpire's *lap*. Mike
Gatting could never be accused of taking a backward
step against fast bowling, and has the nose to prove it,
but if his *arse* ever had *gone* we assume the square-leg
umpire would have moved to point in order to get an
unobstructed view of the game.

Art: *The Art of Cricket* was not a *cricketana* catalogue
but a coaching manual written by Sir Donald
Bradman. The title reflects the way in which even the
most ruthlessly efficient exponents of the game have
tended to view it as an art form rather than a mere
pursuit or pastime. It may or may not be remarkable
also that *art* is a word which attaches itself most often
to the things amateurs used to do in cricket: **batsmanship**, captaincy and leg spin. On the other hand, the
science of biometrics seems to be designed especially to
keep the traditional **workhorses** fit for their toil.

Ashes: Inspired by a mock-obituary for English
cricket in 1882, the *Ashes* have become the symbol for
all sporting encounters between England and
Australia. They were made incarnate by a cremation
ceremony after Ivo Bligh's touring team gained
revenge the next winter, even if forensic evidence still
fails to confirm whether the contents of the **urn** are
the remains of a bail, a veil or a ball. But what is certain is that the *Ashes* never move from **Headquarters**,
even though Australia usually win there.

Assistance: Much can depend, in cricket, on the manner in which the pitch *behaves* and whether it is *docile* or *lively*. The idea of the playing surface *giving every assistance* to the bowlers suggests that it is almost an interested participant in the action. In the same way, a wicket can be described as *seamer-friendly* or said to *encourage* spin. Bowlers will tell you they need all the help they can get – a *true* or *perfect* wicket is always so for the batsmen, not for them.

Asterisk: Traditionally, an *asterisk* appears in cricket scorecards before the name of a captain and in cricket **averages** after the score of a not-out batsman. But *asterisks* may be required in polite journalism when tales of **mental disintegration** are being recounted. The editor of *Wisden* has also registered his exaspera-tion at the way **Super** *Tests* and other ICC initiatives have played havoc with the integrity of the game's records: 'Here we just sigh deeply and knuckle down to deciding how to cope with all the *asterisks* and foot-notes forced on us from on high in Dubai.'

At the death: In fox-hunting, to be in *at the death* is to be present for the final moments of the chase when the game is killed by the hounds; in cricket, to be in *at the death* means to be batting in the final overs of a run-chase when the game is there for the taking. Members of the Countryside Alliance find drag-hunt-ing a pale imitation of real sport; some **members** of county cricket clubs find limited-overs matches *con-trived* compared to **proper cricket**. But *the death* is a concept associated almost exclusively with the one-day game. The pressures of a close finish can make the fielding side feel like the prey, but some of the **death bowlers** are wily old foxes: 'Ray Price, with a very **tight** spell *at the death*, ensured there would be no late-**order** heroics.'

Attrition: This word brings cricket as close as it comes, in the verbal sense, to trench warfare. Indeed, we were already anticipating 'watchword' in the following sentence: '*Attrition* and ***application*** were England's buzzwords.' The adjectival form, in particular, serves to create a mood: 'The afternoon saw more *attritional* batting from Derbyshire.' However, a batsman can win the day by *going over the **top*** every now and then: 'It was Razzaq who sealed the issue with a mix of *attrition* and *blast*.'

Audi: An *Audi* is a modern term for the unlikely event of a *pair* of ***pairs***, suggested by the four interlocking 0s on the German car manufacturer's logo. These *Audi rings* can become *Olympic* if a batsman ***bags*** five successive ***ducks***. The terminology got an airing on the Scarborough Sharks website in 2005: 'Dwaine Miru missed his *Audi Rings* (4 *ducks* in a row) by hitting 26 not out to score his first runs for the club.' Until that point, Dwaine had been 'chasing Matty Davis' *Olympic Dream* from last season with 5 *ducks* in a row'.

Average: No other game is as fixated on this kind of measurement, except perhaps baseball, and even there it supposedly took an English-born statistician, Henry Chadwick, to get the Americans interested in the concept of *averages*. The popularity of fantasy-cricket games proves the sport is particularly suited to the analysis of individual performance, because self-contained figures can be recorded for each *department* of the game. But one of the most damning charges in the professional ranks is that an individual is more interested in his own *stats* than the fortunes of the team: 'Stewart's been *playing for his average*, trying desperately to keep it over the magic 40'; 'Another maiden as Kallis decides to *preserve his average* rather than take any risks.' In lower grades, the charge tends to be bandied about more playfully, especially if one of the bowlers has managed to string together a few *asterisks* without recourse to *sledging*: 'We were all expecting Jezza to have a *swipe* but, after his run of not outs, he's obviously *playing for his average* now.'

B

Back cut: Australasian for *late* cut, logically enough since it indicates where the shot goes: 'When Laxman *back cut* Simon Katich on Saturday afternoon, it looked as lazy as it was full of poise and audacity.' Not an expression endorsed by the *purist*, but it sounds as if Laxman's stroke would have satisfied the connoisseur.

Back foot: 'The Australians like to impose themselves early and are used to having England *on the back foot* from the first day of a series.' In its metaphorical sense, being *on the back foot* always means being 'on the defensive'. This is not necessarily the case in the game itself. Batsmen may indeed *go onto the back foot* to give themselves more time to play fast bowling, but equally they can **rock back** to crash forcing strokes *off the back foot*. In the end, whether a player *favours* the *back foot* may have less to do with his attacking or defensive instincts than the type of wickets on which he has been raised: 'Langer is, after all, a *back-footer* who learned the game dealing with the WACA Ground's *steepling* bounce.' The following headline, typical of the way political reporters use the metaphor, reminds us that the leader of the Australian Labor Party also comes from Perth: 'Latham jibe puts Beazley *on the back foot*.'

Back-to-back: The rigours of the modern international programme, with compressed tours, very few warm-up games and no rest days, has led to the growth in the phenomenon of *back-to-back Tests*. It should not be forgotten that successive Tests at Christmas and New Year had become the norm in Australia and South Africa. However, before the ICC's Future Tour Programme was devised, you would not have seen the following sentence: 'The ruinous stresses of *back-to-back-to-back* Test matches are telling.'

Back up: *Backing up* is a routine act for the non-striker, but risks are involved if he *backs up too far*. He could be **Mankaded** before the bowler releases, or cruelly dismissed if a straight drive is *deflected* onto the stumps, or beaten by a *smart* throw which produces a *direct hit*: 'Andy Bichel was then brilliantly run out by Chris Rogers after *backing up too far* with the score 8–197.' In this example, Chris Rogers will have also taken it as read that mid-off would be *backing up* his throw at the bowler's end. Failing to *back up* is as negligent an act by a cricket team in the field as by the IT department in a large company, and will induce just as much swearing at the guilty man.

Backward: Used of a player's fielding position (with *of square* understood) rather than his mental aptitude, although *short backward square* can still be thought of as *silly*.

Bad trot: 'Hick was having another *bad trot*.' This is the situation of a batsman suffering, not from a nasty attack of the runs, but rather an acute shortage of them: 'Jon Carr was in a *bad trot*, and decided that he would hit his way out of it.' The expression is originally Australian for a 'run of bad luck', no doubt originally experienced at the racecourse.

Bag: The noun is a synonym for **haul** in a match or total wickets in a career: 'The 33-year-old Cairns won

the Man of the Match award with his first *bag* of ten
wickets in a Test'; 'In 21 Tests I increased my "*bag*"
by 131 wickets.' More occasionally it is the hold-all of
choice for batting milestones: 'With 12 centuries and
25 fifties in his *bag*, the former Indian skipper does
not seem to give up.' Although unfortunate batsmen
can *bag a **pair***, the verb is usually reserved for those
with a *safe **pair of hands***: 'Chris Kuggeleijn *bagged*
the catch that gave Sir Richard Hadlee his 374th and
world-record Test wicket.' If a ***chance*** gets ***grassed*** in
Australia, the hapless fielder may be told to *get a bag*.

Baggy green: This cricket cap, awarded on Test
debut, is such a familiar symbol that *baggy green* has
become a synonym for *Australian*: 'The *baggy greens*
are proud, strong and detest losing.' Michael Clarke
sets up a nice antithesis between the ***pyjama game***
and ***proper cricket*** as he explains what playing for
Australia means to him: 'I really enjoy the one-dayers,
wearing yellow clothes, having my name on my back.
But wearing the *baggy green* is the ultimate, the greatest feeling.' Under Steve Waugh's captaincy, such was
the veneration of the *baggy green*, preferably as *battered* as possible, that it was meant to stand for everything good about the game. In a wholly unconnected
development, prices achieved at auction trended
upwards.

Bail out: Facing short-pitched deliveries, batsmen
sometimes *pull out* of an attacking stroke. This results
in less risk to their person but some risk to their
wicket: 'Lara ***spooned*** a catch to Jacques Kallis as he
bailed out of a hook shot off Pollock.' The verb is again
used when a batsman *dancing down* the wicket is
faced with the decision whether to abort a ***big shot***:
'Key might have had an attacking intent but was ***done***
in the air. In that case he really should have *bailed out*
and got something, anything on it.'

Bakerloo: A trade term for a batsman playing down the *wrong line*: 'Anderson's first Test wicket was not long in coming, as Mark Vermeulen played "*down the Bakerloo*", losing his off stump in the process.' Commentators will occasionally make a reference to a more salubrious route like the *Metropolitan*, *Central* or *Piccadilly*, although there seems to be no consensus as to which is the 'right line'.

Ball of the century: By common consent (although many of the best-qualified judges were dead by the time it happened) the *ball of the* twentieth *century* was the one Mike Gatting got *first-up* from Shane Warne at Old Trafford in 1993. Given Gatting's fondness for a good *lunch*, his captain Graham Gooch could not resist a few quips at the time: 'If it had been a cheese roll it would never have got past him.' Martin Johnson, master of the big ripping yarn, has had a few years to work on the variations: 'Gatting's expression in 1993 could scarcely have registered more astonishment had he dialled room service and opened his hotel door to find Shakoor Rana delivering a plate of Ryvita.'

Ball on a string: A suitable figure to describe a bowler's control, especially if he is a spinner, and especially if he relies on subtleties of *flight* rather than *extravagant* turn: 'Tufnell varies his pace cleverly, often luring batsmen out of their crease with a classic *ball-on-a-string* delivery.' As usual, the Indian journalist Rahul Bhattacharya can be relied upon to develop the imagery: 'Kumble trades the leg-spinner's proverbial *yo-yo* for a *spear*, as the ball hacks through the air rather than hanging in it, then comes off the pitch with a kick rather than a kink.'

Ball tampering: A spectator new to the game might be forgiven for thinking that *ball tampering* is the

technical term for how the slip *cordon* passes the time
in between deliveries. But it is in fact the most common way of referring to the offence known, in the
argot of the Laws and the ICC Code of Conduct, as
changing the condition of the ball.

Ballwatching: A cardinal sin in football, and as bad
in cricket when running between the wickets since it
amounts to not trusting your partner: 'Ponting has
only himself to blame as he was *ballwatching* and
probably would have made it if responding to the call.'

Bamboozle: One of a select group of verbs reserved
for the effect a leg-spinner's *variations* can have on a
batsman: 'Mongia was *bamboozled* by a top-spinner,
which had lately been missing from Kumble's *repertoire*.' Compare *mesmerise*.

Banana: This kind of delivery is not to be categorised
with a *jaffa*, as it can be one where the swing, however *extravagant*, is slow and predictable. Indeed, a
banana ball may be as wayward a slice as in golf.
However, the image is also used for more *penetrative*
bowling: 'Gambhir's been out three times to
Chaminda Vaas's special *banana ball* that moves in the
air and *darts in* after pitching.'

Bang it in: An idiom for short-pitched bowling.
Applicable to a short *burst* designed to unsettle a batsman: 'Cork *banged it in* short in the first four deliveries, *glaring* at Dravid as he ducked and just let the
missiles be.' Equally serviceable for a more prolonged
barrage: 'Mohammad Akram insisted on *banging it in
halfway down* for most of his spell.' A bowler who
pitches it in his own *half* for most of his career will be
described as a *bang-it-in bowler*, and his predictable
offerings will be easy for good batsmen to handle
unless he is very fast or receives specialist help:

'Cooley has acted as a sort of sporting version of
Professor Henry Higgins, transforming his bone-
headed *bang-it-in merchant* into a far more sophisticated operator.'

Bar-emptying: 'His performances with the bat during the English summer were rarely less than *bar-
emptying*.' An innings by Flintoff might even become
the latest fashionable excuse for *not* taking a drink,
but the beer tent will always be an integral part of the
social history of the game. Richard Nyren, the captain
of the great Hambledon sides of the late eighteenth
century, was also the landlord of the Bat and Ball Inn,
where there were no restrictions upon the sale of
strong beer. Remembering those good old days in
cricket's first classic text, his son John paints a view
of the *village green* which sounds inebriated as well
as idyllic: 'The smell of that ale comes upon me as
freshly as the new May flowers.'

Barmy Army: The England team's self-appointed
twelfth man, now with over 40,000 members to *carry
the drinks*, provokes diametrically opposed opinions.
Christopher Martin-Jenkins of *The Times* finally lost
patience on the 2004–05 South Africa tour: 'Worthy
souls dwell among them, no doubt. As a group, they
too often demean English cricket. As Betjeman
prayed of Slough: come friendly bombs and fall on
them. Water bombs will do.' Matthew Perry and
Dominic Malcolm, two sociologists from the
University of Leicester, have a different view: 'The
Barmy Army represent a qualitatively new form of
English national identity, its behavioural style
involves a blurring of traditional class-based forms of
spectatorship, and the influence wielded by this small,
deviant group indicates the relatively limited nature
of the cricketing establishment's power.' No doubt the
debate will continue, particularly if sterling continues

to prove strong: 'We're fat, we're round, there's ten rand to the pound.'

Barn door: As a verb, an alternative to **stonewall**: 'Captain Taylor *barndoored* and judged the line expertly, taking an age to score his first run.' As a noun, evidence that the batsman is *seeing it like a football*: 'Hayden's bat was a *barn door* after tea.'

Barracking: An Australian player will probably not mind *barracking* in the slightest, because in his language it can simply mean vociferous support for the home team. In English minds, however, especially after the **Bodyline** tour of 1932–33, *barracking* is the term for abuse hurled (sometimes along with beer bottles) from the popular *hills* (and sometimes even the **members**' enclosures) in Australian cricket grounds. Douglas Jardine devoted a chapter of his book *In Quest for the Ashes* to a study of such '*disgraceful scenes*'. His account reveals evidence of pathology as well as research: 'No doubt a lot of **barracking** is thoughtless, nor is it to be expected that Australia should appreciate the Imperial responsibilities of cricket as deeply as we do at home; but a consideration of these responsibilities should prove a great incentive to action on the part of those who are determined that these painful exhibitions of *hooliganism* shall be suppressed.' While the Imperial agenda may have fallen away, the issues of *barracking* and *hooliganism* continue to raise their heads from time to time. Players like Muralitharan have had cause to agree with Harold Larwood's more laconic conclusion: 'A cricket tour of Australia would be a most delightful period in one's life if one was deaf.'

Bat out: To ensure a draw, or safety overnight, by not taking risks: 'Lancashire's decision to *bat out the game* didn't make for a fascinating spectacle.' Possibly as boring to watch, but more likely to produce a positive result in the end, is the decision of a side with a first-innings lead to grind on remorselessly in order to set a very *unlikely* target: 'Two good sessions with the bat, then a *collapse* and a few days of *leather* *hunting* as India were comprehensively *batted out of the game* by Australia.'

Bat-pad: Classifies catches, usually off spin bowling, where the ball balloons up from a *nick* onto the front pad: 'Neil Foster *prodded* a *bat-pad* to *silly* *point.*' By extension, a reference to the fielders stationed at *silly point* or *forward short leg* to accept such *chances*: 'If I were Ponting I'd put Kat in at *bat-pad* straight away.' The catch can be described as *pad-bat* if the typical sequence of events is reversed, but never the fielder, who is always a *bat-pad man.* In the modern era, now that the *leg trap* has ceased to be such a dominant influence, the *bat-pad* positions seem like the gravitational space in which the batsman versus slow bowler contest is fought. See also ***Boot Hill***.

Batsmanship: Perhaps because it echoes *craftsmanship*, a word which makes batting sound like a skill, an *art* or even a higher calling. Suggestively, there is no equivalent word for bowlers. Furthermore, *batsmanship* signifies *dashing* or aesthetically pleasing play in contrast to mere *occupation of the crease* or *accumulation* of runs. This disquisition on Ganguly's form just before he was relieved of the Indian captaincy sets up a classic antithesis between the stylish and the stolid: 'When someone known to embrace *joyous batsmanship* embraces *ordinary batting*, drudgery hangs in the air.'

Bat speed: A concept more crucial to hitting home runs (perhaps itself suggested by the need for *club speed* in golf or *hand speed* in boxing), but getting through the ball with *fast hands* is an aid to the best *strokeplay* in

cricket too. The word features as the most technical
term in this assessment of Tendulkar's form: 'He needs
to get out of his shell, beat back the spooks and play the
square-cuts, the drives and the pulls with the same
élan, *bat speed*, and that stamp of class which made him
India's greatest modern batsman.'

Batter: The more favoured term for *batsman* early in
the game's history and, following the same process by
which *fielder* has almost completely superseded 'fieldsman', becoming more common again now: 'South
Africa have nine good *batters*.' This trend is unlikely
to reflect the influence of baseball and may seek to
harden the distinction between the *recognised batsmen* and the **rabbits**. Or it may be that *batter* fits more
regularly with the series of terms *bowler*, *catcher* and
fielder. Or it may just be what they've always said in
Pudsey, as Raymond Illingworth used the word before
it became fashionable.

Battery: Collective noun for a group of fast bowlers,
especially when they make up an *all-pace attack*: 'The
familiar *battery* of Holding, Marshall, Garner and
Croft was at Clive Lloyd's disposal.' This kind of
attack then proceeds to launch a remorseless *barrage*
on the opposition batsmen. The phraseology conveys
the distaste of certain commentators for persistent
short-pitched bowling. Indeed, an Australian journalist used the term when predicting trouble before the
Bodyline series: 'If the *battery* achieves success it may
be done by contravening the **spirit of cricket**.'

Beamer: 'Kirby responded to a *beamer* by flinging
down his helmet and marching up to Shoaib.' It is
worth noting that the game suddenly becomes more
serious when a player removes his protective head-
gear in these circumstances. The **lid** can come off
because there is an instinctive understanding that the

most lethal delivery in cricket, the head-high full toss, is beyond the pale. But in terms of regulation, this is one area where the bowler claims the right to the *benefit of the doubt*.

Bean ball: While the English *beamer* may derive from the idea of the ball hitting the *beams* on an imaginary ceiling, the Australian term *bean ball* relies on the fact that *bean* is a colloquialism for *head*. Once *bean ball* could be used interchangeably of a *bouncer* or a *beamer*, but now it refers only to the illegal delivery: 'Sooner or later someone will be *clocked* by a *bean ball* and then will come the day of reckoning.'

Beat the bat: 'Alan Richardson came back at the Pavilion End and *beat the bat* on numerous occasions in the humid *conditions*.' Reporters usually make this observation if there is a good deal of *playing and missing* going on. It serves as a kind of psychological statistic when, instead of capturing wickets, bowlers are moving the ball about *without luck*. If, in his spell from the Pavilion End, Richardson had actually dismissed the batsmen he was bowling to, the phrase *beat the bat* would have become superfluous.

Beat the lot: Here *the lot* means bat, pad, stumps and keeper. Uttered in excitement by commentators – or in exasperation by the fielders – when a good ball gets through everything: 'That one *beat the lot* and will *run away* for four byes.'

Beauty: Synonym for *jaffa*. Perhaps it is our imagination because of the typical Australian exclamation, but the word or its abbreviation seems to be used more when Australia are playing: 'Gillespie to Umar, that one was a *beaut*, on off, seaming just enough and *climbing* as it passed the bat.'

Bed down: A bit like *dropping **anchor***, except for the expectation that once a batsman has *bedded down* his innings will begin to bloom as he gets used to the ***conditions*** or the *conditions* get easier for him: 'The pendulum swung emphatically New Zealand's way during the afternoon as Hamish Marshall *bedded down*, the pitch *flattened*, the outfield quickened and the ball softened.' Batsmen determined to *bed down* sometimes take the precaution of ***booking in***.

Beefy: 'Blackwell again ***punished*** his old county, ***clubbing*** a typically *beefy* 111 to keep the deficit manageable.' An adjective associated particularly with Ian Botham but applicable to any ***yeoman*** capable of *meaty* hitting, particularly if they are on the *stout* side.

Belter: 'On a true Old Trafford pitch, described as a "*belter*" by former Lancashire batsman Neil Fairbrother, bowlers who do not ***hit the deck*** could be *cannon fodder*.' It is not clear whether pitches are so described because the bounce when the ball *belts* into the wicket is so true or because batsmen are expected to *belt* the ball to ***all parts***, but you can rest assured that a *belter* is a very good wicket for batting.

Bend their backs: This phrase has become the standard way of measuring the quicker bowlers' keenness for the task: 'After ***lunch***, for no apparent reason, Botham and Garner *bent their backs* and took eight wickets for 45 runs.' It also works as a formula to suggest that a pitch ought to be responsive provided the bowlers make the approved degree of effort: 'The Jamshedpur track also had some bounce for the fast bowlers if they were willing to *bend their backs*.'

Benefit of the doubt: The standard phrase when an umpire rejects a very *good shout* for leg before. Sometimes it comes with a clear suggestion that the ball was in fact *hitting*: 'Bucknor became the latest umpire in this series to give Thorpe the *benefit* of precious little *doubt* when he turned down a perfectly good appeal from Smith late in the day.' Bowlers, like strikers beating the offside trap in football, never seem to enjoy the *benefit of the doubt*, **beamers** excepted.

Biff: 'The most cerebral chapter in a Flintoff coaching book would probably be something like: "If it's *in the slot*, give it a *biff*."' This may be rather unfair to Freddie, who comes from a chess-playing family, but *biff* is a demotic word for big-hitting that tends to have the *slog* written all over it. Often seen in combination with *bang* and similar alliterative words to give entertaining players or formats a bigger build-up: 'Pietersen is a *biff-bang merchant*'; 'Boyce scored 8,800 *biff-bang-wallop* runs'; 'The *biff-bang-bosh* version of cricket has been a mighty success.'

Big pads: 'He's got *big pads*, lads.' Say this when a batsman comes to the crease if you think – or want him to think – he is a prime lbw **candidate**.

Big runs: The *big runs* can be the fours and sixes which result from **big shots** and which are especially important in order to relieve the **pressure** in one-day games: 'Muralitharan bowls such a consistent line that it's very difficult to score runs – especially the *big runs* – off him.' But the phrase is more commonly used without an article to mean heavy scoring: 'Nick Compton's got *all the shots* but just needs to work out a method of scoring *big runs* consistently.' *Big tons* are the mark of a high-class modern batsman: 'The Windies will need one of Lara's *big tons* to have any chance of staving off defeat.' The days when a Hobbs or a Trumper could *throw away* his wicket after reaching a *milestone* have long gone. Batsmen now like to *go on* and on.

Big shots: In other words, the spectacular strokes played by those who tend to *deal in boundaries*: 'When the new ball is *coming on* to the bat, Hussain can trade *big shots* with almost the best, if not Virender Sehwag'; 'Graham Thorpe was caught in the attempt to accelerate and play the *big shots* which are not a normal part of his game.' A sequence of *big shots* traditionally turns into an *exhibition* of *big hitting*.

Big unit: 'Matty Hayden's a *big unit* and that one *stayed hit.*' A favourite expression of Ian Chappell for a well-built batsman, which he probably imported from American sports, unless he happens to have a very large kitchen. Joe Sillett, managing director of cricket-equipment manufacturer Woodworm, drew on the same terminology to explain why Andrew Flintoff's *flannels* are reinforced: 'Freddie is a *big unit* and likes to get very animated when he is appealing, which puts extra duress on the crotch area of his trousers.' Meanwhile, Ashley Giles might lead us to surmise that Mike Gatting came to the aid of the nation by *tweaking* a few leggies in the *nets*: 'The sharpest-turning spinner in England's *Ashes* camp is a *big unit*, that's for sure.' Giles was in fact talking about *Merlyn* the bowling machine.

Billiard table: 'The Newlands wicket was more like the proverbial *billiard table.*' The trusted metaphor for a perfectly smooth and even-paced wicket, even if a pitch which was actually as *green* as a *billiard table* would in fact be a *seamer's paradise*. The emphasis is, of course, on the track's consistency of pace and bounce, added to the fact that a *grassless* wicket can shine in the sun like baize under the lights. Over a hundred years ago Archie MacLaren was bemoaning 'those *shining billiard table* pitches which would play as well on the last as the first day of the match'. Such surfaces continue to be seen as detrimental to the game, but there is no impulse to update the terminology to reflect the popularity of snooker. Perhaps this is an example of the deliberate anachronism for which cricket commentators sometimes strive.

Bisect: A word which can suggest calculation by the batsman in outmanoeuvring the fielders, although it does not mean that he has literally cut them in half: 'Blakey, scoring mainly from the sweep, perfectly *bisected* the two men on the boundary.' The verb is used more routinely as an equivalent to *pierce*, regardless of where the men are placed: 'Cullinan's trademark square cut *bisected* the field time and again.'

Bits-and-pieces: 'Keith Parsons has been branded a *bits-and-pieces* cricketer for most of his 10-year county career, but the Somerset all-rounder clearly has a big-match temperament.' A *bits-and-pieces* player is the opposite of a *genuine all-rounder*, in that he *fills in* with *useful contributions* in both main departments of the game (usually *seam-up **dobbers*** and *steers* to third man). His bowling ***average*** is likely to be higher than his batting *average*. In the interregnum between Botham and Flintoff, England specialised in putting too much ***pressure*** on *bits-and-pieces* men, to the extent that many players find the term derogatory: 'Ian Bell doesn't want to go down the road of the *bits-and-pieces* cricketer, but will work on his bowling as hard as he can.'

Blackwash: A banner at the Oval, the spiritual home of the West Indies on England tours, immortalised this inversion of *whitewash* in 1984, when they took the series 5–0, a feat they repeated at home two years later. Journalists have, with their usual relish, worked variations upon this theme: a *brownwash* is not a tumble-dryer full of jockstraps but a *3–**zip*** win by an Asian team; a *greenwash* over England was often threatened by Australia in the period between 1986 and 2002–03 but never occurred because of their tendency to take their foot off the pedal in dead rubbers; a *rainbow-wash* indicates any clean sweep by South Africa since their readmission to Test cricket; a *blackcapwash* was one paper's way of describing England's 3–0 victory over New Zealand in 2004.

Blade: The technical term for the part of the bat below the handle, which can come to life in cricket when there is anything *swashbuckling* on display: 'Aravinda's *dashing blade* cut swathes through the New Zealanders'; 'With the *flashing blade* of John Davison leading the way, Canada looked like reaching their target easily.' The opposite of a *bludgeon*.

Blast out: In other words, to dismiss batsmen with sheer pace and hostility rather than consistency or guile: 'While Donald *blasts out* his *victims*, Pollock *snares* them with exemplary *line and length*.' A *blast* is therefore a short, fast spell and can develop into a *blitz*. *Bomb out* places the emphasis on short-pitched bowling, while *blow away* is another alternative (although the quick bowler will not have been *spraying it about*). Fast-scoring batsmen can also be capable of *blasts*, particularly when the word offers alliterative possibilities: 'Byas's 33-ball *blast* came to an end when he *holed out* at long-off.'

Blaze: 'Troughton *blazed* his way to 82 from 67 balls.' This verb is more programmatic than *scorch* when it comes to providing the impetus for a team's batting performance. And yet the *blazer* continues to be such a conservative emblem of a team's identity.

Blinder: Can be used of a wonder ball, a hard-hit stroke or an outstanding general performance, but is usually reserved for a spectacular catch: 'Ijaz dived to his right (he is a *lefty*) and *pulled off* an absolute *blinder.*'

Blistering: 'Ganguly's *blistering* assault on the Kent attack was made in a lost cause.' Along with ***withering***, this adjective seems to epitomise what is meant by *intimidatory batting*, even when indulged in, as in the case cited, for no apparent strategic purpose.

Block: Antipodean for the *square* and a batsman's *guard* (in England, the latter usage is possible north of the Trent). *Blockhole length* is therefore yorker length, and is one of the preferred ***areas*** for ***death bowlers***. The verb usually suggests that a ***stonewall*** is being erected: 'Once Leicestershire were ***reduced*** to seven-down, Millns elected to *block* resolutely.' *Block out* is therefore a synonym for ***bat out*** and *blockers* are defensive-minded batsmen. Mike Selvey has also coined a sprightly word for boring play: 'Only two sides had ever made more in the fourth innings of a Test at the Oval, never to win, and certainly not at a rate that would make Twenty20 look like a *blockathon.*'

Bludgeon: One of the heavier-duty verbs to denote ***hard-hitting***, and typically used to suggest the character of a batsman's whole innings: 'Styris *bludgeoned* an unbeaten 100'; 'Blackwell *bludgeoned* the fastest century of the season.'

Bodyline: Legend has it that the Australian journalist Hugh Buggy accidentally hit upon the precise term *Bodyline* (for Douglas Jardine's unpopular tactics in the 1932–33 ***Ashes*** series) when he was abbreviating 'in the *line* of the *body*' for his telegraphed copy. From Jardine's perspective, 'the term was coined by a sensational Press to explain or excuse defeat, and would have died a natural and speedy death had it not been adopted by the Australian Board of Control in its lam-

entable wire to the MCC'. However popular the
expression became in the Dominion, it seems to have
been studiously avoided – if not *deprecated* – by the
MCC itself, who favoured the terms *fast leg theory*
during the controversy and *direct attack bowling* during the post-mortem.

Bogged down: 'England got themselves *bogged down*
chasing an apparently comfortable target, with Athey
scoring only 20 in 21 overs.' A standard metaphor for
slow scoring which can encourage some inventive
headline-writing: 'Lumb paddles lone canoe as
bogged-down Phoenix batsmen fail to rise.'

Book in: 'Michael Vaughan ran through all his front-
line options to no avail as Salman Butt and Younis
Khan *booked in*.' *Booking in* is not the same thing – to
begin with anyway – as *cashing in*. The phrase indicates that the pitch is of the ***featherbed*** variety and
that the top ***order*** are preparing for a *long stay* in
order to ***bat*** the other side ***out*** of the game. Geoffrey
Boycott and his contemporaries made sure to reserve
their places in these circumstances: 'Players like John
Edrich, Dennis Amiss, Ken Barrington would have
booked in for *bed and breakfast* on pitches like these.
You would have had to knock 'em out to get 'em out.'
Boycott attributes to Barrington the coinage *bed and
breakfast*, sometimes used on the county circuit by
itself to signify a ***flat*** wicket.

Boomerang: Like the ***banana***, the *boomerang* provides a metaphor for ***lavish*** movement: 'Lancashire
collapsed to 12 for three against Martin Saggers's
boomerang swing.' In particular, it has become associated with the *lethal* full-pitched inswingers which
have been the specialism of Pakistani fast bowlers
since Sarfraz Nawaz developed the technique:
'Imran's afternoon spell in Karachi – when he

brought down India from 102–1 to 114–7 with *reverse*-*swinging boomerangs* – is one of the most famous spells of bowling in Pakistan cricket.'

Booming: 'Newman hit some *booming* drives through the covers.' Here the adjective suggests the weight of the shot rather than the sound off the bat. A bowler must do something truly resounding to attract the same term: 'Then came that *booming* leg-cutter to Ponting.' That man Flintoff again.

Boot Hill: The original *Boot Hill* in Dodge City was a cemetery for gunfighters who died with their boots on. For cricketers with **lids** on, *Boot Hill* is the **bat-pad** area very close in and square of the wicket where short leg stands on **sledging** terms with the batsman at the risk of injury to himself. Volunteers for *Boot Hill* tend to be at each end of the age spectrum – either young players first coming into the side or gnarled veterans whose *arm* and athleticism have gone: 'At least Hussain's fielding at *Boot Hill* – where he took an excellent low catch later on in the afternoon – showed that his reflexes and eyesight remain sharp.'

Bore draw: Available in cricket as in football to describe a match unlikely to live long in the memory: 'The Essex v Zimbabwe Vodafone Challenge Match at Chelmsford finished in a "*bore draw*" as both teams took the maximum opportunity for *batting* **practice**.' The interminable progress of a Test match played on a **featherbed** can suggest another rhyme: 'The last three Indo-Pak series were so enthralling and packed with incident that one almost forgot the many *snore draws* that had gone before.'

Bosie: Australian for **googly**, now apparently archaic. Named after Bernard Bosanquet the leg-spinner (who invented what he called the *paradox ball*) rather than

Bernard Bosanquet the philosopher (who was a founder of British Idealism).

Both sides of the wicket: As a batsman, having a range of shots on *both sides of the wicket* is not quite as impressive as having *every shot in the book*. But it suggests a nicely patterned *wagon wheel* and that it might be hard to set a field for the player in question. The captain will have similar issues if his team is bowling *both sides of the wicket*, because this means they will be *spraying it around*: 'Sami was generally inconsistent, erring *both sides of the wicket*, and England took good advantage.'

Bottom hand: 'There was an awful *lot of bottom hand* in that shot from Pietersen.' The *bottom hand* is the dominant one for most batsmen, but if there is a *lot* of it in a shot or *too much* of it in a player generally, *purists* who prefer to see a *high left elbow* believe that the *classical* canons are not being observed: 'Dwayne Smith keeps on playing *across the line*. Runako Morton is also a *bottom-handed* player.' However, there may have to be a choice between playing a correct shot for no runs and *working* it away: 'The *bottom hand* was in control of Pietersen's shots and all but eight of his first 50 runs came through the on side.'

Bounce out: 'Sanath Jayasuriya has urged Sri Lanka's batsmen to ignore talk of being "*bounced out*" of the second cricket Test against Australia in Cairns this week.' A nice conjunction of a technical idea – a batsman being dismissed because he has been unable to deal with or resist persistent short-pitched bowling – with a collo-quialism – *bounced out* can easily conjure up the ideas of being sacked from a job or thrown out of a nightclub.

Bouncer wars: Traditionally *bouncer wars* or *bumper wars* take place when two sides both have

pacemen capable of roughing up the opposition batsmen, and where no truce is called by the *fast bowlers'*
union. However, we have seen the phrase used in
journalism to mean an attack on an individual batsman by one team: 'Ganguly took complete charge,
driving with the fluency of yore, shrugging off *bouncer*
wars by Vaas and Fernando.'

Bouncy castle: The kind of attraction set up to
encourage attendance at day–night games is now
occasionally evoked by journalists to describe a pitch
with *a lot in it* for the bowlers: 'Gallian became
Ambrose and Walsh's *puppet* on a Birmingham
bouncy castle of a wicket.' **Trampoline** is the more
established metaphor.

Boundary rider: *The Boundary Rider* is the title of a
stoic poem by the Australian poet Thomas Heney and
of a reflective song by the Australian band The Go-
Betweens. It is also the most modish term in cricket
for a *sweeper* or any man out *on the fence*: 'Dhoni was
at under a run a ball; two *dot balls* from Harmison
added to his *pressure*; he responded with a *forehand*
smash straight to the *boundary rider* at long-off.'

Bowlers back drive: 'The stroke of the day played
by Yuvraj was *copybook bowlers back drive* for a four.'
This *copybook* is Indian and depicts a shot which the
MCC Coaching Manual would call a *straight drive*
and which an Australian might describe as a hit *down*
the ground. A phrase associated particularly with
Sunil Gavaskar, although it is a matter of debate
whether the correctness of his straight driving
inspired or illustrated it (and whether he would be
happy with the fact that no apostrophe appears to be
required). A *bowlers back drive* always goes *back* in the
bowler's direction but does not always go past him, as
in this example of a *return catch* in the 1999 World

Cup final: 'Azhar left to a *bowlers back drive* which went straight to Moody.'

Bowl-out: A *bowl-out* is cricket's version of the penalty shoot-out, used to decide one-day knock-out games which have been *washed out*. The results of such *lotteries* whetted Dickie Bird's determination to give the ***benefit of the doubt***: 'Look at these *shoot-outs* they have in cup games. Nobody can hit t'bloody wicket. Yer see, it's all about ***angles***.'

Box: Perhaps confusingly, cricketers carry their kit in a *coffin* and protect their private parts by wearing a *box*. If a batsman is caught full on his danger area he is therefore *boxed*. After such an incident in a Test between England and Sri Lanka, Richie Benaud could be heard wincing when the pain-killing ***spray*** was eventually declined by Samarasekera: 'Very wise, Athula, that stuff stings enough on the wrist.' In earlier times, being *caught in the box* was painful only in the sense that *box* meant *gully*.

Boycott test: 'Put two wickets on the score and it doesn't look quite so clever.' A canny saying, borne out by ***collapses*** the world over. But when he was playing we fancy Geoffrey applied a different rule of thumb: 'If I get out, some other booger will score my runs.'

Bradmanesque: A term used 99.94 times out of a hundred when a batsman is in a statistically significant purple patch. It was brought out, for example, to keep up with the prowess of Andrew Strauss, 'whose form since arriving on the Test stage for England has been positively *Bradmanesque*'. Judging from reports once Strauss had *failed* a few times, the opposite of *Bradmanesque* seems to be *mortal*. Now that Kevin Pietersen is established in the England team, we are

on the lookout for the adjective *Jessopian* outside of
Sri Lanka.

Brakes: 'It took the classic pace/spin axis of Snow
and Underwood to *apply the brakes*'; 'Danish Kaneria
was the one bowler able to *put the brakes on.*' In cricket
it is always the bowlers who *put the brakes on*. The one
exception comes when a batsman is sent back by his
partner after starting on a run: 'Gatting sent Atherton
back and he *applied the brakes* too late.'

Breakthrough: The bowling side will be looking for
an *early breakthrough* at the start of their opponents'
innings. If a significant partnership *develops*, they will
be seeking an increasingly *vital breakthrough*, which
will be instantly acknowledged when the partnership
is *broken*: 'There's the *breakthrough*, Billy Bowden's
crooked digit is raised.' If nothing materialises, there
could still be an outside chance of help from an unexpected source: 'Umpire de Silva, who seemed to have
trouble with the law about balls pitching outside leg,
was the only man to look like making a *breakthrough*
all day.'

Break up: Conceivably applicable to great sides coming to the end of their period of supremacy or to
under-pressure captains coming to the end of their
tether, but used invariably to describe the process
whereby a dry wicket begins to crack and take spin.
Usually the deterioration is accelerated by very hot
conditions, although, in the famous example of Jim
Laker's match, the Old Trafford surface proved **helpful** enough without a broiling sun: 'The pitch, which
had shown signs of *breaking up* after only the first day
(leading some to level accusations that the pitch had
been *doctored* for spin, all denied, of course, by the
Lancashire authorities), was again drying out after
the three wet days.' Some surfaces are so *true* that they

are likely to play well throughout the game, whatever might be *read* into them: 'Hussain won the toss and bowled on a Gabba pitch likely to take longer than the Rolling Stones to *break up.*'

Breezy: 'A *breezy* 77 off 66 balls by James Hopes *set up* Queensland.' Not to be confused with *airy*, at least not until the batsman gets himself out.

Brighter cricket: Just as *running rugby* became the Holy Grail for administrators of the oval-ball game, so the MCC and ICC seemed to be forever tinkering with the regulations in search of the forbidden fruit they called *brighter cricket*. Back in 1936 there was nothing necessarily suspicious about the inverted commas when R. W. V. Robins proposed that the new lbw law would 'go a long way towards obtaining *"brighter" cricket*'. But post-war austerity encouraged so much discussion about what C. L. R. James called an 'absurd nostrum' that it became the dullest of clichés. It took Packer's *pyjama game* to fulfil the prophecy of a 1919 *Punch* cartoon which envisaged *Brighter Cricket* to be a matter of multicoloured clothing and painted grass.

Brute: Suggests *unplayable* in the phrase *brute of a ball* or variations thereon: 'Matthew Wood got a *brute of a bouncer* from a fired-up James Anderson.' The adjective *brutish* also applies to bowling, again typically as experienced from the batsman's end when it is nasty and short: 'Sutcliffe received the most *brutish* ball of the day.' Whereas *brutal*, like *savage*, is reserved for batting: 'Darren Stevens *battered* a *brutal* 51 in 30 balls.'

Bucket hands: A *safe pair of hands* – although fielders who experience a *run of the drops* can be said not to be able to catch the ball *with a bucket*, and can even get offered one by Bay 13 at the MCG. At what the local press describes as 'Evenwood Cricket Club's

annual encomium', the joke has been enshrined:
'John Maughan won both first team batting and bowling and also the *bucket award* for the most grotesquely
dropped catch.'

Bucolic: Another adjective which has seen long service to describe *lusty* hitting rather than **studious**
defence. *Wisden*'s reviewer of the 1888 Australian
tour worked up an approximation of rustic patois
even if his subject, Jack Worrall, had not lived up to
the **agricultural** model: 'Worrall is a batsman of the
rural or *bucolic* type. He must be a descendant of that
village wonder who hit "bloomin' 'ard, bloomin' 'igh,
and bloomin' often." But Worrall is degenerate. He
certainly hits hard and high – and seldom.'

Build an innings: One of the motivations for the
introduction of four-day cricket to the county game in
England, as Matthew Engel noted, was to address a
potential decline in this facet of the *art* of **batsmanship**: 'The orthodoxy of the moment is that players
have to be allowed to *build an innings* to Test-match
length.' In **Roses** matches before the war, if Cardus's
description of Holmes and Sutcliffe *getting set* is to be
believed, the sides would have batted for the points on
first innings even if ten days had been scheduled:
'They were like men *building* a stout wall brick by
brick – and on the whole they were as interesting to
look at.'

Bumper: Although the first *Oxford English
Dictionary* citation for what we now call a *bouncer* is
1855, we think the evolution of the word was a grad-
ual process. In late nineteenth-century journalese,
responsibility for the ball *bumping* was normally
attributed to uneven pitches: 'More heavy rain soaked
the wicket on Monday night, and when the Colonials
resumed their innings on the Tuesday morning the

ball *bumped very much.*' Terms evolved to describe a deliberate strategy of what would now be called *intimidatory bowling*: 'Several of Jessop's *bumped-down* deliveries were of almost unexampled short-ness.' Then the *bumper* became established. For example, it was used liberally in the **Bodyline** series by writers as well as bowlers: 'Larwood *bumped* very much.' But gradually the term *bouncer* became more popular, so that references to the *bumper* can nowa-days be self-conscious: 'There is a plague of fast bowlers in English cricket all of whom "love de *bumper*".' The **studious** batsman who wrote this prob-ably came in for suitable *treatment* from bowlers who read his published diary.

Bundle out: To dismiss a side with little ceremony and some haste: 'Worcestershire were *bundled out* for just 77 by South Africa A.'

Bunny: A personalised version of **rabbit**, but extended also to *recognised* batsmen who may have been *softened up* by previous experience of their par-ticular tormentor: 'Atherton is again proving to be McGrath's *bunny*'; 'Warne thought that he had dis-covered a new *bunny* in Strauss.'

Bunsen: Rhyming slang for a wicket which is a *turner*: 'On anything other than a *raging bunsen*, Tufnell is ineffective.' Crumbling wickets always seem to be described as *raging bunsens*, but when play actually starts the burner often seems to be set at a gentle yellow rather than a maximum-strength blue.

Business stroke: Neville Cardus was fond of quoting Wilfred Rhodes on the cut: 'But it were never a *busi-ness stroke.*' Michael Parkinson recorded another frag-ment of the great all-rounder's wisdom: 'Sweeping. That nivver was any sort of shot. Once I was listening to television and a cricketer was coaching youngsters how to sweep. I had to turn it off.' At this rate the schoolboys whom Rhodes coached at Harrow would have been struggling for any scoring strokes let alone *every shot in the book*. But behind these anecdotes lies the serious point that a batsman must weigh up whether a shot's productiveness is worth its dangers. This is a dilemma that has faced many a *hooker*, as well as those who cut and sweep. Andrew Flintoff has addressed such challenges of *shot selection* using modern management-speak: 'The *batters* have all got different strengths and one-day cricket is about *managing risk.*' Compare also *source of income*.

Butterfingers: More a Dickensian than a professional term – Mr Jingle uses it in *Pickwick Papers* to castigate the efforts of some of the fielders, along with *humbug* (no longer used in connection with spilt catches) and *muff* (still permissible in the verb form). *Butterfingers* now tends to be employed as a way of depicting a fielding side's collective inadequacy: 'An attack of *butterfingers* plagued England as Gilchrist had four escapes.'

Buy a wicket: A bowler who serves up some *juicy* balls for the batsman to hit, or a captain putting on a *change bowler* with some *inviting gaps* in the field, are both trying to *buy a wicket*. The precise circumstances will depend on the balance of the game, in which the bowling side might have runs to play with or else little honour to lose: 'Patel could afford to *buy wickets* with *generous flight*'; 'Warne was reduced to *lobbing* the ball into the air in a desperate attempt to *buy a wicket.*' But when the luck is against you, no bribe seems tempting enough for the batsman to take: 'And now a *Chinese cut*. Harmison just *can't buy a wicket* today.'

Buzzer: The trade expression for an *overthrow*, probably because this is the sort of noise to be expected from anything that goes flying past – especially if David Gower is at the controls.

C

Cafeteria bowling: 'England served up *cafeteria bowling* and Smith *bypassed all civilities* by *helping himself* from the very start.' A common term exported from the county circuit for an attack which provides a copious **diet** of *four-balls* for the batsmen to *feast on*. According to Phil Tufnell, who presumably found himself last in the queue, 'It was always better to get in front of Gatt if this type of bowling was *on the menu.*'

Calypso: While there is a proud line of Caribbean wordsmiths who pen *calypsos* to commemorate great victories, like the one at Lord's in 1950, the term *calypso cricket* has sometimes proved rather patronising, suggesting that West Indian cricketers tend to play their **natural game** with a carefree *looseness* that is wonderfully vibrant but not necessarily pragmatic. In the years of their hegemony, Clive Lloyd's team suddenly became *ruthless*. The recent decline in fortunes has suggested more overtly sarcastic commentary: 'It may not be crunch time yet in their Test series struggles but the West Indies, dubbed the *Calypso Collapso Kings*, must be able to feel the jaws of defeat closing tightly.'

Camel: 'It is hard to believe now but those were the days you hid the *team camel* at backward point.' Poor fielders are probably saddled with this name for their ungainliness, although some have been known to get the hump with sarcastic comments made from the slips. Bob Willis, who obviously believes in building up young English players, transferred his similes to summarise Kabir Ali's performance in a one-day international: 'He's bowled like a *camel* and fielded like a *drain*.'

Cameo: This word can catch the eye, especially if it refers to a miniature *gem* of an innings from a major batsman: 'Tendulkar himself warmed up for the Pakistan challenge with an accomplished little *cameo* in the *sylvan* settings of the Bagh-e-Jinnah.'

Candidate: Can specifically single out a *candidate* for a *pair*, but used more these days to refer to a batsman likely to suffer a particular mode of dismissal, especially if he **shuffles** across: 'Vaas bowled **wicket to wicket** not giving anything away and the slightest attempt by the West Indies batsmen to play **across the line** made them a *prime candidate* for an lbw decision.'

Cane: One image conjured by this verb for **hard-hitting** is of a group of wayward bowlers queuing up outside the headmaster's study to take their punishment: 'With the exception of Mohammad Asif, the rest of the Pakistani attack has been *caned* by Indian batsmen ruthless against any waywardness in **line and length**.' *Cane* belongs to a series of verbs including *flay*, *flog*, *lash* and *spank*. In the Caribbean, the colloquial term for a *slogger* has different social overtones: 'Dhoni is just a *cane-cutter*, wait and watch him flop outside the subcontinent.' The term is pejorative but complex, alluding to the **agricultural** hacking motions the player may make with his bat but also to the devil-may-care attitude often associated with such downtrodden workers.

Can't bat, can't bowl, can't field: The disparaging moniker attached to a player or team, especially if they are on tour: 'The England team started slowly against the state sides – *"can't bat, can't bowl"*, it was one of those.' Phillip DeFreitas, here remembering the early stages of the ultimately victorious tour to Australia in 1986–87, was probably a good enough fielder to forget the fact that home journalists had happily appropriated Martin Johnson's assessment of the visitors in full. Johnson later concluded that it had been the right quote about the wrong team.

Captaincy material: Because the captain of a cricket team takes more game-changing decisions than the captain in any other team sport, lovers of the game are always on the lookout for potential candidates: 'A chance remark from new coach Chappell (he will eventually learn to keep his lips sealed) that Virender Sehwag is *captaincy material* has the opening batsman having to fend off questions galore on his ambitions.' In England, where it has been traditional to pick the captain for his leadership qualities first and his worth to the team as a player second, *captaincy material* could often be translated as 'officer material'. Such social niceties may have inspired a Lancashire player to daub the initials FEC on Michael Atherton's locker, a famously colourful reference to Atherton's grammar-school education rather than a prediction that he would be *Future England Captain*.

Captain's innings: Tends to be employed by journalists with a mixture of self-consciousness and hyperbole: 'The phrase *"captain's innings"* is an often-used cliché but rarely can the leader of a team have done so much for his side as Ponting with his 156'; 'Gooch's match-winning 100 against the West Indies at Headingley was the ultimate *captain's knock*.'

Caress: A word reserved for shots that are very well timed rather than hit with brute force: 'While Mark Waugh dominated bowlers and was easily Australia's *longest* six hitter of his period, he always looked as though he had just *caressed* the ball to send it into the wide blue yonder.'

Car keys test: At Test-match level, before groundsmen stopped them doing it, Tony Greig and those great Yorkshire pitch-readers Boycott and Illingworth would stick their *car keys* (but never apparently their house keys) into the pitch to give an indication of how hard the surface was. A similar technique, the *Barrington knife*, was employed by another England stalwart. In club and village cricket, the *car keys test* can be an excuse for players to remind their teammates that they are driving a flash motor.

Carpet: As a verb can mean *drop*, although **grass** is preferred; as a noun, a rather mannered reference to the outfield, especially when stressing the importance of keeping the ball down: 'Despite his **bottom-handed** grip, the ball always seemed to **race away** on the *carpet.*' Harold Larwood's **approach** to the crease was so smooth he was described as *carpet-slippered*.

Carried his bat: 'Mike Hussey *carried his bat* to make a masterful 144.' This classic expression for batting all the way through the innings undefeated recalls the fact that in early forms of the game the heavy bat was left leaning on the stumps by each departing batsman. Originally, to *carry your bat* meant simply to be not out at the end of the innings, but the usage evolved to refer specifically to openers. An example from 1891 shows this nuance to be established and may make the origins a little clearer: 'On the third morning the Australian innings closed for 176, Barrett, who had gone in first, *taking out his bat* for 67.' It is still possible to see constructions such as 'Asanka Gurusinha *carried his bat out* for a defiant half-century.'

Carry: There are three different contexts in which a ball *carrying* on the full is important: first, when it *carries* to a fielder off the bat (often a matter of some dispute); second, when it *carries through* to the keeper (how *good* the *carry* is gives an indication of the pace of the bowler or pitch); third, when it *carries* the rope and goes for a *max*.

Carted: 'Sussex last night defended their decision to put Glamorgan into bat after home openers Steve James and Matthew Elliott *carted* them all over Colwyn Bay.' As many county pros enjoy a flutter, the fact that a headstrong horse *carts* a jockey to post may come into play for bowlers who find they can exert no *control* whatsoever. But the *rubbish cart* probably provides the main connotation.

Cartwheel: The requisite verb to describe Derek Randall's **Ashes** celebrations, or the more common occurrence of a stump sent spinning spectacularly out of the ground: 'Lee sent Strauss's off stump *cartwheeling* with a clever change of pace.'

Carve: This has become the characteristic term for an attacking stroke hit **uppishly** on the off side: 'Paul Hoffman *carved* a winning six over extra cover'; 'Warne often *stepped away* to *carve* the quicker bowlers over point or third man.' The verb indicates a thicker contact than the more involuntary *slice*, although the effect can be much the same: 'Simon Jones *carved* a catch to third man.' But there is a less shot-specific Australian colloquialism where there is no doubt that the bowler has been cut to shreds: 'Harvey's "*carving*" of Tayfield is something that lives in the memory.'

Castle: An Englishman's stumps were traditionally his *castle*. The term has become more or less archaic as a noun, but there is a notable example from the annals, when Bradman once failed to survive a single delivery: 'The great man had his *castle* **knocked** *over* by Bill Bowes for a *golden* **duck**.' The usage has been carried on, though, by the participle *castled*, which offers a more dramatic alternative to *bowled*: 'Yousuf Youhana went first ball, *castled* by an **impeccable** swinging yorker.' An Australian's *castle* can also be his *house*, which is hardly likely to be *castled* but has a fair chance of being *knocked down*.

Catches win matches: One of the oldest axioms in the book, on a par with 'If you're going to *flash*, *flash* hard' or 'Never run on a misfield.' During a game, it usually comes out once the ball has: '*Catches win matches* and if Shane Warne had caught Kevin Pietersen early in his innings England would almost certainly have lost this Test match.' Judging by the following remark from Douglas Jardine, writing in 1957, the maxim was not always expressed so pithily: 'Don't drop a catch and you won't lose the match is an old and tried adage.'

Catch swallows: Roger Harper was a brilliant enough fielder to make even the most difficult catch look easy: 'The Harpoon could *catch swallows* in the slips and was a *gazelle* in the infield.' In phrases praising the *sure* **slipper** the *swallow* can be replaced by the *pigeon* or a variety of other birds. Or *bullets*. Or *hand grenades*. Whereas out in the **country** you might *pick cherries*.

Catch the captain's eye: When a **walking wicket** comes to the crease, ostentatious *loosening-up* exercises may be observed from any of the fielders who can bowl. But whenever Viv Richards was *going* *berserk* in front of his home crowd, nobody on the fielding side tried at all hard to *catch the captain's eye*.

Cavalier: Sometimes the **dashing** approach to **bats-manship** can be taken just a little too far, and in such circumstances it is no surprise to find Sir Leonard Hutton on the side of the roundheads: 'I was very surprised to see Graeme Hole in the first over of the first Test attempt to drive Bedser in the most *cavalier* of fashions. He was bowled.'

Centurion: Perhaps the use of this term for a *century-maker* originally reflected the grounding in Roman history enjoyed by some early writers about the game, but it marches on to describe those who have reached the *milestone* of three figures: 'Queensland were all out for 470 with yesterday's day two *centurions*, Martin Love and Brendan Nash, the backbone to the huge first innings total.' The word is almost mandatory in a statistical setting for multi-hundreds: 'Sehwag was the seventeenth *triple-centurion* in Test cricket.'

Chance: There is an invariable locution – with a little buried double meaning – when a difficult catch is dropped: 'You have to say that *goes down* as a *chance*.' Sometimes, if the ball is really *travelling*, it only *goes down* as a *half-chance*. The description of hundreds as *chanceless* reflects the aesthetics of **batsmanship**, in that **masters** of the **art** are expected to be in total control: 'Sheppard *stroked* a *chanceless* 113.' However, some strokemakers do *give* the bowlers a *chance*, not just in the sense of offering them a *return catch*. Either there is too much adrenalin pumping before they have played themselves in – 'Lara is habitually a *chancer* in his early overs' – or they will always look to be playing shots: 'Tresco *takes the game away* very fast but always *gives* you a *chance*.'

Change bowler: Rather like *utility player* in football, this is not always a particularly complimentary title – especially, it seems, when the adjective *useful* is added: 'McGrath looked just a *useful first change bowler* today.' Sometimes players will have to accept that they must drop a division or two: 'Allan Donald has diminished since entering world cricket in 1992 labelled as "White Lightning". But his control and *late* swing has produced results as a *change bowler*.'

Chappati: The unleavened bread provides a ready metaphor for a *flat* pitch: 'If the light holds for the rest of the game, statisticians could have a tough time keeping up with the run flood on a *chappati-flat* pitch.' There is a similar figure from a different cuisine: 'A *pancake* of a pitch, and an eye-popping assortment of batting onslaughts.'

Charge: 'Bell was stumped *charging* Claude Henderson.' This means *coming down the wicket* to attack the slow bowler, but in terms of *elegance* and safety it compares unfavourably with *dancing*. *Charges* can range from the fairly half-hearted to the well-nigh suicidal, but any report from the field typically has a *victim* to identify: 'Gambhir was caught at mid-on after a casual *charge* at Danish Kaneria'; 'Chris Lewis *gave* May *the charge* and was stumped by yards.' Meanwhile, the *mock charge* is an attempt to fool the spinner into dropping short.

Chase: Batsmen do this to two things in cricket: *wide ones* – 'Prior, *chasing hard* outside off stump, *snicked* to Read' – and *totals*. The concept of the *run chase* has long been established, but the modern idiom, whether inspired by cycling, tennis, hunting or policing, has teams *chasing down* any victory target: 'Waking up to find South Africa had actually *chased down* the total was almost as shell-shocking an experience as waking to find Australia beaten by Bangladesh last year.' Meanwhile, fielders are more usually described as *giving chase* rather than 'chasing the ball'; that phrase is reserved for a metaphor equivalent to shutting the door once the horse has bolted: 'As captain he could dither over field placings, *chasing the ball* and trying to plug gaps in the field.'

Chassé: 'Napier *chasséd* down the wicket to Darren Bicknell and got enough elevation on the ball to *chip* it over the midwicket boundary rope.' The most *elegant* way to **dance** down the track, sometimes attracting the technical observation that the batsman's gliding back foot is the *leading foot*. Geoffrey Boycott uses the word in his written prose, although we doubt whether he will take a winter off to appear on *Strictly Come Dancing*.

Cherry: Popular in Indian-English for the ball, especially when it is *ripe* or *new*: 'Picture a tall, well built man with war paint on his face charging in to hurl the $5\frac{1}{2}$ ounces of the *red cherry*.' Mike Brearley manages to re-motivate the usage when he recommends that a captain should try to take the new ball with half an hour to go 'so that his **quickies** will have two *bites* at the *new cherry*'. In Australian slang, *cherries* can also be the red marks the ball leaves on the face of the bat.

Chinaman: 'Fancy being **done** by a bloody *Chinaman*.' According to the legend, Walter Robins said this walking back to the Old Trafford pavilion after being bowled by the Trinidadian Ellis Achong. Robins would have been referring to the ethnic origin of the left-arm spinner, but the word *Chinaman* became the standard way to describe the ball he got, bowled *over the wrist* so that it spun into the right-hand batsman rather than turning away in the *orthodox* manner. See **Fleetwood-Smith stuff** for further technical discussion. In light of the song by Jamaican-born Carl Douglas, cricket journalists seem to have resisted any temptation to refer to 'funky *Chinamen* from funky Chinatown', although the following piece of internet commentary from Rob Smyth does make the cricket sound like kung-fu fighting: 'Giles just about manages to *squeeze out* a ***reverse**-swinger* from Lee before it does some *Shaolin* on his off stump.'

Chinese cut: One of the ways of cursing a shot intended to pierce the off-side field but inside-edged without hitting the stumps down to fine leg. The outrageous fortune involved can often be demonised as the cunning of an enemy. Hence, in Worcestershire, the shot is known as the *Staffordshire cut*. In Yorkshire, it is the *Lancashire cut*. In Middlesex, it is the *Surrey cut*. In Australia, perhaps thanks to Imperial propaganda, it is the *French cut*. At Eton, it is the *Harrow drive*. Victor Trumper was such a genius he could play a stroke down to fine leg on purpose by cocking his back leg, in which case it was described as a *dog shot*. A case of taking the piss.

Chin music: Music which a batsman will expect to *face* once there is a suspicion that he does not like the ball *whistling* past his helmet strap: 'Unless Sehwag dramatically improves against the short ball, I expect all teams to play *"chin music"* to him in Tests.' The phrase probably came to the West Indies via baseball (the expression *sweet chin music* is also used for a drop kick in American wrestling). It now tends to be used with a degree of playfulness, although it is hard to judge the intended effect of this dispatch from the Kensington Oval: 'On a famous ground with grandstands and ends named respectively for such pace luminaries as Hall, Griffiths, Marshall and Garner, the Gods of the Bouncer and the ***Sandshoe Crusher*** and the Celestial Choir of Caribbean *Chin Music* must have wept to see a centre square so bereft of life.'

Chirp: *Sledging* has become known as *chirping* via South Africa, where the cicada obviously flourishes alongside the cricket: 'Chris Taylor was subjected to plenty of *chirp* during his innings of 176.' The next entry should throw more light on this last example.

Chisel out: The expression required when a batsman or a team is made to *work hard* for *every run*: 'Rahul Dravid *chiselled out* his first century as captain'; 'The West Indies *chiselled out* a further 126 runs from their final five wickets.' The following description of a pur-gatorial innings makes slow sculpture sound like slow torture: 'Chris Taylor took restraint to a devout level as he spent 207 minutes and 173 balls in *chiselling out* 66.'

Chop: Around the turn of the twentieth century, *chop* was being used to distinguish a shot played down-wards backward of square from a full-blooded cross-batted shot: 'George Parr and W. G. Grace made the cut safe by hitting it onto the ground – by *chopping* it; but that is quite a different stroke from the old-fash-ioned cut.' However, the shot still had attendant dan-gers, as we can see in this example from the Edgbaston Test of 1902: 'Jackson ended a beautiful innings by *chopping* a ball from Jones *on* to his wicket, and again England were in a bad way.' It is this usage, synonymous with *played on*, which is prevalent today.

Chorus: 'Carl Gazzard and Andrew Caddick held firm against a regular *chorus* of appeals.' But the degree of orchestration involved may reach *intimida-tory* proportions: 'India, with Kiran More conducting the *choir* as usual, appealed for a catch off the spin-ners almost every ball.' In this case, so we are told,

'umpire Liebenberg finally *succumbed*'. No doubt the
chorus went up *in **unison***.

Chucker: 'If you ask me, that Ghavri is a *chucker*.'
The trade term for a bowler with a *suspect **action***,
often accompanied by an assonant swear word in on-
pitch ***sledging*** or off-mike commentary. Suggestions
of *throwing* can encourage descriptions of a bowler's
action worthy of a nomination. In Jimmy Burke, Ian
Peebles could see 'the chopping *bent-arm* motion of a
constable laying his truncheon on a very short
offender's head'. And those bowlers who come under
scrutiny can be subjected to some fairly cruel
humour, like being no-balled by the entire ***Barmy
Army***. Doug Insole produced a more deadpan effort,
after being defeated in a trial match by Tony Lock's
thunderbolt, when he came back to the pavilion and
asked: 'Was I bowled or run out?'

Circle: Before changes to the regulations of one-day
cricket, any references to *The Circle* would involve the
occasional Sunday League game played by Yorkshire
in Hull. Now it means the area within which a minimum number of fielders must remain as the ball is
delivered: 'The presence of Yuvraj Singh, Mohammad
Kaif and Suresh Raina *in the circle* has created ***pressure*** on the opposition, resulting in run-outs.'
Twenty20, despite not being a format to encourage
the ***wizards*** of spin, even has an *inner circle*.

Classical: We hear speak of a *classic **action*** or a *classic
stroke* when these are of a high order, whereas the half-
twin term *classical* attaches itself more particularly to
the stricter orthodox precepts of ***batsmanship***. Rahul
Bhattacharya has given a classic portrait of a modern
batsman who sets out to uphold the *classical tradition*.
This is V. V. S. Laxman, in thrall to the commandment
'Thou shalt play in the ***V***' and having to will himself to

slog with five overs to go in a one-dayer: 'These were *slogs* of compulsion. They were not VVS.'

Clatter: The recognised sound of the wickets going down, whether in rapid or steady succession: 'The fall of Robinson triggered a *clatter* of wickets'; 'The tempo of Vaughan's innings had been largely dictated by the regular *clatter* of wickets at the other end.' Rapidity is of the essence when it comes to the emerging use of the same word as a verb: 'Pakistan *clattered* an astonishing 353 runs from 58.3 overs.' But only minimal experience is required to sort out the following headline: 'Caddick the catalyst for *quick clatter*.'

Clean: 'You will never see a better example of good *clean hitting* than that.' In this context *clean* means right *out of the **middle***, without any hint of mistiming. The other context in cricket comes when a batsman is *clean bowled* without the ball touching anything else on the way through. Usually worthy of note as in these instances the **batter** has been comprehensively beaten: 'Dravid was *cleaned* by Sami as soon as the ball had been replaced by a drier one.'

Clear the ropes: Periphrastic but quite routine way of saying a batsman has hit a six. Sometimes, though, there can be a hint of suspense: 'Beaten by Ray Price in the air, Lara went through his shot one-handed and the ball just *cleared the ropes*.'

Climb: A verb to describe the trajectory of the ball when a bowler **extracts** extra bounce from the wicket. Sometimes a synonym for **get big** when the hook shot is attempted: 'Kumar Sangakkara hooked one that *climbed on him*, and top-edged to Kaneria at fine leg.' There is also a phrasal verb for very uninhibited batting, included in the following advice given by Matthew Hayden to the specialist **chirper** Andre Nel:

'I wouldn't take a chance and wind up Gilly. He could just get really cross and *climb into* your bowling.'

Clinker: Australian for something *first-rate*, apparently derived from the fact that a *clinker* was the most desirable marble a boy could have, and sometimes seen in cricket reporting: 'The grand final against Baimbridge was a *clinker* with Monivae requiring 18 off the last over and getting them with a ball to spare.' The opposite of a *fizzer*.

Closure: 'At 729 for six wickets, Woodfull *applied the closure*.' As naturally as he would refer to *extras* as *sundries*, Don Bradman uses the Australian for '*declared* the innings closed'. At least in this example, perhaps because the match he was writing about took place at **Headquarters**, he was polite enough not to write the score as 6 for 729.

Cloud cover: Notable in cricket because the ball will probably *do a bit*, especially at grounds traditionally favourable to swing bowling, like Headingley. In the following example the **conditions** are characteristically **two-toned**: 'There was a bit of *green* in the wicket early on and some *cloud cover*, so it was a good toss for Bangladesh A to win.'

Club: Another verb to characterise a *hard-hitting* performance and regarded, it would seem, as more applicable to a shorter innings than a *bludgeon*: 'Gough *clubbed* 51 off 38 balls with two sixes and seven fours'; 'Justin Kemp *clubbed* the ball to *most parts* in his 44-ball *cameo*.'

Coat of varnish: Proverbial unit of measure for the miniscule distance by which a good ball can miss the stumps, although the idiom can be reworked when a batsman only just fails to get any *wood* on it:

'Gunaratne evaded the hat-trick by the extra *coat of varnish* not on his bat, as Lee's next ball – a big swinging yorker – missed the outside *edge* by that margin.'

Collapse: Tradition has it that if the word *collapse* is preceded by the word *English*, then *English* is preceded in turn by the word *another*. In the 2001 **Ashes** series, English journalists were prepared for the worst: 'Ian Ward's downfall, sadly, predictably, initiated the onset of *another England collapse* – they lost their last seven wickets for 22 runs.' Eighty years earlier, even *Wisden*'s correspondent could not altogether hide his depression when England threw away a promising position of 140 for 3 at Sydney: 'So *dismally* did the batting *collapse* that the innings was all over for 190.' However, England are not the only side prone to *collapses* (see **calypso**) as it is an immutable canon of cricket that batsmen are most vulnerable when they first come to the crease. Therefore, it seems, **one** sometimes as easily **brings** six or seven as **two**.

Come off: 'In Kolkata, Afridi *came off* spectacularly in the second innings and had India on the mat before he *gave it away*.' This does not mean that Shahid Afridi had appealed against the light and left the pitch doing handstands or ended a bowling spell by wearing his sweater over his head, but that his approach of *going for* his shots had succeeded. The players can also *come off* for rain or bad light, but this always sounds much less exhilarating.

Come on: 'The ball did not properly *come on* to the bat, as is often the case in one-day cricket at the Rose Bowl.' This is not the sort of wicket on which batsmen can quickly get into their stride and bat *fluently*.

Come out of the hand: 'My first over was a bit **loose** but I've been working on a new run-up and the ball is *coming out of the hand* pretty well.' This may sound like a bowler on a course of drastic remedial action after a case of the *yips*, but in fact it is Glenn McGrath using a common formula to confirm that he is bowling in a good rhythm. How the ball *comes out* when a spinner is bowling can be a more technical matter, both for the batsman trying to **read** him *from the hand* and for the bowler (in this case Harbhajan Singh) striving to perfect his **variations**: 'The "**doosra**" is not *coming out of the hand* properly and there are small things missing.' But even when the ball is *coming out* perfectly, it can be treated as imperfect if there is a **master** batsman at the other end. Doug Wright felt the best over he ever bowled was against the Don at Lord's: 'Every ball *came out of my hand* the way I wanted and pitched where I wanted. I beat him twice. It went for 16.'

Compile: 'Ed Joyce *compiled* 82 in nearly four hours.' This constitutes slow batting but is a relatively neutral use of a verb which is less technical than **accumulate**, less aspirational than *amass* and not quite so basic as *score*. It took Neville Cardus to bring out, or perhaps even to create, a nuance for the word: 'Barnes in an hour could discover three solitary runs; in seventy minutes he *compiled* (*compiled* surely is good!) eight.' Barnes (this time the writer Simon rather than the Lancashire batsman John) used the same verb very deliberately to emphasise how Flintoff **built an innings** in the 2005 Trent Bridge Test: 'He *compiled* – rather than **swatted** or **biffed** or **bludgeoned** – a century of murderous purpose.'

Compulsive: In cricket, as in crochet, this adjective goes with **hooker**: 'When he began his career, Waugh was a *compulsive hooker* – with a motor mouth.'

Concentrate on his batting: 'Badani, who stepped down from captaincy ahead of this tie citing the need to *concentrate on his batting*, played a fabulous hand in Tamil Nadu's revival.' The age-old reason put forward by batsmen to explain their decision to resign the captaincy. Like football managers promising to *concentrate on the league* after being knocked out of the cup, it is not normally possible to believe the players in question had any choice in the matter.

Concrete: Hard, *grassless* wickets can look or behave like *concrete*, but a *concrete delivery* during *net* **practice** is not metaphorical, in that it is *banged* in so short it does not come off the mat: 'Stupidly, while batting in the indoor **nets**, I got too far inside the line and got **sconed** by a *concrete ball*.' *Concrete shot* is a David Lloydism for a boundary hit into the road off the opening bowlers on the basis that 'nothing buggers up t'ball like *concrete*'. This was in the days before **reverse**.

Conditions: Just as pitches have **typical** characteristics, so the *conditions* in a particular part of the world need to be taken into account. Archetypally, English *conditions* favour seam and require batsmen to get on the front foot; in Australia, South Africa and the West Indies *conditions* tend to be *hard wicket*, favouring fast bowling, leg spin and batsmen with a good *eye*; in the subcontinent, dry **dustbowls** with little life in them are the order of the day; on New Zealand's South Island, it tends to be raining. There are many exceptions to these rules but, wherever you are, *exploiting* – or at least *coping with* – the *conditions* is recommended. It also helps to select players with the relevant CV: 'The belief that Gower's left-handedness and skill against the turning ball would be invaluable in the *conditions* peculiar to India had nothing to do with hindsight.'

Confectionery stall: 'Don't bother looking for that, let alone chasing it. It's gone straight into the *confec-*

tionery stall and out again.' Richie Benaud's memorable commentary on a Botham six at Headingley in 1981 is characteristic in that Benaud did keep his eyes on the ball as it *disappeared*. But pointing out where a big hit ends up has long been a trope of cricket reporting. Here is a *Wisden* correspondent in 1891 looking back on a game between Yorks Colts and Notts Colts: 'Tunnicliffe thought the only chance of getting runs on such a pitch was to *have a dash* and he did, sending Bagguley twice in succession into the *little refreshment stand* at the left-hand side of the Pavilion.' Hence the journalese for a big six used to be a *booth ball*.

Conker: Synonym for *ball*, especially when fresh from its casing: 'He always seems to find a *yard* or two *of* extra *pace* with the new *conker* in his hand.'

Constant pounding: What bowlers have to suffer, less from *hard-hitting* batsmen than rock-hard wickets, as Danny Morrison will attest: 'Fast bowling is not a natural function. My lower back and pelvis in particular took the brunt of the *constant pounding* over my career.' A reason many *quickies* give for retirement, so it would obviously lessen the effect to complain of 'intermittent pounding', even if it would be closer to the truth.

Contain: 'I always thought that the best way to *contain* a batsman was to get him back in the pavilion.' This is Alec Bedser reviewing the kind of bowling tactics encouraged by one-day cricket. But the balance between runs and wickets will still need due consideration in longer versions of the game, so that Steve Harmison was right to anticipate some long-haul work on England's 2005 tour of Pakistan: 'If the wickets are *flat* and don't *offer* much bounce, I'll have to fall in line and do a *container job*.'

Conversion rate: Potentially confusing if applied to the Reverend David Sheppard, but the term simply means the number of times a batsman reaching fifty *goes on* to three figures: 'For once Fleming's Test *conversion rate* – past fifty four times, past a hundred twice – kept the critics off his back.'

Coolie creeper: 'I would like to reiterate that the term *"coolie creeper"* in my cricketing terminology means a ball keeping low.' This is an excerpt from Brian McMillan's official apology after he had used this politically incorrect synonym for *daisy-cutter* during a provincial match in 1999. His initial reaction was rather less contrite: 'Does that mean changing a *"Chinaman"*? Some people might take offence at that. I think it's a lot of crap personally.' The whole incident became an interesting test case for the role of language in post-apartheid South Africa, provoking irate leader articles and academic papers. The views of the batsman facing at the time, KwaZulu Natal's Ashraf Mall, do not seem to have been recorded for posterity.

Cordon: A defensive-sounding word for attacking fielders. If the *cordon* of close-catchers numbers six or more it tends to become an *umbrella*, and if it expects to be *in business*, it can be called *Death Row*. There are other variants for ultra-attacking placements, such as an *atom-bomb* field (when there is a mushroom of players behind either side of the wicket) or a *Carmody* field (named after the 1950s captain of Western Australia who liked to *put it up* the batsman). Outfielders are to be found in *rings*, not *cordons*.

Corridor of uncertainty: A phrase ascribed to Terry Alderman and popularised by Geoff Boycott for the *area* just outside off stump where the batsman is not sure whether to play or *leave*: 'Bowling patient *prob-*

ing medium pace in the "*corridor of uncertainty*" combined with a well disguised off-cutter helped "Clem"
claim 19 lbw wickets.' These days everybody is certain where the *corridor* is, even if the full wording is
dropped: 'The transformation of Shaun Pollock from
a *head-hunting* tearaway to a 125 kmh *corridor bowler*
is about more than age: it is a recognition of what it
takes to endure in modern cricket.' Indeed, 'good *corridor*' is now an accepted way of encouraging a bowler
from behind the wicket.

Country: A fielder posted *out in the country* is fielding
in the ***deep***. While the expression may be especially
apt on a big playing area when the groundsman's
mower has broken down, the idea is probably
imported from horse racing, where the *country* is the
section of the course furthest away from the stands.
In Australian cricket, *country* is less likely to be a reference to the outfield than the outback: 'McCabe was
first chosen for New South Wales in 1928 as a *country
cricketer* – a rather unusual honour.' In other words,
McCabe was playing out in the sticks, rather than
grade cricket in Sydney, when first selected for the
state.

Cow corner: 'Ganguly made a tinker with the field,
sensibly calling up fine leg into the ***circle*** to install
extra protection at *cow corner*.' The place on the field,
somewhere between deep mid-wicket and long-on,
where ***agricultural*** shots are traditionally deposited.
The *corner* is not required for the phrase to be understood, especially if a spinner is getting ***carted***: 'Skip, I
need a man at *cow*.'

Crackerjack: Australian slang for something excep-
tionally good, deployed in cricket for ***grenades*** with
the ball or pyrotechnics with the bat: 'The thing about
Warney is that every single ball is a potential *cracker-*

jack'; 'Slater's *crackerjack innings* followed McGrath's six for 85.' Incomprehensible to Englishmen who can remember Peter Glaze and The Krankies.

Cream: Verb used to indicate very good timing from the batsman and high levels of enthusiasm from the commentator. The emphasis can either be on strength or style: 'From then on, anything short was given a *meaty biff*, anything full *creamed* with dazzling power'; 'The right-hander's 133 at Cazaly's Stadium yesterday was decorated with 19 fours, most of which were *creamed elegantly* through the off side.'

Creasebound: For those raised on the *classical* precepts of *coming out* to the spinners, a batsman whose tendency is to be *creasebound* or *crease-ridden* for fear of being stumped may as well stay in bed: 'Against the spin of Harbhajan and Kumble, Sarwan was completely *creasebound* and time and again tried to use his pads as a *first line of defence*.' Nowadays, the term is used as frequently of batsmen who *shuffle* across their stumps to seam bowling: 'Wasim Khan was left *creasebound* when Cousins got the ball to move into him.'

Crouch: Batsmen can *crouch* in their stance – Jessop was the archetypal *croucher* – but this is what close fielders are required to do as the bowler comes in to bowl. Neville Cardus studied their appearance with consummate attention: 'Three slips *crouched* on the batsman's doorstep holding out supplicatory hands.' Oscar Wilde's unique observation on cricket was no less studied: 'It requires one to assume such indecent postures.'

Crowd catch: A *bump ball* which the crowd believes – or wants to believe – is a legitimate catch: 'Full, driven into the pitch and Bharadwaj takes the *crowd* *"catch"* languidly.' In the days of Twenty20, when suitable rewards are on offer, a *crowd catch* can mean one actually taken, rather than just imagined, by a spectator.

Crowd the bat: 'Harbhajan was on a hat-trick, and as many as six Indians *crowded the bat.*' What the fielders are doing in this situation is crowding the batsman and trying to exert *pressure*, but the phrasing recognises that what they are most *interested* in is an *edge*.

Crust: To *crust* a batsman is to hit him on the head: 'Invited to an England *net* in Melbourne, Agnew promptly *crusted* the captain, Mike Brearley.' A *crust* can also form on the *top* of a drying, and therefore difficult, wicket: 'Australia lost their last five wickets on a surface that had been alternately *soaked* and *baked*, and which finally became as *crusty* as an Australian captain.' Compare *scone* for another leftover from the picnic hamper redeployed for figurative purposes.

Curator: Australian for *groundsman* – now apparently used everywhere but the mother country – which somehow makes him sound more meticulous than his English brethren.

Curly: In the late nineteenth century, as swing and swerve in the air were being developed by bowlers, this was one of the common terms used as writers about the game developed their vocabulary: 'Trott says that in bowling his *curly* ball he owes much to the practice he obtained as a pitcher at baseball'; 'Buttress, who was famous for *curly* ones from leg, used to get Parr's wicket.' It is still possible to talk of a ball *curling* in or out, but very unusual to make more generic references to 'curl' or 'curlers', terms which have been superseded by *loop* and *drift*.

Curtain rail: Trade term for the method of a **tailen- der** who aspires to do nothing more than push forward along the same line to every ball: 'Geoffrey Boycott was the first batsman to be *stranded* on 99, against Australia in Perth in 1979–80, when Bob Willis's infamous *curtain-rail* defensive technique failed to hold out long enough.'

Cut in half: 'One ball kicked off length, one **darted** away like a shy kid in the presence of strangers, another **zipped** back in and darned near *cut* the batsman *in half*.' In this boisterous piece of prose, Prem Panicker takes the precaution of confirming that the final ball in the sequence from Wasim Akram did not literally remove Marcus Trescothick's torso from his legs. He is in fact using the standard formula for instances where the degree of *lateral movement* is such that the top half of the batsman's body collapses as the ball **jags** back *through* him (more, in fact, as if he has been punched in the stomach than chopped off at the hip). The following report on a morning's play where it was **doing a bit** at Mohali gives a sense of the undignified positions the batsman can get into in these circumstances: 'Any seaming ball could *cut* the batsman *in half* rendering even an adroit handler of the **willow** into an inelegant waver of a piece of wood.'

Cut strip: *Strip* is one of the many synonyms for *pitch*, but more specific references to the *cut strip* distinguish the actual wicket being played on from the rest of the square, almost always when bowlers are having such trouble with their **radar** that they are struggling to land on it: 'When we finally got to play on grass and off 22 yards, few of them could hit the *cut strip*.' There is therefore often a sense of farce when the *cut strip* is referred to, as in this passage where Derek Pringle describes England's travails in a Melbourne Test: 'Butcher bowled several wides that

barely hit the *cut strip*, while Dawson tried to get
Langer out sweeping to a field more suited to the
beach cricket being played three miles down the road
in St Kilda.'

Cutter: As with the wind, it is the direction from
which the ball comes as it moves off the pitch that
determines whether it is an *off-cutter* or a *leg-cutter*.
In the batting department there are usually players
around who are characteristically good *cutters*, and
often good *pullers* as well. Proficiency in these shots
often seems to be inversely proportional to the batsman's stature: 'John Keeler wasn't the height of two
pennorth of copper, but like a lot of little men he was
a very good *cutter* and *puller*.'

D

Dab: 'The play of Hallows and Makepeace was
mainly interesting for the number of runs scored
through the slips by *late* cuts (or rather "*dabs*" – they
don't cut nowadays).' Reporting on a **Roses** match in
1926, Neville Cardus may be observing the northern
convention that the cut is not a **business stroke**, or
charting the development of an important new **source
of income**. Generations later, one-day cricket has
made the *dab* or *steer* a highly conventional way of
keeping the score ticking over. However, even experienced **accumulators** can *open the face* too much and
angle the bat too little when looking to *lean on* the
ball for a single: 'Damien Martyn attempted to *dab* to
third man, only to become Collingwood's fourth **victim**.' In these situations, the *dab* outside off stump
may be hard to distinguish from a *dabble*.

Daisy-cutter: Originally a description of the action of a racehorse not a bowler, the term is used in cricket for a ball which hardly gets off the ground. Before over-arm bowling became universal, it was a legitimate tactic, even if some found the bowling metaphorically as well as literally *underhand*: 'A *daisy-cutter*, a legal and important part of the **lob**-bowler's armoury, is derisively called a *"sneak"* and thought a caddish trick.' In modern times, unless Trevor Chappell is bowling, such a delivery is acknowledged to be a trick of the wicket: 'The pitch was dry and cracked, but played truly enough bar the odd *daisy-cutter*.'

Dance: The ***classical*** way to deal with slow bowling, if you want to attack: 'Rudolph *danced down the track* to **whip** Giles for six.' Here a compliment is being paid both to nimble footwork and a ***dashing*** attitude. However, in the fully professional age, batsmen are advised that when they *move out* of their crease but miss the ball, they will be accused of *giving it the charge* or having a *rush of blood*, however adroit their use of the feet.

Danger end: Not, perhaps surprisingly, the striker's end when someone like Malcolm Marshall was *steaming in* but the one most likely to receive the throw when a run is attempted: 'Admittedly the call was Waugh's – he was running to the *danger end* – but Martyn's "no" had been emphatic, and Waugh was guilty of disregarding it.' Some partners of D. C. S. Compton, G. Boycott and Inzamam-ul-Haq may have felt as if they were always running to the *danger end*. The *danger area*, contained by imaginary lines on the pitch and now renamed the *protected area* in the Laws, is designed to prevent bowlers **running on the pitch** rather than batsmen running between the wickets, but it does sometimes come into play for the side batting third on a pitch which is deteriorating, especially if they have elected to wear long spikes.

Danger man: The batsman who can change the complexion of a game by scoring quick runs tends to be described as a *danger man* only when the explosive threat he posed has been safely defused: 'Nilesh Kulkarni struck vital blows early, removing *danger man* Yuvraj Singh for a duck.'

Dart: With bowling the usage coincides with *nip* or *jag*: 'Van der Wath immediately began to *dart* the ball off the seam at a *slippery* pace.' As for batting, the corresponding terms would be *dash* and *dip*: 'The last wicket stand had topped 50 when Flintoff could resist a *dart* at Warne no longer and was bowled.' More likely opportunities for bowlers, on the whole.

Dashing: 'Roy Fredericks, always a *dasher*, made 169 in an innings which will forever *leap out* of the scorebook for those who saw it.' Henry Blofeld is always attracted to batsmen who go for their strokes with memorable panache and a refreshingly carefree attitude. This kind of player will always give the bowlers a *chance* though. The adjective *dashing* can be used with rather more emphasis on style, and was a word which lent itself naturally in an earlier age to amateur cricketers and Keith Miller: 'His exploits in the air, as a night-fighter pilot, earned for him a reputation as a *dashing*, devil-may-care fellow which his subsequent approach to big cricket confirmed.'

Dead ball: This is a matter on which the umpire at the bowler's end can exercise discretion. He may have been influenced by his own social commitments in the following case: 'The last man, Mohammad Ali, wandered off to *prod* the pitch before the umpire called "Over" and was run out because the *ball* was not *dead*.' This was just the kind of situation, without regard to context, in which W. G. Grace was happy to demonstrate his own interpretation of the *spirit of the game*. Meanwhile, the provision laid down in Law 23.1 (v), to the effect that the ball becomes *dead* when 'it lodges in the clothing or equipment of the batsman', was directly occasioned by another of the great man's recorded activities.

Dead bat: The traditional method of nullifying pace and, more particularly, of killing the spin. The expression so typifies the idea of defending that it can become an applied metaphor at one remove: 'The England captain *dead-batted* a suggestion that the itinerary will be a very demanding one.' But, according to Marcus Trescothick, on some home Test grounds batsmen get more than *full value* for their strokes: 'The outfields are so quick that *dead-bat* shots go for four sometimes.'

Deal in boundaries: Combines with the adverbs *predominantly* or *exclusively* to describe batsmen who find looking for ones and twos rather beneath them: 'The QAS batsmen *dealt* so *exclusively in boundaries* that, when it came to running between the wickets, they proved rusty.'

Death bowler: Like the *finisher* with the bat, the bowler nominated to send down the closing overs has begun to achieve almost official recognition because of the particular exigencies of the one-day game: 'This season Craig White has happened upon a new role as a *specialist "death" bowler*.' In the last throes of a contest a surprise act of execution can be the best form of *containment*: 'White moved in *for the kill*, mixing swinging yorkers with slower off-cutters.' A more regular *executioner* was Michael Holding, known as

Whispering Death – not even the ever-alert Dickie Bird could hear him coming.

Death rattle: A figure for the moment of being bowled, where the metaphor is driven by the event more than the noise: 'The *death rattle* for Ponting in Perth leaves him century-less as Australian Test captain.'

Decapitation strategy: The verb *decapitate* can be used in colourful reportage to depict the potential effects of **hostile** bowling: 'Edwards almost *decapitated* Trescothick with a **searing** 93mph bouncer that cleared wicketkeeper Ridley Jacobs for four byes.' *Fearsome* hitting can also cause the fielders to duck and weave: 'Jan Berry Berger nearly *decapitated* Andy Flintoff, pulled Paul Collingwood like a hammer thrower and reached fifty with a six.' But modern cricket now well understands the term *decapitation strategy*, lifted by the Australians from the military theory that targeting the enemy's command apparatus can cause their whole infrastructure to collapse. Coach John Buchanan may have read US Army papers on the subject, but with a view to targeting Nasser Hussain rather than Saddam Hussein. The **baggy green** machine has now moved on to new objectives: 'Graeme Smith appears to have become the latest **victim** of Australia's *decapitation strategy*, which has reduced many a touring captain to an ineffective weight for his team to carry.'

Declaration bowling: Distinguishable from **cafeteria bowling** in that the fielding side is serving up **filth** quite intentionally. *Wisden* no longer gives full recognition to any fast hundreds scored off such dross because they were made 'in contrived circumstances when full tosses, long hops *etc* were bowled deliberately to expedite a declaration'. If he was sure that the *etc* was available at *both* **ends**, Geoffrey Boycott would have had every member of his family queueing up for a bat.

Deep: Opposite of *silly*, and indeed fielders posted to *the deep* have been known to be lost in thought as a *skyer* comes their way. While a defensive field may be *far-flung*, it cannot be said to have 'depth' – that term is reserved for a *long* batting line-up or a bowling attack where the captain has plenty of *options*.

Delivery: Richie Benaud, who studied under Peter O'Sullevan, trained himself strenuously to eschew the word 'ball', presumably to avoid committing an involuntary Johnstonism. Johnners used to collect cock-ups in this area committed by himself – 'Now over to Edgbaston for some more *balls* from Rex Alston' – and by his colleagues (Alston included): 'On the outfield, hundreds of small boys are playing with their *balls*.'

Demons: The archetype of the *demon bowler* is F. R. Spofforth, and the torch has been passed down the generations: 'Lillee, Australia's *demon* fast bowler, was the keynote to his side's success.' It is more usual nowadays to hear of *demons* in the plural, but they seem to lurk more in the batsmen's minds than the wicket: 'Australia's **collapse** had little to do with *demons* in the pitch'; 'Both sides batted as if *demons* lurked beneath the surface.' *Gremlins* can sow *seeds of doubt* in the same way.

Deposit: The authentic word for dispatching a ball, or even the bowler, to a point beyond the boundary: 'There was a hint of disrespect in the back-foot *swat* which *deposited* Scott Styris over the **sightscreen**.' The fact that the batsman here was called Stephen Humble, playing for Northumberland against Middlesex, no doubt contributed to the gentle irony in this piece of reporting.

Diet: 'The England bowlers then supplied a *diet* of long hops to Ian Chappell and Ross Edwards.' Against the modern grain, this word seems to be used in cricket only when the batsmen are *gorging* themselves on *cafeteria bowling*. We have not yet seen a reference to a 'starvation diet' when nothing but *dot balls* are on offer.

Dig: An Australian trade term for innings: 'First *dig* we were in all sorts of trouble but recovered to score 250.' *Hit* works in the same way. In phrasal verbs the meaning depends on whether you have a bat, ball or possibly a pickaxe and oil can in your hand. When *digging in*, you are either setting your stall out for long *occupation* or *banging* the ball *in* short. When *digging out*, you are either *jamming down* on a yorker or dismissing an *entrenched* **tailender**. When players try to *dig up* the pitch, they risk censure by the match referee; when anybody else tries it they are either seeking to prevent their team being beaten or aiming to get someone out of prison. George Davis was guilty.

Dirt in the pocket: A phrase forever associated with the *affair* at Lord's in 1994 when the England captain was caught on camera doing some *work* on the ball. Some years later, Michael Atherton had his trousers sponsored by JCB Earthmovers.

Disappear: The regulation word for a big hit which sends the ball *out of the ground*: 'Ian Blackwell's innings contained two huge sixes, one of which *disappeared* over the old pavilion.' The moral effect is almost more dramatic if your figures are such that you would like the ground to swallow you up: 'Tapah Bairya *disappeared* for 87 runs off just seven overs.'

Dislodge: This is the standard term, although not actually used in the Laws, to indicate that a bail has been removed. The matter was expertly dramatised in this piece of reporting by Ray Robinson: 'Gripped by the Australians' struggle for survival, the thousands were so silent you could have heard a bail drop. We did. It was Harvey's, *dislodged* by a swerving yorker from Ramadhin.' On a lesser occasion, a particularly **adhesive** batsman can himself be described as *dislodged*, when eventually **extracted**.

Do a bit: The required understatement when overhead **conditions** suggest the ball will swing or a covering of **grass** on the pitch suggests it will seam: 'I reckon it might *do a bit* in the first session.' A nice way of putting it, first because a bowler may get too excited if he thinks there will be *prodigious* movement and start bowling **both sides of the wicket**. Secondly, it makes sense to want the ball only to *do a bit*, in that few batsmen are good enough to get a **nick** on deliveries that move *extravagantly*.

Dobber: 'He is a "*dobber*".' It sounds like Steve James is being quite rude about Adrian Dale, his Glamorgan teammate, given that the term is probably derived from the older style of delivery in playing marbles. But in modern forms of cricket it is recognised that this type of **trundler** can do a job, as James goes on to assert: 'But he is a mightily effective "*dobber*", especially on the *low and slow* wickets at Sophia Gardens, where he *stymies* batsmen with his **wicket-to-wicket** accuracy.' Double-barrelled variants make the medium pace sound even more fiddly: 'Dale Benkenstein is a *dibbly-dobbly* all-rounder with a name like a New York attorney'; 'We were drawn to play Shropshire at Wellington, an awkward game because minor-county pitches can be poor and suit *diddly-doddly* bowlers.' Perhaps batsmen worry about *dab-*

bling at the first kind of *stuff* and being *diddled* by the second kind.

Dolly: Basil D'Oliveira's nickname, but also the term for a very gentle catch: 'The England captain spilled an absolute *dolly* *offered* by Chanderpaul.' The cricketing usage was probably suggested by the Hindi *dali*, meaning a present of food and flowers served up on a tray, although less romantic etymologists may propose that the nineteenth-century slang for an easy woman could have been applied to an easy catch. *Dolly* was also available as an alternative for *donkey drop* until after the Second World War.

Dolly mixtures: 'In the 1987 World Cup, Steve Waugh started bowling his *dolly mixtures* to disrupt the rhythm of the inevitable *slog*.' It is now standard practice for *death bowlers* to *mix things up* during *happy* **hour** rather than just *spearing* in attempted yorkers every ball. Such variety can also be a feature of the middle period of a one-day game: 'In the twenty-fifth over, Ganguly turned to Sachin's *allsorts*.'

Done: 'I was *done* by his *wrong 'un*.' One of those effective little verbs like *got* and *had* that usually indicates you are out, as in this cheerful example from Division 3NE of the Shrubbery Hotel Somerset Cricket League: 'Holley removed the dangerous Huxtable for 29 with a *jaffa* that *did* him all ends up.' Except when he is *done for pace*, the usage naturally implies an intent to deceive the batsman, but this may not come naturally to the spinner who started his career bowling *military medium*: 'There was a time when a batsman had more chance of being hit by space debris than being *done in the flight* by Giles.'

Donkey drops: High, flighted deliveries which often end up as full tosses. Not normally seen in *first-class*

cricket unless ***declaration bowling*** is being served up
or there is a deliberate policy to *hold* the ball *back* on a
slow pitch: 'Snape's deliveries were often recorded by
the speed clock at about 50mph – *donkey drops* by professional standards – and Vaughan's off breaks
described a parabola not much quicker.' Most club
cricketers will recall an instance of being completely
bamboozled by an apparently innocuous ***purveyor*** of
such ***filth***.

Doosra: Hindi and Urdu for the *second one*, this *mystery ball* is bowled with the same finger action as an
off break but with the back of the hand turned
towards the batsman so that it spins the other way.
The number of bowlers cited for suspect *straightening*
of the arm when bowling their version of the delivery
– Muralitharan, Harbhajan, Shoaib Malik and Johan
Botha are among those reported – has caused some
old pros to suggest that the *doosra* is the off-spinner's
wrong 'un in more ways than one.

Dope: 'I do not hold with the over-preparation of
pitches and the use of various forms of "*dope*" to
achieve perfection and make the batsman's task easier.' From the safety of retirement, Jack Hobbs was
pronouncing on the anaesthetisation of wickets
rather than bowlers. *Pitch-doping* and the dull cricket
so engendered continued to be an issue, especially on
the subcontinent: 'Merchant and Hazare vied with
each other in running up massive scores on the *over-
doped* wickets of the day.'

Dorothy: Australian rhyming slang for six, after
Dorothy Dix, the pseudonymous agony aunt: 'That
was a *Dorothy* from the moment it left the bat.'

Dot ball: 'The *dot ball* has become the Holy Grail.'
Deliveries where no runs result have always been

recorded with a *dot* in scorebooks but, as Colin Cowdrey intimates, their incidence becomes more crucial in one-day cricket and other situations where the build-up of *pressure* is imperative: 'What was particularly admirable was the manner in which Adam Gilchrist was **contained** – he only managed 49 from 69 balls, and was forced to play out 39 *dot balls*.' In this context the opposite of the *dot ball*, as Chris Cairns is painfully aware, is the *four-ball*: 'Although I did OK at Wellington, I'm still *leaking* far too many *four-balls*.'

Double: The only forms of the feat still possible are the *match double* (a century and ten wickets) and the *career double*. The latter is variously defined, but for Test players tends to be recognised as 2,000 runs and 200 wickets. The classic *double* of 1,000 runs and 100 wickets in an English season is now an extinct species, and George Hirst will be the only player ever to achieve the *double double*. Few seem to grow weary of quoting his observation at the end of the 1906 campaign: 'It has been suggested that no one may again do what I've been lucky enough to do this season. I don't know about that, but I do know this – if he does he'll be tired.'

Double teapot: A visual rather than a verbal idiom which replicates the sight of a bowler standing with hands on hips to register his displeasure, whether at his own side's fielding or the umpire's judgement or simply his personal run of luck. The image provided a suitable tribute to Leicestershire's Gordon Parsons on his retirement: 'Grace Road won't seem the same without "Bullhead", steam emanating from both ears, doing a *double teapot* in the middle of the pitch.'

Down the ground: A handy and originally Australian way of referring to the arc between mid-on and mid-off: 'Gooch scored mainly *down the ground*'; 'Graeme Hick played well *down the ground*.' More generally, the ball is said to *go down* to the boundary, obviously because it helps if the square is not situated in a hollow, but also because the ball is psychologically *on its way*. This may help it to *win the race* with the chasing fielder.

Dragger: 'Ray Lindwall was another *big dragger*.' This is not a reference to Lindwall's smoking habits but to his **action** in the days of the back-foot no-ball law. Such was the degree of difficulty caused to the umpires by bowlers with *long drags* that the *front-foot law* was introduced. Batsmen need to be careful not to *drag on*, even when they are not actually trying to *drag* it *from* outside off stump: 'Kirsten drove *hugely*, and *dragged* the ball onto his wicket.'

Drift: 'Kaneria's leg break is quicker, bouncier, but has less *in-drift* and turn than Warne's.' Here the word *drift* occurs in its most specific technical application, which is to the degree of counter-movement that the leg-spinner may be able to achieve in the **flight**. Michael Atherton confirmed the Australian's **mastery** in this dimension: 'Warne was the hardest to come down the wicket to because of the amount of *drift* he used to get in the air.' *Drift* can also be highly effective when uncoupled from the leg break: 'Younis Khan was stumped as he reached forward to a ball by Kumble that *drifted* down the leg side.'

Drinks waiter: 'Lee's total of eight would leave him a few cordials to pour before he outstrips the 19 Tests of perennial *drinks waiter* Andy Bichel, who was on the verge of becoming the poster boy for the Liquor and Hospitality Union a summer or two ago.' This helps convey the frustration of the unlucky player who has been selected in the *original twelve* but left out of the *final eleven*. It refers to one of several menial tasks traditionally expected of a *twelfth man* and to the fact that an experienced player will feel demeaned by the role and a newcomer cruelly disappointed: 'I was struck by the tension and misery on Robin Jackman's face as he still did not know whether he would be playing his first Test for England or *carrying the drinks* (he carried the drinks).'

Drinks wicket: 'Let's have a *drinks wicket*, fellas.' It is axiomatic that any interval can disrupt the concentration of the batsmen, and so the fielding side can sometimes resort to encouraging themselves in this fashion, especially when the score is 80–0 after the first hour's play and the Ribena is as weak as the bowling attack. Now *Test Match Special* is carried on Radio 4 Long Wave in Britain, the *Shipping Forecast* or *Yesterday in Parliament* often seem to work the oracle when England are batting.

Drop-in: Used of pitches prepared elsewhere and then inserted into the square, now common in Australasia where the **block** is churned up by other sports in the winter: 'The *drop-in* surfaces used at rugby-cum-cricket grounds such as Auckland's Eden Park proved as much of a mystery to the home team as the tourists.'

Drop the hands: Jockeys get into very hot water for *dropping their hands* and boxers may get knocked out if they do so, but for top-**order** batsmen this is an important skill, to avoid *gloving* lifters to the slips or short leg: 'Hick's first and natural instinct when a ball rises towards his face is to protect himself with raised hands and bat; Atherton's is to avoid any possibility of losing his wicket by *dropping his hands* lower even as his head sways out of danger.'

Drop zone: The spot on a *helpful* wicket where fast
bowlers should be landing the ball. In 1995, *shell-
shocked* batsmen facing Courtney Walsh and Ian
Bishop were quickly *bombed out* on an Edgbaston
wicket heavily *grassed* just *back of a length*: 'Once a
few early *sighters* had established the relevant *drop
zone*, England were doomed, and the match was over
in just two and a half days.' The two-divisional
County Championship has now introduced another
kind of *drop zone* into English cricket, designed to
eradicate *comfort zones*.

Duck: Derived from the supposed resemblance of a
duck's egg to the number 0. The first *Oxford English
Dictionary* citation dates from 1863, which was, as
chance would have it, the same year that the first
British Poultry Club was founded. The source of the
citation, a novel by Charles Reade called *Very Hard
Cash*, suggests that the term was already in vogue and
that *British duck egg* had replaced *Round O* as the fashionable term for a score of nought in cricket. Though
references to *zip* or a *zero* can be seen occasionally in
Australia these days, being dismissed for no score is
usually an indignity which dare not speak its number,
hence the following catalogue of euphemisms: *bal-
loon, blob, blonger, cipher, daddles, full moon, glozzer,
gozzer, globe, potato, semibreve*. A *first-baller* is, of
course, a *golden duck*, which sometimes leaves the
crowd as well as the batsman disappointed: 'How
short changed do the Gabba fans feel after Gilly's
golden gozzer?' See also *pair*.

Dustbowl: Just as a *gluepot* or *sticky* used to be
associated particularly with uncovered wickets in
Australia, the *dustbowl* is the archetype of the dry,
slow-turning pitch found on the subcontinent. Such
an archetype that touring sides are sometimes
accused of *whingeing* about the way tracks are

(under-) prepared: 'Despite the lack of time that the *curator* had in Ahmedabad, to suggest that the pitch was a *dustbowl* borders on the ridiculous.' The topsoil on a real *dustbowl* of a wicket will not disintegrate quite as quickly as in the American cotton belt, but the *pitch inspection* may still cause great depression amongst the batsmen.

Dyslexic: County circuit slang for batsmen who cannot **pick** wrist spin *from the hand*. Derek Pringle attributed two handicaps for the price of one to certain English batsmen when he observed that Kaneria's **googly** was '*readable* by all but the most *myopic* spin *dyslexic*'.

E

Easy: In cricket, qualifies *singles* (which can also be described as *long* or, if the fielding side accepts that they are *easy*, *agreed*) and the pace of the pitch (which will make life very difficult for the bowlers): 'While the Indians *made merry* with their top-**order** batsmen *feasting* on the *easy-paced* track at the M. A. Aziz Stadium, it turned out to be a day of *hard toil* for the hosts.'

Economical: An adjective which generally indicates *reliability* in a bowler: 'It has been a long time since Mark Robinson, normally the most *economical* of bowlers, was hit for three sixes in one over.' The one-day game has brought the *economy rate* to prominence, although John Woodcock had already been quite fond of the noun: 'Underwood was at his best, causing the batsmen more anxiety than anyone and bowling with *strictest economy*.' Meanwhile, there is an abundance of related terms: 'With Pollock, the watchword was *parsimony*'; 'He bowled the *thriftiest* ten-over spell in South Africa's one-day history.' Obviously, in the wider game, bowlers are happiest when batsmen are being dismissed *cheaply* and wickets are being taken at *scant cost*. But the *economic* factor has no mean place in the lexicon in its own right. See **miserly**, **niggardly**, **stingy**, **tight**.

Edge: The *edge* of the bat is what bowlers are trying to *find* rather than *go past*. If the result of an *edge* is a catching opportunity, it will tend to be reported on as either *thin* (for a **tickle** or **feather** to keeper or first slip), *thick* (especially for the cut) or *top* (typically for a hook or sweep shot). A *bottom edge* is more likely to result in a batsman *playing on* than giving a **chance**. When an *edge* is deemed to be deliberate, as in the *steer* to third man, it may be described as *controlled* or *educated*.

Effortless: 'Michael Hussey made an *effortless* 97 off 120 balls.' While effort is duly acknowledged, *effortlessness* is naturally admired, since it is the hallmark of style. What really makes batting *effortless* is a sense of *timing*, which, once it goes awry, can take time to recover – Angus Fraser described Atherton as a 'natural mistimer of the ball'. David Gower is probably worth consulting on the subject: 'It's hard work making batting look *effortless*.'

Eke out: An old-fashioned verb which conveys the idea of the batting side – often its **wagging** tail – making the best of a bad job given the imperfections of the pitch or the indiscretions of the senior batsmen: 'Croft, Kasprowicz and Wharf *eked out* 80 priceless runs for the last two wickets.' Increasingly, though, we find the term being used as a straight synonym for *grind out*: 'Langer began, as so often, by **scratching**

like a chicken in a farmyard but *eked out* 166 in six
and three-quarter hours.'

Elegant: The adjective which seems to establish batting as an aesthetic activity. Here is a modern example: 'When his timing is so assured, Law does not
seem to hit the ball, but merely to *usher* it to the
boundary with an *elegant swish* of the **blade**.' Neville
Cardus on Herbert Sutcliffe provides a historical
frame of reference: 'His cricket keeps the game in
touch with the great **classical** tradition of the
straight, elegant yet *punishing* bat.' Cardus was himself too *elegant* to bandy the word about, but the point
with Sutcliffe was underwritten by the fact that,
when required to, 'he **stonewalls** nicely, *elegantly*'.
Classical pretensions notwithstanding, *elegance*
should not be indulged in for its own sake: 'Simon
Cook swung the old ball **late** into Bicknell's off stump
as he *elegantly* **shouldered arms**.'

End: One of the game's great attractions is that play
alternates between two *ends*, where the **conditions**,
and the ability of the protagonists, can be dramatically different. Hence the senior bowler in the side
tends to have *choice of ends*, the **stock** *bowler*'s job is to
tie down an end, and a *change of ends* can sometimes
do the trick for both parties. From the batsman's perspective, *keeping an end up* is an expression which has
entered the language more generally to indicate a res-
olute and sustained individual contribution in
defence of the team's interests. A now canonical saying, sometimes ascribed to Len Hutton, decrees that
'the best place to play good fast bowling is from the
other end'. When easier pickings are available, players
with an eye on their **average** itch to be involved in
every ball sent down. Here is a quotation from
another legend of the Yorkshire school: 'My mum
would have scored runs and taken wickets against the

Bangladeshis. She'd have wanted to bat and bowl *at both ends.*'

Enforce: The Laws state that, if a certain number of runs ahead on first innings, the side batting first shall have the *option* of *requiring* the side batting second to *follow on*. Some captains are even imagined politely *asking* the opposition to bat again. But *enforcing* is the standard terminology, emphasising the grip that one side has on the game: 'Brian Lara's West Indies tightened the screw against England in the fourth and final Test as they *enforced* the follow-on midway through the fourth day.'

English length: An *English length* is further *up to the bat* than normal **international length** in order to exploit **conditions** more conducive to swing and seam. Sometimes even the most accurate bowlers take time to adjust their **radar**: 'McGrath's failure to locate an *English length* at Edgbaston was a major factor in Australia's unexpected defeat.' And sometimes a fuller length is appropriate outside the mother country – here is Prem Panicker drawing up the rules of engagement for a one-day tournament played in Sri Lanka: 'Lesson one – rain or no rain, you need to bowl an *English length* if you want your seam bowlers to succeed.'

Essay: Indian-English synonym for *innings*: 'In the third Test at the Oval, Solkar bowled **tightly** in the first *essay* for 3 for 28'; 'Kaif faced 263 balls in his marathon 360-minute *essay*.' Montaigne did not write on cricket, but in these instances the word *essay* is getting back towards its French meaning of 'attempt'. At any rate, it sounds more literary than the Australian **dig**.

Even time: 'Goddard and Bacher *hustled up* their 50 stand in 55 minutes and the innings century was posted in *even time.*' This quotation helps illustrate why it is possible in cricket to score an *even 99*, because *even* means *even time* – a run-a-minute – in such examples. Scoring at a *run-a-ball* is the more relevant statistic in the modern game, now that over rates are slower (and now that scorers routinely count the number of deliveries faced by each batsman).

Every shot in the book: 'Johnson can be a bit *loose*, but he has *every shot in the book*'; 'Haynes swept, cover-drove and *scattered* the field with just about *every shot in the book.*' It used to be safe to assume that the *book* in question would be the **MCC Coaching Manual**, but this tome is no longer sufficient by itself for batting in all the various forms of modern cricket. A quaint and indeed now antiquated way of praising a batsman's range of stroke was to say he hit the ball to *every point of the clock.*

Exaggerated: Used to describe high *backlifts* or *shuffling* around on the crease, especially when such aspects of technique cause batsmen problems: 'Several of us got into trouble against Tyson in the 1954–55 Test series through *exaggerated back-swings*'; 'Flintoff was bowling fast, and forcing Lara to make *exaggerated* foot movements across his stumps.' The same adjective describes *prodigious* movement of a different kind, when the ball is not just *doing a bit* but *doing too much*: 'Countless times they *beat the bat*, but pitching short of a length the *exaggerated movement* took the ball comfortably past the *edge.*'

Exocet: A term which, like the **Harrier**, came into vogue after the Falklands War. It describes a very fast delivery which homes in on the stumps like a guided missile: '*One* wicket so often *brings two*, and Andrew Flintoff never looked *settled* – his lack of foot movement contributed to missing an *exocet* from Shoaib which *clattered* into his middle stump.'

Expansive: An adjective reserved for descriptions of the off drive, usually when the shot is ill-judged or wildly executed: 'Gayle *aimed* one *expansive* drive too many at a Dominic Cork delivery and looked back to see his off stump *cartwheeling* out of the ground'; 'Michael Clarke's *expansive* drive was beaten by a delivery *nipping* back *through the gate*.'

Explosion: Used of bowlers to describe the release of energy that should ideally occur in the delivery stride: 'Now Gillespie *lollops* to the wicket and the *zip* generated from an *explosion* at the crease has largely gone.' Also deployed for dangerous batsmen when they *terrorise* the bowling, although even the *cleanest* of hitters have to get their timing right: 'Klusener rose to the occasion, taking older fans back to the 1999 World Cup with his *controlled explosions*.'

Exponent: Whereas bowlers tend to be *purveyors* of a certain style, batsmen are more often *exponents* of particular strokes: 'The most famous *exponent* of the *scoop shot* is former Zimbabwean international Douglas Marillier.'

Express: 'The Blues have *variety* in the pace attack with Clark, Nicholson, Henriques and Thornley providing right-arm *line and length* options, Bracken providing the left-arm *swing* option and Bird providing the right-arm *express pace* option.' *Express* is the adjective reserved to describe bowlers who are genuinely quick – a rarer breed than the hordes of fast-medium seam and swing *merchants* who pack *first-class* cricket. To nickname a particular *express bowler* as if he were a train *steaming* in all the way from his home town was becoming a rather anachronistic and mannered device until Shoaib Akhtar made the theme and its variations respectable again: 'Those who had contrasted Gul as the *Peshawar Rickshaw* to the *Rawalpindi Express* hung their red faces'; 'The *Rawalpindi Express* has suffered a few *derailments* lately.'

Extract: This verb suggests that, while the pitch may be willing to give **assistance**, the bowlers still have to **bend their backs** to get something out of it: 'Carter *extracted steep lift* to strike Rikki Clarke on his right index finger.' *Lift* or *bounce* is what bowlers are usually said to *extract*, but the word can be used for a *ripper* – 'Stuart MacGill *extracted* his customary five miles of turn' – or even the moment when an **adhesive** batsman is *ripped out*: 'Trego finally *extracted* Dravid for 95.'

Eye in: W. G. Grace had a complete command of the basic principles of ophthalmology as they apply to the batsman: 'When his *eye* is *in*, the cricket ball seems the size of a **football**, and he can't miss it. When his *eye* isn't *in*, then he isn't in long, because he's soon bowled out.' Martin Johnson adjusted the focus to take account of Peter Willey's extremely *two-eyed* stance: 'The Leicestershire vice-captain was a long time *getting his eyes in*.' Willey was clearly working hard to defy the great Doctor's second principle.

F

Face: Cricket is a **side-on** game, but batsmen always *face* the bowling. The **classical** batsman will indeed *present* the bowler with the *full face* of the bat. The methodical **accumulator** will *open the face* for the *glide* or *steer* to third man and *close the face* in order to **work** the ball away to leg. The Indian school is ahead of the game when it comes to manoeuvring the terminology: 'Yuvraj replicated Laxman – two fours and *gone*, *open-facing* Sami to the keeper.'

Facial hair: 'There seems a modern fashion for designer stubble. Some people believe it to be attractive. But it is aggravating to many others. The ECB will imminently be looking into the whole question of *facial hair* on our cricketers.' Ted Dexter's press release after England's 3–0 defeat in India in 1992–93, as well as resisting parody, reflects a common preoccupation of committee men about the *deportment* of the cricketers representing their county or country. The implied correlation between *dapper* appearance and *tidy* cricket has not always held true. In any case, David Gower, not required on the tour in question, probably makes shaving look **effortless**.

Facilities: 'Use all the *facilities*, **Wizard.**' In club cricket this is not an exhortation to a bowler on the away side to have extra egg sandwiches at tea time, a leisurely crap and a luxurious shower. Instead he has just bowled a **rank** *full toss* and is being encouraged by his teammates to **hit the deck**.

Fall away: A technical fault of fast bowlers is to *fall away* in the delivery stride, with the result that they tend to *slide* the ball down leg side. There seems to be no shortage of bowling coaches in the professional ranks ready to point out such failings: 'The word round the county circuit is that Anderson still has the same basic flaw in his delivery stride – head and upper body *falling away* badly towards cover point.'

Fall over: 'Papps was adjudged leg before, *falling over* a full-length ball on leg stump from Stiff.' Although a

Waqared batsman can actually fall to the ground if he is *pinned* by a swinging yorker, in this instance Michael Papps had probably just **shuffled** too far *across his stumps* and not got his head *into line*. The formula is more generally applicable when a batsman is struggling with his technique: 'The footwork was unsure, Ponting's head was *falling over* towards the off side, and he survived countless appeals for leg before.'

False shot: Some credit can go to the bowler for a *false shot* or *false stroke*, which he can induce with a piece of deception or a well-laid **trap**: 'Brown tempted the powerful White into a *false shot* and the former England all-rounder departed 15 runs short of his half century.' But often the expression just means any bad stroke which could have got the batsman out, whether it actually does or not. Rather like a *chanceless* innings, the absence of *false shots* indicates very good batting or a very benign pitch: 'Bichel and Pothas produced some fine **strokeplay** and barely played a *false shot.*'

Fancy dress: Cricket *à la mode* is a whole new subject in itself, a craze which has partly grown up because television prefers to give exposure to fans in costume than to **freakers**. There is now an officially sponsored *fancy dress* award on Test match Saturdays in England, but back in 1997 the Headingley stewards were not seeing the funny side: 'Brian Cheesman, a university teacher dressed as a carrot, was frogmarched from the ground for "drunken and abusive behaviour".' *Wisden*'s account continues with admirable impartiality: 'He vehemently denied the allegations.'

Farm the strike: The technical expression (interchangeable with *farm the bowling*) for stealing a single towards the end of each over in order not to expose a weaker batsman: 'Mascarenhas *farmed the strike* so effectively that there was a period of five overs in which Taylor did not *face* a single delivery.' *Farming the strike* amounts to the same thing as **shepherding** the tail, whereas *pinching* it amounts to *harvesting* the bowling for individual benefit.

Fast and nasties: Used of aggressive linebackers in American football and **hostile** fast bowlers in cricket – especially, in the second case, if they hail from the Caribbean. The expression is rarely employed these days without a degree of self-consciousness. Jonathan Agnew did not need his **armour** when chatting to Franklyn Stephenson in the pavilion: 'Like all the West Indian "*fast and nasties*" who seem intent on death and destruction on the field of play, Franklyn is a lovely, almost comical, character off it.' Nor, judging from this piece of internet commentary on a Sydney Test, did the English batsmen really need their **lids** when the **change bowlers** came on: 'A series of *fast-and-nasty* bouncers from, er, Steve Waugh.'

Fast bowlers' union: One minor indication of cricket's urbanity is that the English players' collective is called the Professional Cricketers' *Association*, an organisation once described as the only trade union more right-wing than its employers. But there are more unofficial cooperatives, such as the *fast bowlers' union*. Their main restrictive practice used to be to avoid bowling short-pitched balls at each other. However, you can no longer **whistle down the mine** for a quick bowler, and modern professionals like Brett Lee have no concept of solidarity: 'I wasn't trying to hurt the fella, or cause any sort of malice. My job is to get him out. There's no such thing anymore as a *fast bowlers' union.*' The idea only survives as a kind of honorary club, as in this piece on Lee and Shoaib: 'Both carry the usual baggage for a modern-day *quickie*, questions over their actions and the back injury without which membership of the *fast bowling union* would probably be turned down.' To be a fully paid-up member of the *keepers' union*, you should be under five foot eight and speak loudly at 100 words a minute.

Fast hands: When Marvin Hagler challenged Alan Minter for the world middleweight title in 1980, Henry Cooper predicted the outcome (TKO third round) in one sentence: 'Hagler's got *fast hands* and Minter's a bleeder.' Against bowling attacks liable to **haemorrhage** runs, a player with *fast hands* is likely to settle the contest in equally clinical fashion: 'Karen Rolton is probably the best **striker** of a ball in women's cricket. She has very *fast hands*, gets in *great positions* – against South Africa she went in in the ninth over and the game was over in the 25th.' Mohammad Azharuddin was a male cricketer but he had '*hands faster* than a Chinese masseuse'. Compare **bat speed**.

Fast twitch: Derek Pringle, when looking into the mechanics of fast bowling, turned up the suggestion that West Indies *quicks* were ahead of the rest because they had 'more *fast-twitch* muscle and relatively shorter backbones'. Since then we have come into the era of '*intimidatory batting*', as Simon Hughes has called it, and the scientific terminology looks set to change allegiance as well. Here is Ed Smith on the muscular potential just waiting to be released by Andrew Symonds: 'He stands still at the crease, upright and uncomplicated, a stationary mass of *fast-twitch* muscle ready to *explode* at the ball.'

Feather: In snooker, *feathers* are the smooth practice strokes a player makes at address before actually striking the cue ball; in cricket, contact with the ball *is* made – albeit registering the lowest possible reading on *snicko* – and the batsman is usually *trudging* back to the pavilion as a result: 'The target was down to 51 when Cottey *feathered* a catch to James Foster.'

Featherbed: A classic cliché for a docile pitch with predictable and probably low bounce: 'Chanderpaul won the toss and elected to bat on a *typical* Bellerive *featherbed*.' Meanwhile, the Middlesex attack were soon feeling homesick playing an *out match* away from *Headquarters*: 'They could get nothing out of a *typical* Uxbridge *featherbed* and must have longed for something more conducive at Lord's.'

Feed: 'A *diet* of deliveries pitching on middle or leg – especially from Cork and White – *fed* Mark Waugh's insatiable appetite for on-side runs.' In this example, the unfortunate bowlers are cast in the role of *pie chuckers* providing an endless flow of *four-balls* for a *master* batsman to *tuck into*. But sometimes the *feeding* of a debatable strength or penchant can be deliberate, in the hope of the stroke being played *uppishly*: 'Botham ostentatiously set three gullies and *fed* Wayne Phillips his favoured cut shot.'

Feeling: In the same way that goalkeepers want to have an early touch, it is understandable that batsmen like to *get bat on ball* as soon as they can. This can make them play at deliveries in the *corridor of uncertainty* that they should be leaving: 'Jayawardene initially *played and missed*, *feeling* for the ball outside the off stump.' And sometimes the foot movement remains minimal throughout a batsman's stay at the crease: 'Ramesh spent much of his tortured tenure tentatively *feeling* for the ball outside his off stump.'

Fence: *Fencing*, rather than constituting a stylish use of the *blade*, is likely to produce only a fatal *stab* at the ball: 'Darren Stevens, *fencing **loosely*** outside the off stump, was the ***victim*** of extra bounce.' The noun *fence* is also applied loosely in the modern game, in the sense that when a batsman *strokes it to the fence*, the ball will usually strike the boundary *boards*.

Fend: Related etymologically to 'defend', but in the event always an unsuccessful attempt to ward off an awkward delivery: 'Kamal's *doughty* resistance ended when he *fended* Kumble to short leg.' Compare ***spar***.

Fetch the ball: The fielding side will be *fetching the ball* from over the boundary rope if their bowlers have not been putting it in the right ***areas***: 'Avishka Gunawardene is always going to *give you a **chance*** but if you bowl half-volleys and long hops you are going to be *fetching the ball*.' Greg Thomas once had to *go and fetch it* after giving Viv Richards some unsolicited ***chirp***.

Fidgety: Describes a batsman who never looks ***settled*** even when he is ***set***. Neurotic characters like Jack Russell, classified by Martin Johnson as 'a *fidgety* and near unwatchable ***nudger*** and *nurdler*', fit this bill. In effect, the word stands in antithesis to the serene ***classical*** manner: 'Croft, a *fidgety* picture of *inelegance*, ***clubbed*** anything he could swing his arms at.' But, as pictures go, it would be hard to beat the Australian suggestion, as reported by Matthew Engel, that 'Randall bats like an octopus with piles.'

Fiery: This adjective is applicable to any fast bowler who is *fired up* or *firing* on all cylinders, but it will always be associated with Freddie Trueman, who appreciated the alliteration: 'People only called me "*Fiery*" because it rhymes with Fred, just like "*Typhoon*" rhymes with Tyson.' Pitches with a bit of *devil* in them can be described as *fiery* (although this is unlikely to 'rhyme' with Faisalabad): 'India's worst display of the series came on a *fiery pitch* at Durban when it was bowled out for 100 and 66.'

Fill-in bowlers: 'Richards is the hardest batsman to *contain* in modern cricket, while King tore our "*fill-in*" bowlers to shreds.' In abbreviated forms of the game, the *fill-in bowlers* are obliged to turn their arms over if there is no specialist *fifth bowler*. In Test matches, such duties will be far more *occasional*: '*Fill-in bowlers* Anthony McGrath and Mark Butcher shouldn't be required against Zimbabwe.'

Filth: 'Ponting bowls what is politely known in the trade as "*filth*".' In cricket this term means 'rubbish' rather than 'unsportsmanlike', and indeed it may be the prelude to a *sporting declaration*, as Steve James reports: 'I eventually reached my hundred, Glen Chapple bowling one *proper* ball, before some *filthy declaration bowling* set up an intriguing match.'

Final frontier: In the most recent period of Australian domination of international cricket, the *final frontier* was a Test series win in India. The Border-Gavaskar Trophy eluded Mark Taylor and Steve Waugh, but in 2004 it was left to Ricky Ponting's side (under Adam Gilchrist's captaincy) to boldly go where no man had gone before (or at any rate for thirty-five years). Other Test-playing nations also travel to India viewing it as the most *difficult place* to tour: 'South Africa have the added burden of living up to the standards they set on their last tour of India in 1999–2000, when they conquered the so-called "*final frontier*" by winning 2–0.'

Finger: *Dreaded* by batsmen, *raised* by umpires, occasionally *given* by pumped-up bowlers.

Finisher: The ultimate accolade for a batsman in the
limited-overs format who is renowned for clinically
putting away the bowling during the final *happy
hour* overs: 'Mike Hussey's extraordinary season continued last night as the best *finisher* in one-day cricket
blazed Australia to an *imposing score* on a *wearing*
pitch at Melbourne's Telstra Dome.' In this example,
Hussey has *run riot* to *post* a challenging total, but the
role of a *finisher* is even more crucial when a target
needs to be *closed out*. See also ***Terminator***.

Firecracker: Can serve as a metaphor for explosive
operations with bat and ball: 'Hodge has been selected
after his *firecracker* Twenty20 innings'; 'Boycott
enjoys saying that the new ball goes through like a
"*fire-cracker*".' Real *firecrackers* sometimes appear on
the field of play, but they are certainly not permitted
at ***Headquarters***.

First-class: 'Naved was a *newbie* but *averaged* 25 *in
first-class.*' This clipped Indian-English way of putting
it may suggest for a moment that Naved-Ul-Hasan has
played all his cricket in a railway carriage. But it is
entirely characteristic of the sport that it insists on a
segregation between cricket recognised for the purposes of career *averages* and lower forms of the game
in a way which suggests university honours or the
cabins set aside for the gentlemen. Here is the editor
of *Wisden*, writing as Attlee's Labour government
was embarked on a second term, eulogising the captain of the MCC's touring party to Australia in
1950–51: 'Brown follows the tradition of the great
amateurs who made this game of cricket as we know
it in the *first-class* sense. There is always room for the
talented professional but the amateur brings the
essential *spirit* of adventure.' The ocean liners on
which touring sides used to make their passage to
Australia were floating pavilions in which class sensi-

bilities could come to the fore. On the 1958–59 tour Jim Laker had an alternative view of Mr Brown's effect on team spirits, once all alcohol except beer was prohibited during the team's weekend social evenings: 'At the very first Saturday Night Club the manager, Freddie Brown, set a splendid example to one and all by drinking whisky. This presumably is what the military men call Leadership.' Compare *captaincy material*.

First drop: A synonym for the number-three batsman, who can also be said to go in *first down*: 'Ponting joins the game's most celebrated *first drop* as the only other man to raise three double-centuries in a calendar year.' It is possible to substitute the cardinal number for the ordinal, although the effect can be momentarily disconcerting: 'Adam Bacher, all of 19, came in *one drop*, and from the first ball he faced, looked a very fine player.'

First use: Cricketers have always had a *first-use* policy, even during the Cold War. The sound captain will already have his initial strategies worked out: 'Taking *first use* of a slow, *drop-in* MCG pitch, Pakistan shaped up aggressively to Australia's bowlers'; 'Sachin Tendulkar opted to give Debasis Mohanty *first use* of the new ball.' Having *last use* of a *wearing* pitch doesn't sound like an initial strategy.

Fish: Batsmen who *fish* are themselves the bait, because they will be playing well away from their body, as if casting a rod. The chances of a *nibble* are high: 'Yousuf *fished at* an away-going delivery and only succeeded in edging it to Parthiv Patel behind the stumps.'

Five-for: 'Hoggard had only taken two Test "*five-fors*" before this match.' The speech marks seem to indicate that this is still a wannabe expression for a five-wicket return in an innings, but it seems to have gained common currency, so much so that the slang term for it – *Michelle* – is readily understood by aficionados of cricket websites. In a campaign for equal rights, Australian bowlers held the ball aloft each time they took a *five-for*, seeking to give the achievement a similar status to that of a batsman's century.

Fizzer: A *fizzing* delivery can be a *firecracker* from a fast bowler or a *grenade* from a spinner: 'Shoaib just gets his glove out the way when a Flintoff *fizzer* goes through to Geraint Jones'; 'Left-handed Wavell watched aghast as he played a Stuart MacGill *fizzer* back onto his stumps.' But a *fizzer* of a contest will not be at all exciting, as this is Australian slang for a damp squib: 'The largest cricket crowd in Gabba history were on hand for the historic encounter, though in the end the match was a *fizzer* as South Africa stumbled along to be all out for 114.'

F. J. Titmus: See *Titmus, F. J.*

Flag: In the professional game, the boundary was once marked by *rails* or *pickets* and now is designated by a *rope*, a *fence* or advertising hoardings described as *boards*. But at club level the painted line tends to be indicated by *flags* placed along it at intervals. These can be quite useful markers for a captain making subtle adjustments to his field: 'Guy, move five yards finer. Yes: right *on the flag*.' This does not of course mean that Guy tries to balance on top of the *flag*, in the same way that *being on the 45* means you are backward of square trying to *save* a single rather than cueing one up on the turntable.

Flail: Akin to *flash*, but the reference to the implement suggests a hyper-extension of the batsman's arms in order to reach the ball at all: 'Warwickshire removed Scott Newman, *flailing* at a wide one from Dougie Brown, before the close.' The aesthetic effect is remarked on in this other example: 'Taufeeq Umar combined *ungainly flails* with some *sublime* straight drives.'

Flannels: The game of cricket has happily appropriated the allusion in Rudyard Kipling's 1902 poem 'The Islanders' to '*flannelled* fools'. Not only does the reference sound more playfully self-deprecating than the same verse's designation of rugby players as 'muddied oafs', but the context of the poem has long been forgotten. 'The Islanders' was not intended as a tribute to Ceylonese cricket but as a critique of the leisured class's commitment to the Boer War. Although even *big units* now wear state-of-the-art cricket clothing rather than *flannels*, the word survives happily in journalistic formulae: 'The question whether Dravid would *don the flannels* in Ireland, on a short-term basis, began doing the rounds.' And Kipling's coinage continues to be reworked, especially if it offers exceedingly good opportunities for alliteration: 'To be among the 15,000 present at Edgbaston on a balmy Wednesday night in July 1997, for English cricket's first floodlit *flannelled foolery* of any consequence, was to wonder why the counties had dallied for so long. Here was cricket without an exclusion zone, a family affair complete with crèche and *bouncy castle.*'

Flash: If you are going to commentate on a fierce *edge* over the slips by using one of the most over-used clichés in the game, *go hard* – with as much conviction as the batsman who has played the shot: 'The Queenslander is broad-shouldered enough to power himself out of difficulties, the maxim "if you *flash*, *flash* hard" taking on a brutal new aspect.' Like *catches win matches*, a canonical saying.

Flat: 'Malcolm's second five-wicket *haul* of the match was a splendid effort on a *flat* pitch.' Ideally, all cricket squares should be *flat*, although there are some celebrated examples of *ridges* or *slopes* at major venues, including *Headquarters*. In standard usage, *flat* means *batsman-friendly*, indicating that the bounce is neither variable nor disconcertingly high. Extremely *flat* pitches qualify as *billiard tables* or *shirtfronts*, and sometimes reporters can share the bowlers' frustration: 'Neither side could force a result out of an Adelaide pitch that could have been Exhibit A in the case for the *Flat Earth Society.*'

Flat-batted: Used for a shot somewhere between a cut and a *carve*: 'The Sri Lankan reached his half-century with a *flat-batted* six over cover.' This kind of stroke, which can also be smashed *down the ground* or to *cow* depending on the amount of *bottom hand* in the shot, is now so familiar in the one-day mode that it seems less improvised than the verb: 'Tendulkar came down the wicket and *flat-batted* Blignaut over his head for a one-bounce boundary.'

Flat-footed: 'First to go was Virender Sehwag, well caught by Tikolo at second slip, after a *flat-footed drive* at an outswinger from the *bustling* Thomas Odoyo.' The adjective is usually deployed when a batsman has not brought his front foot *to the pitch* of the ball, although it is possible to describe a failure to move back and across in this way: 'Russell Warren aimed a *flat-footed cut* to be taken at the wicket.' If a batsman is actually successful with a *stand-and-deliver* shot, it suddenly becomes an example of *clean hitting* rather than *flat-footedness*. More old-fashioned terms are still readily available to suggest a more concrete-like rigidity at the crease: 'Tim Tweats sliced a *fast-footed* drive'; 'Trescothick *bashed* the ball *firm-footed* over deep wide mid-wicket.'

Flat-track bully: The canonical application of this term is by John Bracewell to Graeme Hick, after he had *cuffed* century after century for Northern Districts on allegedly *easy* pitches against allegedly *friendly* bowling. This is one of the most recent examples of a cricket phrase finding a wider currency. Sports journalists now refer routinely to those who fail to shine in adversity or on the big occasion as *flat-track bullies*: we have seen so described the footballer Francesco Totti, the athlete Hicham El Guerrouj, the tennis player Serena Williams and the racehorse Keen Leader.

Flay: 'Upcoming batsman Venugopala Rao *flayed* the bowling to *all corners* of the ground in his brilliant *knock* of 156.' *Flay* is one of a series of verbs, like *flog*, which depict a savage onslaught. Perhaps this is as close as the batsman can actually come to *knocking the cover* off the ball.

Fleetwood-Smith stuff: Whereas the English generally use the word ***Chinaman*** to refer to the left-arm wrist-spinner's normal delivery, which turns from off to leg, for Australians the *Chinaman* is the left-armer's ***wrong 'un***, which turns from leg to off. This could all get so complicated that it was common to describe left-arm wrist spin in general after a well-known previous ***purveyor*** of that style: 'Wardle was a bowler of uncommon skill, with the ability to bowl *orthodox* English left-arm spin and also the *Fleetwood-Smith* type of *stuff* out of the back of the hand.' Len Hutton chose a different model when he described the young Gary Sobers as bowling wrist spin 'in the *Jack Walsh fashion*'. In the modern game, with Fleetwood-Smith and Walsh long forgotten by many, *Chinaman bowler* seems to do the trick after all.

Flight: 'Bedi remained a master of *flight* and *guile* but *spin* seemed to be in decline.' The three terms supplied

here by Peter Roebuck are helpful towards a definition of the finger-spinner's art. But the control of
flight is crucial if this kind of bowler is to succeed on
all types of wicket. The great exponent was Wilfred
Rhodes, whose 'beautifully *curved*' as well as 'beautifully *curving*' flight was consistently admired by
Cardus, along with his 'imperturbability': 'The way
he persisted in *tossing them up* was delightful to see.'
Hutton noted the effect from a batsman's point of
view: 'With Rhodes the ball was *never there* when you
arrived.'

Flipper: 'Kaneria is armed with *ripping* leg breaks,
an excellent *flipper* and the best disguised *googly* of
the modern era.' This account gives a useful inven-
tory of the wrist-spinner's ***repertoire***, give or take
the *top-spinner*. Michael Atherton noted the effect of
Ian Salisbury never having acquired a *flipper*: 'It was
like being a fast bowler without a bouncer.' And yet
Bobby Simpson makes the basic ***action*** for the delivery which ***scuttles*** on sound so simple: 'It's like click-
ing your finger to attract a waiter's attention.' Bobby
hasn't eaten out in London recently.

Floater: The traditional way of describing a spinner's
arm ball if it is tossed up quite slowly to ***drift*** in the
air. But *floater* seems to have moved on in certain
quarters to mean ***doosra*** as well: 'Saqlain's main
weapon is his "*floater*", the "*mystery ball*".' On seeing
the new (and in his opinion *suspect*) method of turning the ball the other way by means of elbow and
wrist action, Bishan Bedi proudly recalled the more
classical methods he employed: 'In the good old days,
it was called the *floater*. It was bowled using the
shoulder, like an outswinger. You bowled it with the
off-spinner's action, but without imparting any spin.'
Less controversially, a *floater* can also refer to ***gentle***
swingers pitched up to the bat: 'Trevor Jesty took five

cheap wickets with his little *floaters*'; 'Anthony McGrath provided a vital spell of *floaty* medium pace.'

Floating slip: 'McGrath has two regular slips, a *floating slip* and two gullies.' A *floating slip* is any man in the **cordon** who leaves more room than is orthodox between himself and the man inside him. Although the practice of *staggering* the slips is long-established, this is one of the very few new terms for a fielding position in recent times. Marcus Trescothick has taken many catches at *floating* first *slip*, but sometimes the ball goes where a more old-fashioned slip *would have been*: 'The Blues needed more luck, watching Carseldine reach his century with an **edge** between wicketkeeper Brad Haddin and *floating slip* Michael Clarke.'

Flog: Probably the most **punishing** verb in its category, especially for putting the students in their place: 'Blackwell *flogged* Durham UCCE's bowlers for 191 off 138 balls.' It might be inhumane, though, to treat a **strike bowler** like a **workhorse**: 'We would not *flog* Daniel on an *unhelpful* pitch.'

Flurry: Indicates a lively development in the action, whether achieved with bat or ball, but probably not enough in itself to alter the course of a match: 'A *flurry* of wickets gave Middlesex hope'; 'Only a *flurry* from Warne took Australia beyond three figures.'

Flyer: Used in cricket for two distinct purposes. Firstly, it refers to a *flying start* to an innings: 'The Royals had got off to a *flyer*, crashing 37 from the first four overs.' Secondly, it indicates a very fast *track*: 'I was edgy with trying to work out how to bat against Hadlee on a *flyer*.' The diarist definitely *not fancying it* here is Jonathan Agnew.

Flypaper hands: Guaranteed to make catches *stick*:
'Simmons made runs, took a lot of wickets with his
deceptive pace, and had *flypaper hands* in the slips.'
Potentially applicable also to wicketkeepers: 'James
Knott had his father Alan's genes but not his *flypaper
gloves.*' The potential opposites in the second case are
cymbal gloves and *Teflon gloves*.

Football: What batsmen *see it like* when they are in
really good *nick* or have been in a really long time:
'From the moment the new ball was taken DeFreitas
saw it like a football'; 'By the close Tim Ambrose was
seeing it like a football.' Alternative spherical objects
available to journalists include *pumpkins*, *beachballs*
and *basketballs* – and other objects can be suggested if
the batsman cannot seem to **lay bat on ball**: 'At the
other end Jefferson was seeing the ball as if it were a
peanut.'

Freaker: 'We have got a *freaker* down the wicket now,
not very shapely as it is masculine.' Being a poet as
well as a commentator, John Arlott may have been
remembering one of the dictionary definitions of
freak – 'to sport, gambol, frolic' – when Michael
Angelow became the first person to run naked onto
the pitch at Lord's in 1975. More likely Arlott had
misremembered the new word for taking your clothes
off in public (first attested by the *OED* in 1973). The
rest of his commentary qualifies as a *champagne
moment* (Angelow managed to get his *leg over* when
he vaulted the stumps): 'And I would think it has seen
the last of its cricket for the day . . . He has had his
load, he is being embraced by a blond policeman and
this may be his last public appearance. But what a
splendid one. And so warm!' *Streaking* reached epi-
demic proportions on English cricket grounds in the
1970s and 1980s. But whereas some cricket fans once
needed no second invitation to disrobe, the craze for

fancy dress now sees them decking themselves out in all manner of costumes.

Freddied: 'In recent months West Indies captain Brian Lara has been *Freddied*, along with most of his players. New Zealand has been *Freddied*, and Flintoff's Lancashire teammate, Stuart Law, has been *Freddied*, too.' This passage was written in an Australian newspaper preview the summer before Flintoff's arched-back celebration after taking a wicket, not bad for a *big unit*, became the symbol of England's pursuit of the *Ashes*. It is not entirely clear whether Stuart Law was *Freddied* in the Old Trafford *nets* or on a big night out in Knutsford.

Full value: 'The fast outfield and short boundaries gave England *full value* for any strokes that pierced the 30-yard *circle* in the first 15 overs.' A common way of suggesting that there will be more fours and sixes than normal. Experienced batsmen try to *cash in*, because they know that *value* reverts to the mean over time: 'Butcher looked far more *comfortable* and timed the ball well from the start, but the slow out-field failed to give him *full value* for his shots.'

G

Gardening: This is something all *proper* batsmen seem to do, and they are therefore imitated by average club players and professional *tailenders*: 'Harmison calmly dispatches Bravo over point for four, and then promptly does *a bit of gardening* on the *highway-flat* wicket.' There is often a genuine need, especially in English *conditions*, for batsmen to effect some makeshift *repair work* to the pitch. However, a cricketer's soft spot for *gardening* may simply betray his nerves or his intention to waste time. In other circumstances kidology is at work: if the batsman wants to make clear that he has been defeated by the pitch rather than the skill of the bowler, or that the wicket is unplayable if the other side are about to go in on it, or – to return to our first example – that he can **hold a bat**. At Ebbw Vale, Peter Walker was simply curious to know if the miners were working on the seam: 'When I tap the pitch with my bat, someone else taps back.'

Gentle: Suggests innocuous **dobbers** or **rollers**, particularly when such bowling presents more difficulties than it should: 'Binny's *gentle* medium pace claimed match figures of 7–58'; 'Amarnath, often battered and bruised during his defiant 5 and ³/₄ hours at the wicket, eventually fell to a *gentle* off break from Richards.'

Get: This little word tends to appear when the batsman is on the receiving end of a nasty delivery: 'Peter Hepworth *got* one that *reared* straight up on his gloves'; 'Gavaskar *got* an **unplayable** one *first-up*.' The word appears twice in W. G. Grace's straightforward dictum suggesting that the batsman should retaliate first: '*Get* at the bowler before he *gets* at you.'

Get big: A trade expression for when a delivery **climbs** too sharply for the batsman to adjust. This happened to Jacques Kallis when he tried to repeat a successful pull shot: 'The ball *got big* on him and looped off the **splice** to Muralitharan, standing near the square-leg umpire.' 'I suppose it just *got big quick*' was Mike Kasprowicz reflecting on how he was last man out in a famous Test match.

Get-out shot: Get-out clauses are a useful thing in business, but there is no upside in *get-out shots* unless the batsman has a *lunch* appointment: '*Opening the face* to a spinner is nothing but a *get-out shot*. The best you can get is a single.'

Gimme: 'Neil Johnson bowled a *shabby* first over (four wides, one no ball, and one *gimme* ball promptly put away through long-off for four by Klusener) and there was no looking back.' Like *free hit*, which sounds as if it has come from hockey, *gimme* is another word for a *four-ball*, definitely borrowed from golf. A *walking wicket* might also be imagined as a concession, this time to the bowlers: 'Panesar, by repute anyway, is a hapless batsman, a *gimme*.'

Give it away: The unprofessional action of a batsman who has got himself *set* – and hence has *done all the hard work* – only to get himself out with a poor shot. Depending on the context of the game, the batsman in question can be criticised even if he has reached a personal *milestone*: 'Bashar's 108 had spanned almost five hours, but the manner in which he *gave it away* took some of the sheen.' The same can be said for a player of whom much was expected, even if he hardly managed to *get a start*: 'Gilchrist *gave it away* with a dreadful shot off Giles when Australia needed him to produce something special in their chase.'

Glare: In the modern game *glares* and *stares* seem to be the gestural accompaniment to *sledging* or else sufficient of themselves, judging by the way Ramachandra Guha described Javagal Srinath in 2002 as 'the only new ball bowler now playing who does not regularly swear or *glare* at the batsmen opposite him'. Andre Nel has developed a reputation for the fullest range of facial expression, even when under caution: 'After a word from Bucknor Nel mixed his *verbals* with mere pantomime villain *stares*.' Nowadays a batsman can have a *mid-pitch conference* with the bowler as well as his partner, and fast men like Mohammad Sami are likely to pitch much further up than the deliveries they bowl: 'His *follow-through* on the next ball ended inside Yuvraj's nostrils.'

Glove: 'Stuck on 99 for 20 minutes, Fidel Edwards gave Alfie one to hook, and he simply *gloved it* to Ramdin.' This usage as a verb is virtually unique to cricket, just as financial reporting knows all about 'trousering a profit'. Meanwhile, the noun features in one of a series of matching phrases – **hit the deck**, *hit the bat*, *hit the gloves* – which follow the action *through to the keeper*: 'A couple of overs Bond bowled to Tendulkar were *genuine quick*. He looked in good shape and is certainly *hitting the gloves* very *hard*.'

Glovework: The term which gives wicketkeeping its proper ranking among the higher arts: 'Gareth Cross showed swift footwork and quicker *glovework* to *whip off* the bails.' *Whipping off* can be the indispensable rite of ceremony in this context.

Gluepot: An extreme case of a **sticky wicket**, archetypally at the Gabba in Brisbane, when the sun dries out an uncovered track rapidly after a tropical storm. Batsmen will have to *sniff* everything off a *gluepot* to have any chance of survival. The era of *covered wickets* has consigned the phenomenon and the expression to the history books, so that you are more likely to hear football or rugby pitches described as 'gluepots' in contemporary journalism.

Gnat's pace: 'Usually we had to assure Tufnell that Walsh/Donald/Ambrose was bowling at *gnat's pace* that day'; 'Devon tried to bowl the way they wanted him to bowl and hit the side of the net. At *gnat's pace*.' Used in the trade in preference to 'snail's pace' for bowling which is by no means at full speed, no doubt by association with *gnat's piss*, English slang for weak beer.

Go: Primarily, a synonym for *swing*: 'Dukes don't *"go"* so much as Readers, and they do it later'; 'In the humid **conditions** several deliveries *went* like a **boomerang**.' But also refers to the fate of balls which amount to *free hits* – 'When I saw it up **in the slot** it *had to go*' – and batsmen reluctant to be *sent on their way*: 'Iqbal was unlucky, but despite returning to the pitch to appeal to the umpires, he *had to go*.'

Go hard: Means to bat with attacking intent and noticeable intensity: 'Slater wants to show people he can play one-day cricket so he *goes* really *hard* early.' This is a quality much admired in Australia, although there may be a risk in not playing with **soft hands** at the start of an innings: 'Ponting *goes hard* at the ball when he is new at the crease.'

Going off out there: 'I don't know what's *going off out there*, Brian, I really don't.' The signature phrase of Fred Trueman, whenever **side-on** principles were breached or whenever an English bowler did not carry out his precise instructions. The *new Freddie* is taking up the mantle, if Mike Selvey is to be believed: 'From midway through the afternoon until the New Zealand innings came to its conclusion, the media pod periodically shook with a rumbling noise. This had nothing to do with earthquakes or the Jubilee line, and all to do with Ian Botham doing his Fred Trueman *not-knowing-what's-going-off-out-there* impression when asked why England had not bothered to take the second new ball.'

Golden arm: In the 1955 Otto Preminger film, *The Man with the Golden Arm* was played by Frank Sinatra. On cricket pitches around the world, the role is taken by any **change bowler** who has a reputation as a partnership breaker: 'Malcolm and Gough struggled to get anything past the bat, but with the total on 260 the *golden arm* of Joey Benjamin struck once more as Richardson ***feathered*** one through to the waiting gloves of Rhodes.' The *golden over* is not one in which a *golden arm* takes a hat-trick but was a short-lived experiment during the development of the Twenty20 concept: 'There was even the idea of a "*golden over*" where runs would count double, signalled by umpires waving a big gold-coloured card in all directions to the sound of a hooter.' Perhaps one day the umpires will recycle the card to signal a *golden* ***duck***.

Googly: One of cricket's defining terms, particularly because if you cannot explain what a ***wrong 'un*** is and how it is bowled you may fail to be accepted as a true lover of the game. Nobody is quite sure where the word comes from (Maori and Aboriginal roots have been suggested) but it has gone on to symbolise a difficult challenge: 'If President Chandrika plays Mr Wickramasingha's *googly* safely without getting out, then Mr Wickramasingha has to try some other trick to de-stabilize President Chandrika's position.' *Google* used to be available as noun and verb, but is now trademarked elsewhere.

Go on: 'All of the top eight got good starts without *going on*.' In other words, they failed to *go on* to a big score, as distinct from simply carrying on batting. Above 50, the ***conversion rate*** comes into play: 'Thorpe, not for the first time, failed to *convert* a fifty into a century.' The idea of the *big hundred*, evoked fondly by Geoffrey Boycott, begins to kick in above 150.

Go-to bowler: 'Flintoff is now not only England's main "*go to*" bowler for wickets but also the man most likely to keep the runs down'; 'Glenn McGrath, Australia's other *go-to* bowler, was shaking his head ruefully after perhaps the worst five-wicket **haul** of his illustrious career.' The phrase looks to be an import from American sports via Australia and is fairly new to the lexicon (as evidenced by the speech marks in the first example and the uncertainty as to whether to hyphenate). The *go-to guy* in NBA basketball is the man you want to be shooting for two or three points right at the death. Other ways of describing a team's main **spearhead** include *gun bowler* and *pole bowler*.

Gozunder: In certain English schools, a chamberpot kept underneath a boarder's bed; on Australian tracks, a yorker-length ball which sneaks beneath the batsman's defence.

Graft: 'Bicknell *grafted* for 69 overs before a short ball from Kirtley finally *blasted* him out.' This usage is expertly glossed by Mike Brearley as to 'fight it out by *orthodox* batting'. Our second example goes for a more oblique definition: 'Michael Powell *grafted* in the old-fashioned way.' Related expressions like *gritting it out* and *grinding out the runs* suggest the kind of clenched concentration required. Such an approach may not please the **purists**, but used to be admired, especially when **conditions** were difficult, and especially by Yorkshiremen and Australians. The game has now moved on to a new era, or perhaps back to its golden age: 'Having started as a *grafter*, Langer changed his ways to accommodate the times and started **carting** the ball around like a latter-day Clem Hill.'

Granny's pinny: A Boycottism to describe an absolute **sitter**: 'That was such an easy catch my *granny* could have caught it in her *pinny*.' As in other sports, *grandmothers* can be wheeled in when there is any other task on the agenda which turns out to be ridiculously simple: 'It was a day when Sussex would have got out to their *grannies* bowling underarm.' It has been known for *mothers-in-law* to be put on standby for a tour to Pakistan.

Grass: As a verb, probably Australian in origin: 'Normally a *safe slipper*, Trescothick *grassed* a sharp **chance** from Adams.' Perhaps this way of denoting a dropped catch has a connotation of the fielder letting his mate down. Meanwhile, the amount of *grass* left on a pitch is considered to be a fairly sure indication of how it will *play*. If the wicket is *well-grassed*, the faster bowlers will be in business, and possibly in heaven: 'The *healthy covering* of *grass* in Nagpur made the track a *seamer's paradise*.' On the other hand, a *grassless* wicket can be a distinctly unappetising prospect for the bowlers, who will not have appreciated this Sabina Park pitch report from Prem Panicker: 'Watered and rolled to within an inch of its life, so bare of *grass* as to give a stray cow the impression that it had wandered into bovine hell, this wicket was made for batsmen.'

Graze: Fast bowlers are expected to go in for the kill, but when resting between spells they often become herbivores, especially if they are fielding in the **deep**: 'Michael Vaughan had tended to use Hoggard in short bursts with the new ball, and then leave him to *graze in the outfield* while the old ball specialists did their work.' Sometimes the economics of the situation force bowler and captain to ruminate earlier than anticipated: '5–0–51–0, and surely time to *chew the cud* at fine leg for a few hours.' It would be possible to say in this context that a bowler getting long in the tooth has been *put out to pasture*, although this might also mean his contract has not been renewed one year before his *benefit* is due.

Green-tinted spectacles: What a captain might be wearing if he convinces himself that a pitch which looks like a *shirtfront* will in fact be *helpful* to the side bowling first. A phrase ascribed to Bob Barber, after Mike Smith *inserted* South Africa at Johannesburg in 1965. Close of play score on a *rain-affected* first day: 192–2.

Greentop: '*Greentops* at Chelmsford are usually mirages that tease the thirsty bowler and vanish the moment the ball leaves his hand.' A *greentop* that is not a mirage will be *well-grassed* and will provide *assistance* to the seamers. It is the opposite of a *dust-bowl*, as Harbhajan Singh appreciates as he remembers defeats at Wellington and Hamilton in 2002: 'In India, we don't play in *gardens* like they do in New Zealand.' We think he is alluding to the lushness of the *cut strip* rather than the size of the playing areas.

Grenade: Whereas *exocet missiles* tend to do their damage in the air, *grenades* explode on contact with the pitch, often when a spinner *extracts* extra bounce: 'Kumble's deliveries burst like *grenades* on the faintest hint of a crack.' During the Gallipoli campaign, the Number 15 spherical hand grenade was known as a *cricket ball*, but in those days *throwing the cricket ball* was still a recognised activity on the curriculum.

Grope: This word used to occur regularly in cricket reporting: 'Iddon was nearly caught in the slips while *groping out* at Verity like an old lady looking under the bed.' We had begun to think that the implications of men behaving badly might have rendered it unfashionable. Even Brian Johnston might have been nonplussed by another example of Jack Iddon's uncertain batting: 'Iddon spoiled a valuable innings by *groping half-cock*.' However, the expression turns out to be still alive and well in cricket to denote tentative footwork or hesitant batting in general: 'The Australians *groped* in the dark against veteran Anil Kumble'; 'Sri Lanka *groped* to 2–25 in reply by stumps.'

Grouping: A term borrowed from target sports like shooting and darts to describe the accuracy of a bowler hitting the same spot on the pitch. Increasingly popular now that technology allows commentators to illustrate in diagrammatic terms a bowler's *grouping* in an over or spell.

Guillotine: An occasional synonym for *bat*, when the person holding it has a high backlift and is ready to *dispatch* a delivery in summary fashion: 'Then Lara's *guillotine* would fall, sending the ball *flashing* to the boundary.'

Gun-barrel straight: This expression is fundamental to the '*You miss, I hit*' strategy: 'Mike Smith bowls *gun-barrel straight*: he *skids* the ball up to the bat without any *width*, demanding that you take risks against balls that will hit the stumps.' *Cannonball straight* serves as a perfectly interchangeable equivalent: 'Spinners would turn the ball adequately on the *flat plasticine* wickets of Sydney grade cricket, but in Adelaide or Perth the ball would go through *cannonball straight*.' Since a *cannonball* can be a very fast delivery or throw, like a *thunderbolt*, the term might seem incongruous with reference to spinners. But the concept of *dead straight* is essentially one-dimensional.

H

Hacker: A term for *slogger* probably imported from baseball, where it is used for a batter swinging from the heels for a home run. Certainly it is now current in all cricket-playing parts of the southern hemisphere. It is harder to say whether the same influence is at work in Andrew Strauss's explanation of why he tried a *big shot* on 98 not out in a one-day international: 'Twos don't count if you need one to win but going for a massive *hack* is probably not the best way to do it.'

Had: In the nineteenth century, specifically a synonym for *caught*: 'Mr Hornby was *had* at cover-point for 29'; 'Daft was *had* at wicket for 3.' *Taken* serves as the modern equivalent: 'Macmillan, seeking one *booming* drive too many, was *taken* at slip.' But *had* is still functional in an instrumental sense, and not only for catching: 'Patel *had* Ramprakash *taken* in the gully'; 'Sami faced 33 deliveries before Hoggard *had* him lbw.'

Haemorrhage: More critical on the scale of fluid loss than just *leaking* runs: 'Durham *haemorrhaged* 239 on the second afternoon.' *Avalanche* serves as a more traditional metaphor for an irresistible flow of runs.

Half: The pitch is sometimes divided into *halves* when dissecting the bowler's length: 'Michael Mason kept the ball up in the batsman's *half* and gave away no *width*'; 'Ashraful didn't get much in his own *half* from Brett Lee.' During the hegemony of the West Indies' *pace battery*, some self-appointed custodians of the *spirit of the game* suggested that the imaginary line halfway down the pitch should be actually painted on the wicket, with no deliveries allowed in the *bowler's half*. Such measures are now considered unnecessary, especially when Harmison and Flintoff are *banging it in*.

Hammer: The most familiar item among the various tools and implements of the batsman's trade. Hence this agreeably functional sample of prose: 'Ben Smith *hammered* anything short.' Compare also *club* and *bludgeon*, as well as *flail* and *scythe* in the more *agricultural* section.

Hang around: *Hanging around for a bit* is how a *tailender* might first think of venturing into *obduracy*. But on a bad day even the *recognised* batsmen can struggle for recognition: 'Damien Wright and Johann Louw ensured that Lancashire's top *order* did not *hang around* too long.'

Hang the bat out to dry: A visual metaphor for an *airy* shot played with minimal foot movement outside off stump. Sometimes in such a case it is acknowledged that the batsman is demonstrably not *in nick*: 'The out of form Alistair Brown *hung his bat out to dry*.' But with a *prize scalp* the reporter may want to publicise the washing in a more extravagant way: 'Sachin *hung his bat out to dry* on the *Polly Clothesline* in the fifth over and found one *nick* and plenty of pain outside off.' Here we discern that Tendulkar has been *undone* by Pollock.

Happy hour: 'Both Hinds and Reifer counted four fours and one six as they set the stage for the *happy hour* onslaught.' Having batted through the middle phase of a one-day innings, Hinds and Reifer are *dealing in boundaries* rather than rounds of drinks here as they prime themselves for the closing *slog*. Traditionally, *happy hour* begins when there are ten overs to be bowled, although the introduction of fielding restrictions means that the opening fifteen are another time when batsmen must try to fill their boots.

Harbour bridge: Australian for the moment when a fielder dives over the ball and doesn't even manage a *milkman*: 'A real *harbour bridge* from Pietersen there and it will *run away* for four.'

Hard-hitting: 'Hall tore the attack apart with a brilliant, *hard-hitting* and unbeaten 99 to put the game beyond England.' Means what it says, and has been rather taken out of the cricket arena by politicians or anybody else who wants to claim that they are telling it how it is.

Harrier: The RAF jump-jet used as a metaphor for one which lifts sharply without necessarily having been *banged in*: 'Then came a *"harrier"*, a ball which *climbed* almost vertically from a length and was taken by Bob Taylor jumping high into the air – a most unsavoury delivery.'

Harsh: 'Langer and Hayden were particularly *harsh* on left-arm spinner Murali Kartik.' While a spot of *mental disintegration* may also have been in order, in this example the Australian openers are understood to have been *carting* Kartik round the ground – he *went* for 33 in his first three overs – rather than making acerbic criticisms of his bowling action. Strangely, batsmen never seem to come in for such *harsh treatment*, even when they have taken many blows to the body, although they can be the *victims* of *harsh decisions* by the umpires.

Haul: The usual collective noun for a statistically significant number of wickets taken: 'Heath Streak claimed his third five-wicket *haul* for the county.' The cultivation of statistics encourages other regular alternatives, like *bag* and *return*. Meanwhile, *five-for* has emerged as the players' own preferred variant.

Have a look: Batsmen do this when they are sizing up an attack. More often than not such circumspect play is the prelude to *fireworks* later: 'Sehwag *had a look* at the bowling and then unleashed a barrage of shots that brooked no answer from the Kiwis.' Selectors are also said to *have a look* at players that they are keeping in mind: 'In 1981, we left Downton out of the last match, to *have a look* at Colin Metson as wicketkeeper.'

Head of steam: A reminder, in its way, of the fact that *first-class* cricket became established in the railway age: 'Gough, working up a decent *head of steam*, took the first two wickets to fall.' The game also grew up in a time of sterner views on education: 'Flintoff worked up a *head of steam* and twice *rapped* Hasan Raza on *the knuckles*.'

Headquarters: Still Lord's, even though the International Cricket Council has moved to Dubai. Lord's is also at one and the same time the *Cathedral of Cricket* and the *Mecca of Cricket*.

Heave: An ugly shot to leg which may result in dismissal but which can be a successful tactic in shortened versions of the game. These two examples from an evening of Twenty20 are illustrative: 'Ian Thomas soon departed after *heaving **across the line*** to Greenidge'; 'Bilal Shafayat *heaved* each of his five fours on the leg side.'

Heavy ball: This expression does not imply that a bowler has somehow introduced a *replacement ball* that weighs a few more ounces (although in the light of various **ball-tampering** controversies perhaps this once did happen). Instead, it commends the efforts of those who can get something extra out of the pitch: 'Roger Telemachus bowls a *heavy ball* and he surprised us a little'; 'Pedro Collins was bowling the *odd heavy ball*, and getting a few to bounce rather nastily.' The phrase tends to be used when reporting on bowlers whose pace is *deceptive* rather than *raw*: 'Michael Kasprowicz bowls a *heavy ball* but will not get many English batsmen **hopping** about.'

Hector: 'I took a hit full on the *Hector*.' Australian for *box* – via *Hector Protector*, the nursery-rhyme character (or Prix de l'Arc de Triomphe winner, depending on who was bringing you up).

Helicopter wrist: One of two pieces of anatomical freakery associated with a particular spinner: 'Muttiah Muralitharan sends it the other way with largely the same *helicopter wrist* and *crackling elbow*.'

Helpful: 'The Gloucester seamers did not make the most of a *helpful* pitch.' When this word is used of the wicket, it is always understood to be *helpful* to the bowlers, not the batsmen. The pitch can, however, be described as *batsman-friendly*. Compare ***assistance***.

Hide: What a captain tries to do with the *team **camel*** or a player carrying an injury: 'It is unlikely that Smith would be happy having to *hide* Langevelt, with his broken hand, *in the field*.' Since one-day cricket revolutionised fielding standards, it is accepted that there are no longer any obvious hiding places. Another comparatively modern development, since a change in the Laws, is for batsmen to pretend to be playing a shot when they are actually *padding away* a spinner outside off stump: 'Darryl Hair has a reputation for losing his patience when left-handed batsmen *hide* their bats behind their pads.'

High: Unless you have locked yourself in a disabled toilet in Christchurch, as a cricketer you will always be praised for getting *high*. The coaching manual decrees that a *high elbow*, along with a *still head* and ***straight bat***, is one of the tenets of ***classical** batsmanship*: 'An ***elegant*** player to watch, Atapattu's *signature shot* is his *high-elbow* cover drive'; 'A third of Flintoff's runs came through the cover region, the favourite area for players of *high elbow* and *straight bat.'* A *high arm* or a *nice high action*, often following a rhythmic **approach** to the crease, will enable a bowler of whatever speed to **extract** more from the wicket: 'Jack Hearne had a long run for the time and a *classic high* action that gave him higher bounce on hard, very fast wickets than most bowlers of the 1890s.' The icing on the cake is a *nice high seam*, because the more upright it is the more chance the ball has to move in the air or off the pitch: 'Anderson ran in with his usual youthful enthusiasm and *presented* a *beautifully high seam.'*

High and dry: How a *recognised* batsman is *left* once he has run out of partners, especially if the innings closes when he is just short of a significant milestone. Sometimes, though, the phrase seems to be a hyperbolic way of saying 'left not out': 'Supersub Chandana was *left high and dry* on 19 after Muttiah Muralitharan missed with a wild shot'; 'With Chris Silverwood unable to bat, Stewart was *left high and dry* on 66.' Compare **marooned**.

Hit the deck: A cricket pitch only ever seems to become a *deck* when somebody is running in and trying to pound the ball into it as hard as he can: 'With the effort that Bichel puts in, *hitting the deck* over after over, you can understand why the spectators love him.' A *deck* or *hit-the-deck bowler* is therefore one who relies on **extracting** extra bounce rather than producing prodigious swing: 'The young giant at Kent, David Stiff, is a *hit-the-deck bowler.'*

Hoick: Like the **heave**, a shot to leg which belongs eminently in the unaesthetic category: 'Chaminda Vaas top-edged an attempted *hoick* off Oram and **holed out** to mid-off.'

Hold a bat: This phrase works on the assumption that anybody who can *hold a bat* also knows how to *wield* it: 'Daniel Vettori has scored a Test century and even Daryl Tuffey and Shane Bond can *hold a bat*.'

Hold one back: 'Bandara cunningly *held one back* and Agarkar's drive ended up in a tame return catch.' The sense here is of the bowler disguising his pace so that the batsman finds the ball is *not there* for the shot (although it may also be possible to think of the bowler reserving the delivery especially for a particular customer). When a batsman consciously *checks* his shot, even if he is Donald Bradman, he may regret it: 'I did restrain myself and in so doing "*held*" a shot against my better judgement and was out caught-and-bowled by Hedley.'

Hole out: Whereas in golf *holing out* is the point of the exercise, and requires steady nerves, in cricket it is not so clever and often results from a *rush of blood*: 'Geraint Jones rashly *holed out* to Kasprowicz at deepish mid-off.' The suspect stroke may be less injudicious if a batsman has enough runs on the board to try a *chip* over the infield: 'Prior *holed out* to wide mid-on for 104 off 106 balls.'

Hooker: Titters may still need to be suppressed in the *Test Match Special* box when a summariser says something like 'Farokh was always a *hooker*.' But because of the danger to body and wicket, especially against Test-class fast bowling, many players try to *cut out* the shot, even if they are *instinctive* or ***compulsive*** hookers.

Hoop: The vital component in a classic expression with which to disparage a bowler's ability, especially if the venue is north of Watford: 'The South Africans include someone called Andre Nel, who when I saw him playing for Northants last season looked as though he *couldn't bowl a hoop* downhill.' There are more imaginative ways of saying someone can't bowl for toffee: 'They're mere *pie chuckers* who *couldn't bowl* a good length *with twine*'; 'He couldn't get a *bowl* in a Chinese restaurant.' But *bowling a hoop* is more respectful of a tradition which can look back to the *trundlers* who bowled underarm.

Hop around: The requisite image for batsmen troubled by pace whose footwork is at best *hurried* and at worst *shy*: 'Shoaib had both batsmen *hopping around*, and *softened* Ganguly *up* for Razzaq, who got him lbw very soon.' Although batsmen can really *hop around* in their attempts to *duck and weave* away from bouncers or to avoid *sandshoe crushers*, the expression is often used merely to suggest that they are having an uncomfortable time. But it is more sharply focused than usual when the *Rawalpindi Express* is in full steam: 'In his *swaggering* pomp – hair flapping, *batsmen hopping*, stumps flying – Shoaib remained the most visceral experience in world cricket.'

Hostile: What an attacking bowler needs to be in order to achieve a *breakthrough*: 'Misbah-Ul-Haq, the *well-set* captain, received as *hostile* a ball as any in the match.' A more standard formulation can be found in 'Kasprowicz bowled with *sustained hostility*.' Compare *friendly*.

Humpty: What an attacking batsman promises to *give it*, usually the ball before he is comprehensively bowled. Botham's declaration of intent to his partner Graeme Dilley at Headingley in 1981 provides a famous exception. Perhaps, in view of the nursery rhyme, there is sometimes a suggestion that the ball is *smashed* so hard there is a risk of it or the bat being broken: 'Hinds, tall, domineering and oozing machismo, simply planted his front foot and *gave it some humpty.'*

Hurry: A standard term in cricket reporting for when a bowler is uncomfortably fast: 'Roberts consistently ***beat the bat*** and *hurried the batsmen.'* In these circumstances the batsmen can find the ball *hurrying on* to them off the pitch and can find themselves *hurried into* shots. They can be *given* the *hurry-up* in a different sense when a declaration is due and their captain gives them some ***humpty*** signals from the balcony. But the strike rate may already be frenetic enough for the team's purposes: '***Hard-hitting*** Ricardo Powell made a *quickfire* 34 off 23 balls as West Indies *hurried the score along.'*

Hustle out: An alternative to ***bundle*** or ***skittle*** out, describing the quick and sometimes shock dismissal of a side: 'Andre Adams took five wickets as Essex *hustled out* in-form Durham for 196.' The connotation is of the batting line-up being ***undone*** by pace – indeed, *hustle through* is a routine description of the way a quick delivery behaves. Perhaps curiously, as spinners have more of a reputation for deception, they never seem to *hustle* teams *out*.

Hutch: The *pavilion* tends to become a *hutch* when the ***rabbits*** are being *sent back* to it or are ***padding up*** in it, in which case the bowling side will want to behave in suitably predatory fashion: 'Ripley was *deceived* and dismissed for 58 by Robert Croft, which *opened the hutch* for Waqar's ***thunderbolt.'*** The term may be hard to resist, though, whenever there is a quick ***tumble*** of wickets and the pavilion gate is swinging regularly: 'Pakistan were in a spot of bother at 7–2 in 2.5 overs with both openers *back in the hutch.'*

I

Impact player: The fleeting appearance of *supersubs* in one-dayers encouraged the appearance of this term in the dailies: 'Prior fits the bill as an *"impact" player* who will come into his own when England bat second.' But once discovered (no doubt via rugby), the expression can itself play a substitute role, on the grounds that *impact* suggests *strike*: 'Giles is the key to their strategy of resting their *impact bowlers.*'

Impeccable: Cricket being a *noble game*, the conduct of the teams should be as *impeccable* as their *flannels* – although such pure attitudes and pristine whites might last only as long as a disputed diving catch in the first over of a match. Touring sides are traditionally complimented on their *impeccable behaviour* by their hosts, especially if they have been soundly beaten. *Impeccable* can be used more straightforwardly, along with *immaculate* and *unerring*, to describe a batsman's *defence* or a bowler's *line and length*. Only the wicket, though, would be referred to, when appropriate, as *blameless*.

Imperious: An epithet which may once have hinted at cricket's higher purpose of 'consolidating the Empire', but still used to mark out a dominating batsman: 'While his driving was *imperious*, Hick was no less *devastating* off the *back foot*'; 'Flower, rated the best batsman in the world three years ago, showed that he has retained his *imperious* form.' The fact that both the batsmen referred to hail originally from Zimbabwe is perhaps another historical accident.

In-and-out field: This consists, according to Michael Atherton's almost casual definition, of 'plenty of *close* *catchers* and the odd ***sweeper*** and nothing much in between'. But the point is to make allowance for a batsman's *aggressive* intentions while at the same time maintaining ***pressure*** round the bat: 'As V. R. V. Singh walked out at 8/169, Ganguly turned defensive, with an *in-and-out field*.' The more conventional type of field settings *saving the one* will still be appropriate for the more conventional type of batsman, as Mike Brearley noted: 'Bedi placed an *in–out field* for Greig and a ***ring*** for me.'

Incision: An apposite word with reference to a bowler who provides his team with a cutting edge: 'Srinath *made incisions* with his surprise *inducker*.' The term is useful also because, even if ***one brings two***, a ***breakthrough*** will begin to lose its value in the currency if used too often in the plural: 'Caddick made early *incisions*.'

In front: 'Chris Nevin was *trapped in front* by Bracken off the second ball of the match for a *blob*.' Whenever a batsman is said to be *trapped*, *pinned* or *nailed in front*, then *of the stumps* is always understood. Also understood is *definitely out*, even should the umpire fail to *raise the **finger***.

In harness: Bowling *in harness* often amounts to the same thing as bowling ***in tandem***, but sometimes the implication is that a captain's hand has been forced: 'Australia nearly blew it on Thursday because the *make-up* bowlers, Moody and Mark Waugh, bowled *in harness* for too long.'

Insert: *Inserting the opposition* now seems preferred to merely *asking* them or *putting* them *in* to bat. The expression emphasises that *opting* to field first should be a purposeful decision based on the belief that the other team will be ***hopping*** around on a *lively surface* or ***groping*** *around* on a *seamer-friendly track*. The decision sounds even more purposeful with the opposition already dismissed from the phrase: 'The Centurion pitch looked *green* and it was no surprise when Vaughan chose to *insert*.'

Inside out: It is possible for a batsman to be *turned inside out* by a ball which really ***squares*** him ***up***: 'Heath Streak was *turned inside out* like an old sock by Zaheer Khan bowling around the wicket.' However, it is more usual for batsmen to *go inside out* deliberately when they are aiming a calculated slice over the infield: 'Clever play there by Langer *going inside out* against Giles after two ***hoicks*** with the spin.' The operation often involves ***making room*** for the shot: 'Youhana *leant back* and once more made his rapacious *inside-out* loft, for six.'

In tandem: The standard way of reporting on two bowlers operating ***unchanged*** is to say they *bowled in tandem*, especially if they happened to be dovetailing well: 'This started an amazing period of play where Nadif and Enamul Haque jnr *bowled in tandem* for 22 overs.' One unseasonably hot Easter at the Oval, the *Guardian*'s Paul Weaver could not resist the obvious pun: 'Saqlain and Ian Salisbury had ***wheeled away*** *in tandem* in the warm sunshine as the Lancashire batsmen prospered on a traditional Kennington ***belter***.'

Interested: 'Bicknell and Guy Welton survived for 45 minutes, although both batsmen ***played and missed*** on a number of occasions to keep the four slips *interested*.' The slips are understood to remain *interested* in this context because of the likelihood of an ***edge*** *coming their way*, even if they are probably all chatting between balls about the barmaid in the team hotel.

International length: What Ken Barrington used to call **two-man's-land** New Zealand coach John Bracewell calls *international length*: 'Harmison has found *international length*, that *middle length* where as a batsman you don't know whether to go forward or back.' It must be said that over the years several great bowlers – as long as they **hit the deck** hard enough – found great success bowling *back of a length*.

In the slot: Means *there for the drive*: 'Michael Lumb *chased* a ball not quite *in the slot* for driving.' If the ball really is *in the slot*, a batsman *in the groove* will duly *dispatch* it: 'Four, *top shot*, a cover drive from the top shelf, it was *up in the slot* to be hit, and hit it he did.'

In two minds: How the slow bowler wants to *get* the batsman. Neville Cardus described the process meticulously: 'Norbury *dropped* his off break just at the length that draws a batsman forward, only to *get* him unpleasantly *in two minds* at the crucial moment.' The classic anecdote goes back to the same era, when Arthur Wood is alleged to have observed, while Cameron was hitting Verity for 30 in an over: 'Go on, Hedley, you've got him *in two minds*. He doesn't know whether to hit you for four or six.'

In waiting: 'Under no circumstances should Sarwan, the captain-*in-waiting*, be seen in a party stand'; 'The 26-year-old Irishman looks more and more like a Test batsman-*in-waiting*.' While players who are **captaincy material** can get into hot water for drowning their sorrows after a defeat, in the second example the terminology covers the possibility that Ed Joyce's first role in five-day cricket may be to *carry the drinks*.

Irish: Australian for **reverse**, as in this observation from Damien Martyn: 'Flintoff has been their big one with the ball going *Irish*, and Jones bowls well with the *Irish* ball as well.'

J

Jack-man: When hyphenated, not a reference to the Surrey and England seamer but a trade term for a cricketer who *plays for his **average***. Perhaps Imran Khan learned the term during his time at Sussex: 'I have played in Pakistani teams with more talent and experience, but half the players were what are known as *"Jack-men"*, as in "I'm all right, Jack".'

Jaffa: 'Hoggard produced an absolute *"jaffa"* that drew Kallis forward and swung away *late* to *find* the ***edge***.' It is now unusual to see inverted commas round this word, so common is it to describe an outstanding delivery. Whether they take wickets or not, *jaffas* are understood to cause the batsman conspicuous difficulties: 'Greatbatch survived a couple of early *jaffas* from McGrath.' A *jaffa* was an orange by antonomasia in the early post-war period (Outspan came later from South Africa), so perhaps it could have been used as a metaphor for the ball itself (compare ***cherry***) before coming to mean a very good ball in particular. Or perhaps oranges were such a rarity in the years of rationing that this idea was carried over to describe exceptional deliveries. Whatever the case, the adjective ***juicy*** is nothing to do with cricketing *jaffas*.

Jag: A likely verb to describe significant movement *off the seam*: 'The Australian batsmen never exuded the same degree of permanence as the ball *jagged around*.' In the typical case, it records the effect of the off-cutter: 'Topley got a couple to *jag back* into Humpage.'

Change *back* to *through* for a more incisive suggestion: 'Glenn McGrath got ball after ball to *jag through* the defences of the England batsmen.'

Jam: An old-fashioned term suggesting *cafeteria bowling*, although sometimes batsmen are best advised to concentrate on preserving their wicket: 'Jameson bowled slow right-arm from an enormous height which appeared absolute *jam* from the ringside but had even the best batsmen in a pother.' An alternative to *jam* in this context is provided by an Edward Kamau Braithwaite poem which depicts Clyde Walcott threatening to put the England attack *out of business*: 'Feller name Wardle/ was bowlin'; tossin' it up/ sweet sweet slow-medium *syrup.*'

Jam down: 'Caddick was denied a hat-trick when Hylton Ackerman *jammed down* on a yorker-length ball, which flew to second slip and was *spilled* by the diving James Hildreth.' When a batsman is faced with a yorker, he is often said to *jam down* on it, whether he manages to *keep it out* or not.

Jazz-hat: 'Not all of our matches were *first-class*, and the so-called "*jazz-hat*" *games*, against the likes of the Free Foresters and the Cryptics, provided some light relief.' The colloquialism used by Michael Atherton recalling his time at Cambridge derives from the fact that the club caps of wandering amateur sides tend to be patterned and colourful. Pro's pros have been known to use the moniker to avoid more colourful language, even if they cannot completely disguise their contempt: 'Asked how many of his 183 *victims* in 1949 came through *googlies*, Roly Jenkins replied: "About 14 – and they were all *jazz-hats.*"' *Fancy caps* is a similar expression, with inverse snobbery even more to the fore. The following example involves another Worcestershire stalwart, who in this case proved to have a more *classical* technique than the amateur batsmen already back in the pavilion: 'Don Kenyon meanwhile had been *negotiating* the turning ball with great skill, which in itself was a model lesson to the "*fancy caps*" now departed.' Perhaps the last word should go to Michael Parkinson, who remembers being taught the virtues of *line and length* by an ex-Yorkshire pro: 'T'only time tha' forgets this golden rule is when tha'rt faced by one of them *fancy* buggers wi' a *striped cap*. Then tha' forgets what I've just told thi' and aims straight for his head.'

Jerk: A term which survived in the Laws of Cricket long after it ceased to be directly relevant as a technical usage, because *jerking* originally referred to **lob** or round-arm bowlers knocking their elbows against their bodies. However, the verb remained serviceable for *suspect actions*: 'If Sonny does not "*throw*" his off break he certainly "*jerks*" it a good deal.' You may still therefore hear an occasional reference to a *jerker* in the sense of **chucker** but, if the stump mike is turned up high enough, sentences ending in *jerk* will be short, colourful and not necessarily directed at the bowler.

Jessopian: 'Jayasuriya was jet-propelling the scoreboard with some *Jessopian* hitting not seen for a long time in Adelaide'; 'One can only attribute India's easy win to the near *Jessopian* hitting by Indian keeper Mahendra Singh Dhoni.' One of the few adjectives in the lexicon derived from a player's name which has not fallen stillborn from the press. According to our research, it now seems much more popular in Sri Lanka than Gloucestershire.

Join the dots: '*Join the dots* now, Thommo, *join the dots.*' A way of encouraging a bowler to close out an over without conceding a run. It arises from the fact that the outside staves of an *M* in the scorebook are by tradition drawn over two columns of **dot balls**. However well-meaning such support from the field, it can put extra **pressure** on the bowler and he may promptly serve up a **juicy** *offering* after five **impeccable** deliveries.

Joke bowling: Usually the same thing as **declaration bowling**, and a practice that was becoming beyond a joke for some observers of the English county game before four-day cricket was introduced. Even now, a few *rain-affected* games can provoke the **purist** to complain about the shenanigans required to *engineer* a positive result: 'The fevered argument over *"joke" bowling* and *contrived finishes* raised its head again at Basingstoke yesterday as Hampshire *force-fed* Derbyshire a *nourishing* mixture of long hops and **donkey drops**.' As a Test against India at Old Trafford in 1982 petered out into a draw, Graham Gooch once indulged in real *joke bowling* by impersonating the bowling **actions** of several of his contemporaries.

Judge for the shot: 'There was a suspicion that Barry Meyer was *judging for the shot*, as the ball was probably **missing leg**.' Sometimes umpires can seem so unimpressed by the way a player has tried to **give it away**, especially playing the sweep, that they can be accused of making their decision on moral rather than factual grounds.

Jugalbandi: 'The Younis–Yousuf *jugalbandi* for the third wicket, raising three-figure partnerships in each of the three innings the hosts have batted, has been a real thorn in the Indians' flesh.' Although *jugalbandi* may mean no more than 'pair', there is a fitting allusion here to the genre of Indian classical music in which two players on different instruments perform a call-and-response duet. Good partnerships in cricket also combine a contrast in styles with mutual understanding.

Juggle: Fielders who do this are not showboating but trying to pouch the ball at the *second attempt*: 'Rogers *miscued* a hit off a *fizzing* Cullen off break, where Jason Gillespie at mid-on *juggled* the catch.' It is difficult to count the attempts in this piece of reporting by Rahul Bhattacharya: 'Akmal popped up a *dolly* off Irfan to Yuvraj at short leg and Yuvraj *gargled* it between his hands, forearms and chest before letting it fall.' Here the coded message to Yuvraj is that the *chance* should have gone *straight down his throat*.

Juicy: Good or bad news for a batsman, depending on whether the adjective refers to a friendly ball or an unfriendly surface. While *tempting* half-trackers or balls *up in the slot* can lead to a run-starved batsman's downfall, they are *meat and drink* to the best players: 'Greg Chappell kindly served up a *juicy half-volley* that Boycott emphatically *drilled down the ground* for four to reach his *milestone*.' However, if the pitch has been *juiced up* by some *moisture*, it will be full of *demons* rather than runs: 'Trapped on a *juicy pitch* after losing the toss, Warwickshire could only muster 123 for seven.'

K

Kick away: 'England will claim their tactic of Giles bowling monotonously into the *rough* outside leg stump, for Tendulkar to *kick away* ad nauseam, worked.' The dilemma for the batsman in these situations is that there is always a degree of risk to playing shots against balls pitched in the footmarks. Before the lbw law was changed to prevent *padding up* outside off peg, the tactic of *kicking away* could be used there also – and could prove excruciating for bowler

and spectator alike. Here is Tom Graveney reminisc-
ing on Cowdrey's *pad play* against Ramadhin in 1957:
'Colin *kicked* him to death. He never tried to play with
the bat.'

Kiss the badge: A celebration imported from football, with the differences that the event is a *ton* rather
than a goal, and that the *badge* is located on your
brain basket rather than your breast: 'Slater *kissed the
badge* on his helmet in 1993 once, but Pietersen positively slobbered over his – three smackers for the
three lions.' Here is David Hopps on the same *champagne moment*: 'A South African scoring a maiden
hundred for England and celebrating with virtually a
French *kiss*: you don't get any more internationalist
than that.' The pejorative term *badge-kisser* will probably be the next import from the beautiful game, especially as the alternative would be 'helmet-kisser'.

Knob-ender: Trade term for *sitter*, perhaps suggesting that the ball has come off the *toe end* of the bat,
perhaps something else.

Knock: A colloquialism for an innings, usually that
of one batsman – though you can say 'the Foxes
scored 350 first *knock*' – and usually with the implication that, however useful or entertaining his contribution, the batsman did not reach the officially
estimable three figures: 'It was a ***breezy*** *knock* from
DeFreitas'; 'The gritty fifty from Whitticase turned
out to be a valuable *knock*.' Meanwhile, there is an
abundance of phrasal verbs. *Knocking in* refers specifically to the process of preparing a new bat for use. In
English club matches during April, the batsmen's
concentration is less likely to be interrupted by the
first cuckoos of spring than by a teammate bashing
the ***sweet spot*** of his new Kookaburra concussively
with a bat mallet. *Knocking up* – less indigenous than

in tennis – means a gentle ***practice*** before play, usually a few ***throwdowns***. *Knocking off* is what the batsmen try systematically to do to the ***shine*** at the start of an innings or what they rather casually do to the runs when the target is not particularly exacting. *Knocking over* is what bowlers do to their ***victims*** when they dismiss them in quick succession, especially if the stumps are *knocked out* of the ground, rather than just *knocked back*. All this activity assumes that the ***batters*** have not already *knocked the cover* off the ball.

Kolpak: The Slovak Maros Kolpak was at least a *keeper* – but for Ostringen in the second division of the German handball league. A *Kolpak* has become cricket's equivalent of a *Bosman* ever since his successful restraint-of-trade case in 2003 had every county secretary scurrying around for a list of cricket-playing countries who have a trading agreement with the EU. A press release would then follow making the right noises about nurturing local talent: 'Our decision to sign Murray as a *Kolpak player* was not taken lightly due to the need to keep places available for our own home-grown players.'

L

Lace: One of those many verbs available to a cricket journalist when he wants to say that the batsman gave the ball a good belt. This particular option lends itself particularly to shots played through the offside ***ring***: 'Gilchrist *laced* Simon Jones through the covers for a succession of boundaries'; 'The Sri Lankan memorably *laced* Cork with utter finality through mid-off for four.' Also, especially in Indian-English, the participle is used in the same way as *studded* to indicate the number of boundaries which have decorated an innings: 'Pinal Shah's 512-minute effort consumed 355 deliveries and was *laced* with 25 boundaries.'

Laconic: 'Fletcher was his usual *laconic* self – just scoring runs when absolutely necessary.' The subject in this example is not Duncan but Keith, and the suggestion of a terse, no-frills approach has been transferred from his style of public speaking to his style of batting. We have also seen the adjective used of players who stay very still before the ball is bowled: 'Motionless and *laconic* at the crease, Inzamam has so much time in which to play any given delivery, it often seems he has dozed off with the ball in mid-trajectory.' Walter Hammond was also by all accounts *laconic* at the crease, but the word was returned to its normal context in a revealing anecdote from Ben Travers, who lent Hammond his binoculars every lunchtime during a Sydney Test: 'There he would sit, taking a detailed tour of the Ladies' Enclosure, until a few minutes before play was due to start again, when he would hand me back my field-glasses, say thanks and disappear. *Laconic*.'

Landing strip: 'With the series intriguingly poised at 1–1, the Antigua Recreation Ground and its *landing-strip* of a wicket was the last place that such a crucial encounter deserved to be held.' A metaphor for a very *flat batsman-friendly track*, which ignores the fact that the runway at certain airfields can be potholed or otherwise uneven. The same might be said for the other surfaces used as metaphors for a pitch which is *like a road* (except perhaps the first one): *Autobahn, highway, macadam, motorway*.

Languid: Somewhere in between *lazy* and *elegant* when it comes to describing a style of batting. Indeed, a *cameo* of an innings can exhibit all of these traits: 'Harvey induced a *lazy* back-footed *waft* from Aftab Habib, who had shown glimpses of his *class* with a couple of *languid* drives through the covers.' Again, the *laconic* Pakistan captain is a modern archetype: for Mike Selvey, Inzamam's batting 'at its *languid best* can make Marcus Trescothick's footwork seem like a qualification for a starring role in *Riverdance*'.

Larrup: Suffolk is not a *first-class* county, but its dialect has lent the game a word for *agricultural* hitting. We will not speculate on what other language might have been used in this next exchange before the batsman's fun was ended: 'Gough even *larruped* Waqar for three offside boundaries, which drew a predictably tart response from the Pakistan captain.'

Larry: 'He's given it some *Larry* there.' Australian slang for *hammer*, alluding to the nineteenth-century bare-knuckle boxer Larry Foley. Richie Benaud sometimes refers to a batsman *giving it the Larry Dooley* – a version which is attested elsewhere in Australian English, even if nobody seems to know who Larry Dooley was. Perhaps he was Wade's great-great-uncle.

Lash: 'Sohail *lashed* 26 off 10 balls in a boisterous *cameo*.' One of several violent words available to describe *flogging* the attack to *all parts*. In some particularly quickfire innings, the onslaught is so carefree it sounds like the batsman might also have been 'on the lash' in the pavilion beforehand.

Last man in: 'There's a breathless hush in the Close to-night –/ Ten to make and the match to win –/ A *bumping* pitch and a blinding light,/ An hour to play and the *last man in*.' Bishan Bedi, a *confirmed number eleven* if Chandrasekhar wasn't playing, might have gone *absent hurt* with some justification in the

famous scenario imagined by Henry Newbolt's jingo-
istic poem.

Late: 'He played extremely *late*, the mark of a great
player.' This is Clyde Walcott on George Headley, and
his judgement is supported by the more memorable
coaching maxims, like *late and straight* (rather than
'early, *across the line*, and head *falling over* to the
offside') or *see it early, play it late*. The quick bowlers,
meanwhile, will be looking to find *late* movement,
which is a further reason for *playing it late*, even if
you don't manage to see it early. Finally, the *late cut* is
a *classic*, if not *exquisite*, stroke, but it has its own cau-
tionary axiom, attributed to Maurice Leyland of
Yorkshire: 'Never *late cut* before June.' We can recall,
even more finally, that John Arlott once described a
shot as being 'so *late*, it was *posthumous*'.

Lavish: The knowing qualification from the press box
when a batsman gets out attempting an overambitious
drive: 'Phil Weston played on driving *lavishly* at Jason
Lewry.' *Expansively* and *flamboyantly* come into the
same bracket. *Lavish* can also spell trouble for the batsman in a different way: 'The ball swung *lavishly* and
there was seam movement too.' *Prodigious* and *extravagant* are the close cousins in this case.

Lay bat on ball: *Laying bat on ball* is very different
from *putting bat to ball*, because it is a formula which
turns up when batting is no fun whatsoever: 'Sarwan
could hardly *lay bat on ball* in a 55-minute stay.'
Sometimes, when a bowler is moving the ball about
extravagantly, it is not always clear what the batsmen
are trying to hit: 'Leicestershire could hardly *lay a bat
on* Heath Streak at the City End.'

Leading edge: Produced when a batsman has gone
through too early with a forcing shot to leg: 'Warne's

work across the line resulted in a catch to mid-on off a
leading edge.' Since in these circumstances the ball
will naturally *dolly* up slowly into the fielder's hands,
the *victim* will often have an agonising few moments
in which to contemplate – and curse – his downfall.

Leather on willow: The sound which encapsulates
the essence of the game and which will be invoked
periodically, perhaps over a *warm beer*, by retired
politicians nostalgic for the England of *village
greens* and maps of the world coloured pink.
However, given that the Laws of the game still insist
on the traditional specifications, both nouns are
ready to stand in for *bat* and *ball*. With *leather*, in particular, the situations are fairly predictable. Tired
fielders find themselves *chasing leather* or, in a more
archaic usage, are forced on a *leather hunt*; batsmen
under fire must *smell the leather*; and *watchful* occu-
piers of the crease will want to *sniff the leather* as they
smother the spin or get *right over* a backward defensive shot. The use of *leather* as a verb is more
unusual: 'Virender Sehwag *leathered* a devastating
309 at Multan last year.' Here it might seem that 'wil-
lowed' would have been the more apposite choice of
word, except that the real distinction at work is
between *spanking* and *flogging*.

Leave: A *good leave* can be as valuable as a *good shot*.
Sometimes a batsman's judgement of *where his off
stump is* is taken to be *impeccable* until the internet
commentator looks at the replay: 'Jones to Richardson, no run, outside off, swings back, *great leave*, or
was it a *brave leave*, maybe a *bad leave* as that *shaves*
the off stump.' An indisputably *bad leave* can have a
notable effect on morale: 'Crawley played especially
limply, possibly with Stewart's fatal "*leave-alone*" in
mind.' The notion also has an ambivalent role to play
in *sledging*. '*Good leave*, mate' can be a sarcastic com-

ment on a batsman repeatedly *playing and missing*, or an attempt to sow seeds of doubt in his mind about the location of the off stick.

Left elbow: John Nyren used this expression as early as 1833 when considering the best method of keeping the ball down. Today, it seems to have been superseded by the *high elbow*, which does not discriminate against left-handers. But even in times when the phrase was accepted, its influence could prompt a degree of scepticism. This was Cardus in 1928: 'Mitchell gets well over the ball with a **straight bat** – perhaps too straight. The *left elbow* makes the inverted "*V*" rather elaborately.' Viscount Cobham, in 1967, was altogether more emphatic: 'English cricket, for as long as I can remember, has been bedevilled by the cult of the *left elbow*.'

Legging: The old-fashioned term for **padding up**, as in this complaint lodged in the 1888 *Wisden* by the umpire Robert Thoms: 'This very unsightly play cannot be termed batting, 'tis simply **scientific** *legging*.' Pads can still be called *leggings*, but the only time *legging up* can be a cricket expression is when a batsman is unexpectedly promoted: 'Gillespie was given a *leg up* the **order**, and joined the last real Aussie batsman at the other end, Hayden.'

Legs: A cricketer is described as *strong off his legs* not because he is good at turning ones into twos but because he is adept at **whipping** balls directed down the leg side into the area between mid-wicket and fine leg. But batsmen must also beware not to be bowled *off* their *legs* when an inswinger deflects off pads onto stumps, or *behind* their *legs* by what Shane Warne calls the *pickpocket ball*: 'When Benaud bowled May *round his legs*, the game had clearly changed complexion.'

Lid: Trade term for *helmet*, now imported into commentary: 'That's Katich under the *lid* at short leg.'

Liking: All around England, pub-restaurants offer 8oz sirloin steaks 'griddled to your liking'. This is a promise that can sometimes prove hard to keep. When batsmen are *tucking in* to the bowling with 3lb bats, the word seems more in order: 'Karthik took a special *liking* to Danish Kaneria'; 'Kaluwitharana slammed a 32-ball 50, taking a particular *liking* to Glenn McGrath.'

Limpet: A word for a determined batsman which seems to have stuck in the consciousness of Martin Johnson: 'Cork's first wicket yesterday was the invaluable one of that well-known *limpet* Jimmy Adams'; 'Hick's historic innings would not have been possible without a succession of *limpet-like* lower-*order* partners.' Any other shellfish on show have surely been attracted by the potential alliteration, as with 'Chanderpaul, back to his *crustacean* best' or the archetypal *Barnacle Bailey*. But *lobster* is an extinct term for someone who bowled **lobs**.

Line and length: This phrase serves as a mantra for any faster bowler embarking on a career or his next spell: 'Everyone's got a chink in their armour if you bowl *line and length*.' The twin virtues are so commonplace, in fact, that cricket reporters have taken to tacking on an appendage. The reference could be to the *miserly* Shaun Pollock 'dispensing *line, length* and *maidens*' or to a *shell-shocked* Australia 'relying on conventional warfare – *line, length* and *crease occupation*'. We should not omit to record the liveliest offering in this particular vein: 'McGrath produced his usual challenging mix of *line, length* and *lip*.'

Lines: A bowler will seek to produce *tight* lines if he is concentrating on giving the batsmen no *width*; he will create *dry lines* if he is bowling negatively way outside the off stump; and he will probably be offered *hard lines* if he is **carted** to **all parts**.

Lob: Designates the old-fashioned mode of underarm bowling, Mr G. H. Simpson-Hayward (Worcs) being, reportedly, 'the last of the *lobbers*'. Nowadays the term will be used only with reference to very *flighted* **stuff**: 'With his *lobbing* off breaks Powar would *prise out* two wickets just when the game was slipping away.' In fact, it will just as likely occur when a batsman *lollies up* a catch as the result of a **false shot**: 'Flintoff found an Asif delivery *stopping on* him and was *lured* into *lobbing* to mid-off.'

Lofted: When playing the *lofted drive*, the batsman will presumably have calculated the degree of risk involved: 'Inzamam **danced** down the pitch to *loft* over long-on.' But the verb is also used for unintentionally **uppish** shots: 'Smith *lofted* one straight into the hands of the waiting Michael Hussey.' Or sometimes the batsman gets a bit too much *loft* on the ball when he **underclubs**: 'Paul Collingwood was caught on the midwicket boundary using a seven-iron when a six was needed.'

Lollipop: 'Well, that's just a *lollipop*, that is. He'll smash those back past you all day.' Boycottism for a very bad ball. The shortened form can be a variant of **dolly** in Australian and Indian-English: 'Srinath should have got the 300th in New Zealand but he dropped a *lolly*.'

Long ball: 'Pietersen hits a *long ball* in the manner of Ian Botham.' Perhaps more at home in baseball or golf, but a fashionable way of saying that a batsman can **carry** the boundaries at most grounds. In his assessment of Imran Nazir, Prem Panicker goes to some lengths to describe what goes into the batsman's *big shots*: 'He's a very *clean* hitter, with lovely extension into his *lofted* shots, very quick to *pick* the ball to *loft* and hitting *clean and fluid*, getting a lot of distance on his *long ball*.'

Long half-volley: 'Get the yorker wrong and it becomes a *long half-volley* or a low full toss.' The difference between a *long half-volley* as opposed to a *half-volley* is, at first sight, the same as that between a *rank* long hop and a *long hop*. In other words, there should be no doubt that it is a very bad ball to be dispatched to the boundary. And yet it can sometimes happen that a batsman can get himself out, whether through eagerness or casualness, when the ball is right *in the slot* for driving. Therefore, the *long half-volley* can become a yorker after all: 'In the end Leyland was bowled by what is known in Yorkshire as a *long half-volley*, hitting a little too late and over the ball.'

Long handle: This stereotyped expression indicates a definite policy of *hitting out*, as once when Victor Trumper had been beaten twice in the first over of an innings: 'After that he gave them the *long handle* and made 100 before *lunch*.' Sometimes the batsman will be sure to wield the *cane* at both ends: 'To use a cliché, Singh gave it the *long handle* and got a six off Rao. Nadeem got the taste of the *handle* as he too was hit for a straight six.' A longer handle or a high grip will in theory allow a freer swing of the bat, but the technical origins of the phrase are almost always submerged beneath the idiom.

Long stop: It took some time for traditionalists to accept the demise of this fielding position in the late nineteenth century: 'The whole *science* of wicket-keeping does not consist in dispensing with the *long* *stop.* But a throwback to the good old days is possible when the wicket is lightning fast: 'Geoff Arnold was posted so fine he was almost a *long stop*.'

Loop: Any spinner worth his salt will want to cultivate or, if necessary, replenish his *loop*: 'Marks *lured* the batsmen to their doom with his *hanging loop*'; 'Giles has discovered the *teasing loop* that had been missing since he remodelled his **action** during the winter.' Phil Tufnell makes it sound too easy when reviewing a job well done against the West Indies: 'All I have to do is bowl *loopy-doopies* to them and they commit suicide.'

Loose: In the contest between bat and ball the batsmen will want to avoid producing too many *loose strokes* and the bowlers too many *loose deliveries*. Sometimes the bowlers succeed in *keeping it **tight***, whereas at others the batsmen are able to *cut loose*. The Caribbean has the expression *it's loose*, which might sound like a directive to the bowlers to stop **spraying** it around. In fact, it serves as a message of encouragement on the grounds that the batsmen are playing too *freely* and that the fielding side is in with a **chance**.

Loosener: The term combines the idea of a stiff bowler getting his muscles into full working order with the prediction that the deliveries sent down while he is warming up are not likely to be accurate. Slow bowlers don't qualify for a *loosener*, even if it may be hard for them at first to *drop on* a length. But the batsman, too, may have yet to get into his stride: 'Andre Nel's *loosener* cut back to *trim* Matthew Wood's bails.' What Wood obviously needed is called a **sighter**.

Lose the ball: While a game is in progress, the verb *lose* has the specific meaning of not *sighting* the ball:

'The catch fell to earth after Panesar *lost* it in the sun';
'There were no **sightscreens**, and Bradman *lost the
ball* in the crowd.'

Losing draw: 'There is nothing in sport quite like the
joy of the *losing draw*.' This observation by Simon
Barnes recognises the fact that there are few other
games – exceptions might include chess – where a
draw can feel so much like a win. If the last man survives for an hour to *save the game*, it is the batting side
who will celebrate wildly, even if they have been con-
summately outplayed over several days' play. A *losing
draw* is only a cause for disappointment, not rejoic-
ing, if it occurs in the grand final of certain domestic
competitions, decided on *first innings lead* if there is
no positive result to the game overall. This rule is a
foolproof way of snuffing out **brighter cricket**, as the
game will almost certainly *meander* or *peter out* into a
tame draw.

Lunch: *First-class* cricket used to be tightly gov-
erned, in the social historian's phrase, 'by the meal
times of the leisured'. Indeed, Neville Cardus saw it as
his prerogative to pass comment intermittently on the
luncheon interval: 'Rather a fanciful term this at
Sheffield, at least this was my experience on
Saturday.' Report has it that George Gunn once **gave
it away** deliberately when informed that the recess
he was playing towards would be later than usual: 'I
always have my *lunch* at 1.30.'

M

Majestic: An epithet of the highest possible order:
'Lumb's *majestic* six over long-off from a length ball

by Ben Phillips was the shot of the match.' *Regal* is on a par: 'Astle *regally* cover-drove Wright for a breath-taking six.' The closest journeymen pros on the county circuit get to the *majestic* and the *regal* is when they are looking for their overnight B&B.

Make inroads: This phrase will usually apply to bowlers *getting amongst* the top **order** early on: 'Three of the new Somerset players came to the rescue after Worcestershire had *made inroads.*' But it can also mean 'taking wickets' in a more general way: 'Essex's recruitment of Alex Tudor highlights previous lack of *penetration*, but Danish Kaneria should *make inroads* in late summer.' Compare **breakthrough**.

Make room: A standard phrase to register the footwork required when a batsman is looking for runs on the off side. This exercise is always dangerous against an off-spinner who is **extracting** some turn. There could even be an element of risk when Vic Marks was bowling: 'Trying to *make room* to cut, Randall succeeded only in playing on.' *Step away* is a regular variant, as in this comparable example: 'Chris Taylor *stepped away* to the leg side once too often and was bowled.' Batsmen who deliberately *back* or *draw away* towards leg in order to *manufacture* scoring strokes like the **inside-out** should be distinguished from those whose **arse** has *gone*.

Maker's name: A traditional piece of advice to batsmen early in an innings was to *show* the bowler the *maker's name* – in other words, to *present* the *full* **face** of the bat and play as straight as possible in *the* **V** between mid-off and mid-on. This exhortation is heard less these days, perhaps because the manufacturer's advertising is now plastered over most parts of the cricket bat. The phrase can also be used more ironically of the ball when it is hard and new (with the print on the *leather* intact) and it *hits* a batsman a *painful blow* on a fleshy part of the body: 'That looked a nasty one and Rodney might be able to see the *maker's name* in that bruise when he has a bath tonight.'

Mammoth: 'Middlesex prepare for *mammoth* run-chase.' *Mammoth* is certainly the headline word for a total of huge proportions. *Amass* and *pile on* also come ready to use as the relevant verbs. Huge scores constructed by an individual batsman tend rather to be thought of as *monumental*. Indeed, a really *big one* can be more than just a *milestone*: 'Sehwag took 497 minutes and 364 balls for his *monument*.'

Man: In certain contexts a member of the fielding side always seems to be a *man*: 'Cook was unlucky to *pick out* the *man* at point'; 'The *man* at backward square leg had just been moved five yards finer and Smith obligingly hit the next ball *straight down his throat*'; 'A 6–3 field with a *man on the drive*.' A predictable contraction of the old-fashioned *fieldsman*, handy for old-school summarisers still getting to grips with the names of the summer tourists: 'They all look the same under those sunhats, Richie.'

Manhattan: The bar chart now shown routinely in televised one-dayers to provide viewers with an at-a-glance breakdown of runs scored off each over. The ideal progression of a one-day innings tends to start quite high with some *pinch-hitting* (it might perhaps take fifteen overs to walk through the Financial District), then aims a bit lower as the batsmen *consolidate* (once the field goes back, a gentle stroll up to Greenwich Village is in order) before the final *slog* goes as *aerial* as possible (given enough room, you would want to get the Chrysler and Empire State Buildings onto the graph).

Mankad: To *Mankad* is to run out a non-striker who has ***backed up*** too far. Derived from the first recorded instance of the practice in Tests, when Vinoo Mankad removed the bails in his follow-through to get rid of Bill Brown. The mode of dismissal is considered very unsporting, especially by those who do not recall the fact that Mankad did issue a previous warning to the batsman. The shorthand for such run-outs remains common, especially in Asia and Australia, and is even applied to instances which occurred before Mankad was born: 'Ranji caused a stir when he *"Mankaded"* a batsman in what was essentially a social game between the Maharaja of Patiala's team and that of the British Residents of Simla in India in 1898.'

Manoeuvre: 'Kallis and Gibbs added 134 in 26 overs on a slow pitch, providing a lesson in how to *manoeuvre* the ball *into spaces*.' A vital skill in one-day cricket, especially for batsmen *consolidating* in mid-innings. Tactically astute captains and bowlers are said to *manoeuvre* their *fields*, while club cricket at its most frustrating can seem to be an endless round of *manoeuvring* the *covers* and the ***sightscreens***.

Marooned: Usually equates to *stranded* or left ***high and dry***, in that the batsman in question has run out of partners close to a *milestone*: 'Shah was left *marooned*, as one batsman after another ***perished*** in a ***blaze*** of rash shots.' More occasionally the verb may indicate that a *well-set* batsman has himself abandoned all attacking intentions and got stuck on a certain score: 'Moxon became *marooned* in the nineties before being caught at first slip one short of his hundred.'

Master: Before the Second World War, the most common method of signalling which side had got on top in the battle between bat and ball was to say whether the batsmen had *mastered* the bowling or not: 'Duleepsinhji and Hendren obtained the first real *mastery* over the attack, adding 104 runs in ninety minutes'; 'Blanckenberg bowled with such effect that the England innings was finished off for 183, no batsmen obtaining the least *mastery*.' It followed that Jack Hobbs became *The Master* and, since that title was already taken, Don Bradman became *The Complete Master*. Though the idea of achieving *mastery* became more ideologically unsound, the title of *Little Master* has been awarded in turn to Hanif Mohammad, Sunil Gavaskar and Sachin Tendulkar, while Vivian Richards *swaggered* to the fore as *The Master Blaster*. This last moniker may have been suggested also by the volume at which Viv liked to play his reggae, but it is so synonymous with *destructive* hitting that in South African Pro20 games it has become the title of an official prize: 'Kleinveldt was named *master blaster batsman*.'

Masterclass: A feature so well advertised in various sports these days that it would be impossible to attend them all: 'Cottey gave a *masterclass* against spin'; 'Above all, Tendulkar's innings was a *masterclass* in pacing.' Indeed, the *Little* **Master** is now expected to become the *little wall* as soon as Rahul Dravid has been dismissed.

Mateship: A word which John Howard wanted to enshrine in his country's constitutional Preamble. It encapsulates the team ethic of the Australian national side, an environment in which others might have found themselves at home: 'Brash, athletic, hard-living and born to win, Botham would have thrived in the *mateship culture* that drove their game in the seventies – assuming he could have coped with being in the same dressing-room as Ian Chappell, that is.'

MCC Coaching Manual: The tome which you reach for if you want the authorised version of the *textbook*. Some shots come *straight out* of said manual, while other techniques suggest more homespun instruction: 'Emburey's unbeaten 55 demonstrated a variety of improvised strokes hinting at a *DIY batting kit* rather than the *MCC Coaching Manual*.'

Meat: Corresponds approximately to the *middle* or *sweet spot*. Sometimes the term is used to emphasise brute power: 'Flintoff drives right out of the *meat of the bat*, sounding like a gunshot in a wooded glade.' At others it is employed to distinguish *genuine* strokes from *false* ones: 'Dilhara Fernando's bouncers were daringly pulled away – some off the *meat of the bat*, others off the *edge* – and Vaas and Murali weren't allowed to cast their *pressure net*.' For *meaty*, see *beefy*.

Members: Usually worth a sidelong glance in cricket reporting: 'Shahadat Hossain is not much shorter than Harmison and delivers the ball with a grunt that will shake the *members*' gin and tonics on the pavilion's new roof terrace.' *Egg-and-bacon* ties, rather than being a spluttered response to the same phenomenon, carry the recognised MCC colours.

Mental disintegration: 'Our job on the field is to always exploit a weakness in the opposition. If we find somebody is susceptible to *mental disintegration*, we will quickly apply the *pressure*.' John Buchanan is not necessarily referring only to the *art of sledging* here, because the *baggy greens* have other techniques, like delaying declarations, to make sure their victims feel truly shattered. But the expression, ascribed to Steve Waugh, has become the high-sounding way of referring to polite enquiries about the batsmen's parentage or bedtime preferences.

Merlyn: 'Born in a barn overlooked by the Black Mountains' (says the blurb), *Merlyn* is the name of a *wizard* new *bowling machine* which, reportedly, 'can spin it more than Alastair Campbell and as much as Shane Warne'. The English team therefore used it to prepare against leg spin in the 2005 *Ashes* series, although, again reportedly, the contraption jammed a few times when used in the *nets* at Lord's before the first Test. Older members of the groundstaff may have been reminded of the first bowling machine installed at *Headquarters*. According to Mike Brearley, this became 'known as the "Chris Old", since it kept on *breaking down*'. Before the invention of such devices, old *workhorses* like Alec Bedser may have been soured by their ceaseless toil: 'Bowling machine? I used to be the bowling machine.'

Mesmerise: One of those words, like *bamboozle*, used in classical descriptions of the leg-spinner's mystical *arts*: 'Qadir *mesmerised* the Australians in their second innings with a superb display of bowling.' But a passage by Cardus on Wilfred Rhodes suggests that spells of this kind are not always conjured from the *back of the hand*: 'The batsmen promptly gave themselves up to his *mesmerism*.'

Metronome: The moniker for a bowler who *drops it on the same spot* with *unerring*, *hypnotic* accuracy. In recent times, Glenn McGrath, 'the Outback's own *automaton*', is the archetype. Even he can have the odd day when he cannot find his *rhythm*: 'You don't see the *great metronome* with figures of 9.4–0–76–1 too often.'

Mexican wave: 'Another highlight was a *lengthy Mexican wave* during England's innings involving the use of torn newspapers, which ended abruptly with the dismissal of Alec Stewart. As a spectator behind me commented, "We've been distracted by the cricket."' This would now be called a *dirty Mexican wave*, because of the detritus thrown into the air, a manifestation which is very common in Twenty20 games. Like the **Barmy Army**, the *Mexican wave* is either viewed as an unbridled force undermining the very traditions of the game or some harmless fun being enjoyed by spectators who have availed themselves of refreshments. The difference of opinion often gets played out between the **members'** enclosure and the more popular areas of the ground, as in this example from Australia: 'While the ener-gised crowd propelled their arms into the air, the *members* wanted nothing of it – booed by the rest as the *Mexican wave* almost died as it reached their quarter.'

Michelle: 'Magic Matthew Hoggard's latest date with "*Michelle Pfeiffer*" stunned India's batting galacticos.' This line from the *Daily Mirror* on Hoggard's 6–57 return at Nagpur helps explain why *Michelle* is now a trade term for a *five-for*. As well as the rhyming slang, there may be some continuity with more estab-lished vernacular in that once a bowler has taken four wickets in an innings he traditionally starts thinking of *jugs*.

Middle: *Middle* works as an abbreviation three times over in cricket. When a batsman takes guard he may ask for *middle* (stump). To play himself into form he may need time *out in the middle* (of the pitch). And, once he is **set**, the ball will find the *middle* (of the bat). In the last instance the term can be applied a little more creatively: 'Flintoff's *edges* were as hard-hit as most people's *middles*.' This encourages us to read a dictum of Colin Ingleby-Mackenzie in a new light: '**Thrash** on with the *edges* and the *middle* will come.' But, back in Lancashire, an *orthodox* batsman like

Charlie Hallows impressed Neville Cardus in a different way: 'His bat seemed all *"middle"* from the match's outset.'

Middle of next week: Where you can get hit if you are being *dispatched* to **all parts**. However, batsmen who consciously try to put the ball well over the international date line may be sending the wrong message: 'Thorpe just *used the pace* on the ball and great placement to score more quickly than others who tried to *blast* it into the *middle of next week.*'

Military medium: *Brisk military medium* was a description commonly used in the early post-war years, if only to sustain the morale of the *change bowlers*. Any occurrence of the expression nowadays is likely to be disparaging in tone: 'Phil Mustard made Yorkshire's army of right-arm fast bowlers look *distinctly military medium.*'

Milkman: Trade term for a bit of botched ground fielding when, instead of getting down with the *long barrier*, the fielder tries to pick up on the run but succeeds only in taking the top off the imaginary milk bottle and a little bit of pace off the ball.

Milk the bowling: To take the ones and twos on offer rather than playing unnecessary forcing shots, because the bowling is so easy to pick off: 'Hemang Badani and new man, Vijay Bharadwaj, rightly decided to eschew flamboyant strokes, preferring instead to *milk the bowling.' Milking the bowling* is certainly distinct from *creaming* it.

Mind the windows: What Freddie Flintoff said to Tino Best from the slips, encouraging him to aim at the Lord's pavilion. Tino duly got himself out shortly afterwards having an *almighty slog*. At less exalted club venues, the instruction can be given less play-fully by irate house or car owners.

Miserly: The most standard way of referring to very *economical* figures, as in this suitably spare example: 'Dale Benkenstein proved *miserly*.' The word is defin-itive enough to encompass an attitude to bowling: 'The England seamers must aspire to match the *miser-liness* of Shaun Pollock and Glenn McGrath, who have thrived in Pakistan.' It can even be used, almost epigrammatically, to sum up a whole career, as in this remark attributed to Ray Robinson: 'Mailey bowled leg spin like a *millionaire* and Grimmett like a *miser*.'

Missing leg: 'Sarwan survives two Hoggard lbw appeals, the first one not worth the effort but the sec-ond a very good *shout* which umpire Koertzen pre-sumably feels is *missing leg*.' A one-size-fits-all way of explaining why an lbw appeal has been rejected, unless it has been ruled out *for height*. In club cricket, *missing leg* is sometimes uttered by home umpires when the ball would have *taken out all three*.

Mix and match: The phrase describes strategies developed to meet the demands of limited-overs cricket. Applied to both main departments of the game, there is an underlying sense of *rotating* the strike or the bowling. More specifically, though, bats-men must develop the flexibility to combine **big shots** with less ambitious **manoeuvres**: 'Katich, Hussey and Clark are high-quality front-line batsmen who *mix and match*, *consolidating* in mid-**order**.' To combat such tactics, especially if there is little variety in the attack, bowlers bring out the **dolly mixtures** to keep the batsmen guessing: 'Central Districts' charge to the semi-final came on the coat tails of a *mix-and-match* seam bowling attack **spearheaded** by Lance Ham-ilton and Ewen Thompson.'

Mop up: This idiom lends an air of brisk routine to the process of taking the last few wickets: 'Mark Ealham *mopped up* the innings'; 'Tate took three in the final *mopping up.*' *Clean up* and *polish off* provide support in this department. Real *mopping-up* exercises used to take rather longer, before the groundstaff became equipped with *Waterhogs* and *Whales*.

Mosaic: A colourful description of a pitch which is already riddled with cracks and likely to **break up** quickly: 'The more immediate talking point is the *biscuit-dry mosaic* of a pitch at Galle's International Stadium.' Modern landscape gardening can take over from ancient interior decorating when it comes to sourcing the relevant imagery: 'England's novice pace attack should all receive huge credit for the way they ruthlessly exploited the *crazy-paving* pitch.'

Motsa: Australian slang for a large gambling win, applied in cricket to big *tons* and significant **hauls**: 'I remember McGill got a *motsa* against the Bangers last year.'

Move about: 'Dilley bowled well in **conditions** which helped him *move* the ball *about.*' Here the verb is content to remain unspecific about which way the ball was deviating, in the same way that *lateral movement* is an expression which can comprise both swing and seam. The phrase can also be qualified so that it becomes virtually synonymous with **wobble**: 'He wasn't a bad bowler, Amar Singh. He *moved* it *about* a bit.' *Moving about* is not so clever if it is done behind the bowler's arm: 'SIDDAHN!'

Mow: Belongs to the same range of **agricultural** shots that includes the **heave**, **hoick** and the occasional *haymaker*, without being altogether distinguishable: 'Both batsmen played calmly against the two leg-spinners except for one inappropriate leg-side *mow* by Pietersen.'

Mullygrubber: An Australian term which can be used either for execrable *filth* which bounces several times before reaching the other end or alternatively for a dangerous delivery which shoots along the ground after pitching. Perhaps it is because batsmen are so wary of the ball which *keeps low* that they have so many words for it: *ankle-grabber*, **coolie creeper**, **daisy-cutter**, *mamba*, *scuttler*, *shooter*, *sneaker*, **submarine**, *torpedo*, *uruttal*, *worm-burner*.

N

Nagging: Derek Underwood was once described as a 'pitiless bowler' for his 'remorseless accuracy'. But *nagging* is the adjective used most remorselessly in this connection: 'Peter Trego bowled an excellent ten-over spell of *nagging* outswing.' As Piers Morgan intimates, this is not so much *asking questions* of the batsman as asking the same question over and over: 'McGrath just chunters away like the worst kind of hectoring mother-in-law. *Nag, nag, nag.*' After the entry on **granny's pinny** we will resist the temptation to tell any more mother-in-law jokes.

Name on it: What the captain sometimes shouts when a massive **skyer** is at the highest point of its trajectory. Helpfully, he usually doesn't put a *name on it* himself, sometimes leaving keeper, point and third man wondering who should *claim* the catch or whose name is going to be on the hospital bed if they collide.

Natural game: *Natural* means *uncovered* in the context of the pitch, and *uninhibited* in the context of a batsman's approach: 'Batting *behind* the top six in Tests is a wonderful position, I can come in and play my *natural game.*' Adam Gilchrist's *natural game* basically amounts to *giving it some **humpty***. We suspect that there are players whose natural inclination, even before they received formal coaching, was to *occupy the crease* and **compile** an innings carefully. But, while this method may be dignified with the term ***proper cricket***, it is only players who want to **knock** *the cover* off every ball who seem to qualify as *natural cricketers*.

Neck-and-crop: An equestrian term for falling arse-over-tit redeployed in cricket when the stumps have been sent well and truly ***cartwheeling***. Raffles, the anti-hero of E. W. Hornung's novels, was a crack gentleman cricketer before he became an amateur cracksman. During a bad few days in the Boer War, when the British army suffered three quick reverses, he reached instinctively for a cricketing metaphor, while also attesting that *peg* can be a synonym for ***pole***: '"All three *pegs*," groaned Raffles on the last morning of the week; "*neck-and-crop, neck-and-crop!*"'

Negotiate: Used, most predictably, when players are required to go in to bat at a difficult moment: 'Left with an awkward hour to *negotiate*, Australia lost three *cheap* wickets'; 'Riki Wessels *negotiated* a hat-trick ball, then took apart some woeful Somerset bowling.' Gooch and Boycott, like most opening batsmen, preferred to avoid *negotiating* tricky passages in the early evening – unless these were clauses in a ***rebel*** contract.

Nelson: Always *dreaded*, particularly in some quarters over recent years because of the media obsession with umpire David Shepherd's *superstitious jig*. The

West Country *yeoman* has at least provided a plausible explanation for why 111 is known as *Nelson*: 'Because he had one eye, one arm – and one cup of tea for breakfast.' Australia were bowled out for 111 at Headingley in 1981 after Botham had *given it some humpty*, although their *devil's number* is supposed to be 87, as if to reflect the fact that there the water goes the other way down the plughole.

Nervous nineties: The latitudes that a potential *centurion* can get *stuck* or *becalmed* in if he doesn't sail through to his *milestone*. One of those adjectival combinations that has become a noun in its own right: 'De Villiers surrendered to a fit of the *nervous-nineties*.'

Nets: 'The guys look in *top nick* in the *nets*. I know it's different in the middle but the *conditions* in the middle are also a lot different to the *nets*.' James Anderson's observation is not as confused as it may appear at first sight. Professional cricketers expect to be praised for the *hard work* they put in during *net practice*, unless they are attending *naughty-boy nets* in the aftermath of a heavy defeat or breach of curfew. Yet every cricketer will tell you that no amount of *netting* truly replicates *time in the middle* with or against fielders, especially if practice involved *net bowlers*. A withering piece of *sledging*, therefore, after an easy victory batting second, not advisable if you are planning to have a drink in the pavilion afterwards, is to say 'thanks for the *net*' to the fielding side as they *trudge* off the pitch.

Neutral umpires: In 1994, the ICC finally accepted that the concept of *neutral umpires* was not necessarily a tautology.

New Botham: Even while the great all-rounder was still playing, the English press were desperately trying to find the *new Botham* and awarding the title to any medium-pacer who could *hold a bat*. An entire squad can be constructed from the procession of *bits-and-pieces* players with *averages* the wrong way round who were saddled with this burden: Ellison, Pringle, Capel, DeFreitas, Lewis, Cork, Chapple, Ealham, White, Reeve, Hollioake A., Hollioake B., Hamilton, Irani. Darren Gough only had to score a fifty to be put forward for selection, while Andrew Flintoff took some time to reach full maturity and recognition in his own right. Flintoff is no longer the *new Botham* but Marcus Berkmann has suggested that as Botham gets older he is becoming the *new Freddie*. See *going off out there*.

Nibble: We all know what it's like to take a bite against our better judgement, but maybe the time of day just gets too much: 'After tea Lancashire lost Mark Chilton, *nibbling* at an outswinger'; 'When Spearman finally *nibbled* a catch behind on 341, he had batted nearly nine hours.' Batsmen can also *fish* outside the off stump, in what might sound like a curious reversal of roles.

Nick: Seems to have taken over almost entirely from *snick* to indicate an outside *edge*: 'Ben Hutton *nicked* one that left him from Neil Carter.' Typically fatal, although Peter Roebuck used the word to describe his early technique against spin: 'I had to rely on *nicks* and *tucks* to pick up some runs.' This was before he gave his game a lift via the *aerial route*.

Niggardly: 'England found runs desperately hard to come by on a sluggish pitch against *niggardly* bowling, *backed up* by a *prehensile* performance in the field.' *Niggardly* seems to be the favoured word to describe an opening spell that *gives nothing away*. Otherwise not as frequent as *miserly*, but just as mean. We are reminded of the Yorkshire motto 'Give 'em *nowt*.'

Nightwatchman: An occasional job in cricket, but still serious and potentially dangerous work, especially if it goes into overtime the next day: 'Billy Taylor batted through the two and a quarter-hour morning session in a dogged demonstration of the *nightwatchman's art.*' Jason Gillespie's double century at Chittagong was more Rembrandt than Pratchett.

Nine, ten, jack: A way of referring to the last three men in the batting *order*, usually in the hope or expectation that they will *collapse* like cards. But sometimes the tail is made of sterner stuff: 'There is *depth* in the batting, so much so that even the *nine, ten, jack*, Waqar Younis, Saqlain Mushtaq and Shoaib Akhtar, are not *bunnies* and can add some *useful runs* in their own way.' Within this particular trio, traditional *tailenders'* methods would be favoured by *nine* and especially by *jack*, leaving the *ten* to play *proper cricket*.

Nine-to-five job: This could be a reference to playing hours during the Pakistani winter (if the light holds) or a reflection on the staleness caused by the county circuit, but instead Duncan Fletcher was talking about *regulation* catches: 'If Jones was putting down *nine-to-five jobs* then you probably would be worried, but they were difficult *chances*.'

Nip: In the eighteenth century, to *nip* meant to *nick*, and into the nineteenth fielders could be placed in positions like *cover nips*, presumably in order to collect such edges. The word then evolved to describe turn off the wicket, a precursor of *rip*: 'Tyldesley bowled a clever length without spinning the ball with the "*nip*" that kills.' It could also be employed as a sharper term for pace off the pitch, usually combined with some *lateral movement*: 'Bedser *cut* the ball either way with marked *nip.*' This is the main sense today: 'Sheriyar *nipped* the ball both ways.' The usage also allows for an ironic reference to the weather: 'The autumn has brought more *nip* than the Derby bowlers.'

Not a man move: When Gary Sobers was in good form, this was one way of suggesting that his cover drives were so well struck that the fielders remained rooted to the spot. David Bratt of the *Trinidad Guardian* has adopted the formula to pass comment on the timing of Carl Hooper and the sportsmanship of crowds at **Headquarters**: 'Hooper could make the *latest* of *late* cuts, *not a man move* and not an Englishman clap.'

Not cricket: Seeking 'to spread the gospel of British fair play' as MCC manager on the 1932–33 tour of Australia, Pelham Warner proudly recited the commonplace that the game was associated with the highest moral standards: 'To say "that is *not cricket*" implies something underhand, something not in keeping with the best ideals.' Later on that tour, Warner went to the Australian dressing room to enquire after the health of Woodfull, who had been struck over the heart by Larwood. The Australian captain's celebrated response, as reported at any rate, is interesting in that it told Warner **Bodyline** was *not cricket* while studiously avoiding the actual establishment phrase: 'There are two teams out there but only one is playing cricket.' It would *not* be *cricket*, however, to conclude without adding that Warner became uncomfortable with Jardine's tactics and that Woodfull might not have been so ready to take the moral high ground if he had possessed a **battery** of fast bowlers on his own side.

Not there: 'The runs were flowing and I saw the *width* and went after it. But the ball was *not there.*' By this Mahela Jayawardene does not mean the ball has

disappeared, either to the boundary or into thin air. Instead, it was not quite up ***in the slot*** for the drive.

Nudge: The verb that best illustrates the style of an ***accumulator*** such as Neil Fairbrother, whom Michael Atherton recalls as '*nudging* here and there and rarely *becalmed*'. It tends to be accompanied, almost indiscriminately, by *nurdle*, as when Andrew Strauss tried to give just a tactful *nudge* to the selectors back in 2003: 'We have enough players in our squad here who can hit the ball over the ropes. So, hopefully, at some stage there will be a role there for a *nudger* and *nurdler* like me.'

Nuggety: 'In his playing days, Border was the epitome of the tough, *nuggety*, Aussie battler'; 'It was a *nuggety* innings from Langer that *glued* the innings together.' Although the glue may be 'universal', such instances suggest this as being an Australian (and even a left-handed) quality. This third example ends up rather by corroborating the point: 'Whenever England needed him, Thorpe was at the height of his *nuggety* powers, except for his back – and his slip fielding.'

O

Obdurate: Denotes stubborn batting carried to an extreme degree: 'Peter Trego played an *obdurate* innings of 92 minutes for three.' Batsmen wishing to specialise in self-denial are advised to study the history of Indo-Pak Tests and ***Roses*** matches. According to legend, the latter encounters were so *fiercely contested*, especially between the World Wars, that the top ***order*** was instructed not to risk fours before

lunch. Derek Birley relates how, if Holmes and
Sutcliffe (the Yorkshire openers of this period) happened to fail, 'the next man in was Edgar Oldroyd,
who had raised *obduracy* to an art independent of out-
ward events'. Cardus described the same batsman as
'unmistakably Yorkshire', adding for good measure
that 'he bats with an accent'.

Occasional: Cricket needs to find alternatives to
'irregular' for a bowler who *turns his arm over* only
sporadically: 'Simon Katich *occasionally* **purveys**
unorthodox left-arm wrist spin'; 'Owais Shah took
four wickets with his *part-time* off breaks.' The
Tsunami Appeal match was a special occasion, when
everybody wanted to contribute: 'Brian Lara employed ten bowlers, including his own *ultra-occasional*
dobbers.'

Occupation of the crease: Cricket is measured not
just by runs and wickets but also by time, which
means that *staying in* may become the tactical imperative: 'De Villiers is proving as adept as his captain at
crease occupation.' There is another form of the noun
which makes the batsman sound more like a tenant
than a soldier: 'Katich's five hours of *occupancy* across
two innings was an invaluable effort.' Some of
cricket's greatest innings have been heroic exercises in
sustained resistance, but sometimes *mere occupation of
the crease* is not sufficient for the needs of the team or
the spectators. Don Bradman saw slow play as a good
argument in favour of one-day cricket: 'It rids the
game of the unutterable bore who thinks *occupancy of
the crease* and his own personal aggrandisement are all
that matter.' It so happened that these lines were written in the year of Geoffrey Boycott's retirement.

Offer: Batsmen can get out *offering* no stroke,
although when they play at the ball it is extremely

unusual to be told that they 'offered' a shot. Meanwhile, deliveries can *offer to swing*, a way of saying that the movement was minimal or that the batsman has been *set up*: 'Martin-Jenkins produced a **beauty** which *offered to swing* into Adam Hollioake only to leave him off the pitch.' Umpires regularly *offer* the light and batsmen almost as regularly **accept** it. There is no shortage of other routine examples on offer: 'Irani *offered* no discernible **chance**'; 'The pitch was a **belter** and *offered* only some slow turn.' But only the noun really invites us into idiomatic territory: 'The visiting team's *wayward offerings* were *hungrily* accepted.' **Cafeteria bowling** is just around the corner.

Off the mark: Bowlers spend much of their cricketing life going *back* to their *mark*, whereas batsmen are only concerned with *getting off the mark* as smartly as possible. This is hardly a *milestone*, but it can still be a challenge even to the experienced batsman. Raymond Robertson-Glasgow recalled, of the *impish* Patsy Hendren, that 'to the end he was a *nervous starter*; and it was, surely, the character of boyhood, which he never quite threw off, that caused him such visible emotion over the first run of each innings.' Since Hendren **compiled** 170 centuries, we tend to think that he was not a major sufferer of the **nervous nineties**.

One brings two: A little rule of cricket, which gives rise to the **Boycott test**. Because batsmen are usually at their most vulnerable when they first come in, one **breakthrough** will often lead to another: 'The cricket cliché that "*one brings two*" was proved accurate when Agarkar removed Hussain with his next ball.'

One-cap wonder: Writing a tribute to the Yorkshire bowler Alec Coxon, Frank Keating mourned the passing of the 'unofficial president of cricket's *one-cap* *wonder* club'. Coxon's only Test appearance was at Lord's in 1948, a year when England narrowly escaped a whitewash by Australia. It is usually in such circumstances, when the selectors *chop and change* throughout a series, that the number of one-off selections increases. The players in question then return to their counties, waiting for a recall more in hope than expectation. Most of them are not left hanging on as long as Khalid Hassan, *discarded* by Pakistan after one match in 1954: 'As a *one-cap wonder*, his last day of Test cricket came at the tender age of 16 years 356 days.'

One-day shot: 'Trying to hit it *on the up* there was a *one-day shot* and he should have been getting his *nut* down.' The traditionalists have their way here in the sense that *one-day* almost always seems to be a pejorative adjective when combined with *shot*. Compliments to *one-day shots* actually played in one-day games seem to be considered redundant. Complaints about 'five-day shots' in Twenty20 cricket are also never heard. But, if a slip *cordon* remains in place after the fielding restrictions have been lifted in a one-day international, a commentator might say: 'Looking at the field Gillespie is bowling to, it's almost like a Test match.'

On the up: Refers to driving without *getting to the pitch* of the ball, although this may be something of a relative concept, as John Arlott noted of Clive Lloyd: 'His great reach enabled him to drive "*on the up*" deliveries to which ordinary men would play back.' Not a shot to delight the *purist*, but nevertheless there are *few finer sights* in cricket.

Oomph: An imitative term for how hard a bowler *hits the bat* or for acceleration in a one-day innings: 'Hussain had given the Essex innings *oomph* with a rapid 35 – including 18 *larruped* from an especially *wayward* Sheriyar over.' In Bollywood they are still calling actresses with sex appeal *oomph girls*, which may or may not be relevant to the following example: 'Suresh Raina is probably amongst the top 10 fielders in world cricket and would add real *oomph* to the Indian side in Tests.'

Open the shoulders: Like *freeing the arms*, an idiom for *hitting out* or going on the attack: 'Symonds contented himself with playing **second fiddle** but once Flintoff had gone he *opened his shoulders.*' First violinists might be wise to eschew such a dramatic change in tempo.

Open up an end: What the fielding side does when it gets through all but one of the *recognised* batsmen and *exposes* the tail. The idea is that they then concentrate on **containing** at one *end* and *firing out* the **rabbits** at the other. Depending on the strength of the middle **order**, an early **breakthrough** can be enough: 'The **collapse** began with a suicidal drive by Gayle and, roared on by the capacity crowd, England's bowlers *swarmed through* the *opening.*'

Optional practice: David Gower's characteristic euphemism for *naughty-boy **nets*** on the 1985–86 tour of the West Indies. As far as we know, he gave it a miss.

Order: The batting *order* is conventionally divided into *top*, *middle* and *lower*, with an occasional glance at the class system: 'The *middle* and *lower-middle order* had *melted* away.' Jonathan Agnew, when playing for Leicestershire, had the feeling that umpires could be a bit more inclined to give an lbw if the **victim**'s career was not at stake: 'It seems often to be the case that *lower-order **batters*** get *fired out.*' Bowlers can be just as fussy about taking wickets: 'Billy Taylor sliced the *bottom* off the Gloucestershire batting yesterday, as he had the *top* the previous evening.' This is also known, somewhat less graphically, as *topping* and *tailing*.

Outer: In Australia, the open sections of the ground where you can down a tinnie; the world over, an umpire who is liable to *shoot up* the **finger**: 'He's always been an *outer*, that one.' *Outers* are usually retired bowlers.

Out of business: The phrase puts a mercantile perspective on the ramifications of failure: 'If I played a spinner like Laker or Wardle, one of the stroke-makers like Weekes or Walcott might put him *out of business* for the tour.' Sometimes a captain like Len Hutton can fear one of his key bowlers may have to be given a very long **rest** if he is hit out of the attack on an unhelpful wicket in a confidence-draining way. But sometimes it is the batsmen who may feel underemployed. This observation by New Zealand's Shane Bond during the Videocon Cup seems to be suggesting that the **fast bowlers' union** remains fully operative: 'It was nice from our point of view that Zimbabwe could keep India's top **order** *out of business* once again.'

Over the bar: 'Although *missed* on 30, when Mark Butcher *palmed* a catch at second slip off Caddick *over the bar*, Bichel played well.' Here the terminology has come from football because of the opportune analogy with a goalkeeper conceding a corner. In the cricketing case, a boundary will have been the likely result.

P

Padding up: 'Fancy *padding up*, Dom?' This is more likely to be a captain clarifying who is next but one in the **order** than a bowler ironically suggesting that a batsman should *offer* no stroke. *Padding up* can be risky against swing or seam – 'Windows was beaten by late movement as he *padded up*' – but stubborn *pad play* remains a legitimate method of keeping the spinners more in line. See also *hide* and *kick away*.

Paddle: The shot (also known as a *lap*) amounts, in effect, to a sweep played like a glance: 'Lara moved across his stumps and *paddled* the ball fine.' But the batsman needs to do a bit more than just *help it on its way*: 'John Francis *paddled* a leg-side ball from Mark Davies to the wicketkeeper.'

Pair: *Of spectacles* was once understood, but the term is so universal for the occurrence of two *blobs* by one batsman in the same game that no imagination is required to work out what being *on a pair* means. A *king pair* is comprised of two *golden **ducks***.

Pair of hands: Usually described as *good* or *safe*, although there are alternatives, especially for wicketkeepers: 'He's got a *lovely soft pair of hands.*' *Safe pair of hands* is another expression that has passed into everyday use, as these headlines illustrate: 'Ben Bernanke: A *safe pair of hands*?'; 'New Pope – *safe pair of hands.*' Even the Fed Governor and Benedict XVI probably understand that it is advisable to do their catching with both hands rather than one.

Palpable: Saw service in the past as a synonym for *definite* or *rank*: 'Douglas mistimed a *palpable* long hop that he tried to pull and was *clean* bowled.' Nowadays the word is reserved for a clear lbw: 'Knight tried to cut and was *palpably* leg before.' Compare *adjacent* and *plumb*.

Paltry: The favoured term for any score that is going to be uncompetitively low: 'Bangladesh's batting crumpled inside 37 overs for a *paltry* 90'; 'Surrey were left a *paltry* 40 to win.' *Meagre* and *scanty* come in as respectable runners-up, but the traditional preference for *paltry* can be sensed also in Cardus's adoption of the abstract noun: 'The innings was saved from *paltriness* by Sutcliffe's superb **batsmanship**.'

Park: Forms part of the address of many cricket grounds and therefore used routinely as a synonym, especially when a bowler is being **hammered** to **all parts** of it: 'If you couldn't put the ball in the right place, you'd be hit *all around the park*.' In Australia, *park* is used as an adjective in the same way that the English would use *club*: 'Key reminds me of your standard tubby *park* cricketer.' Bill Lawry is once reported as saying, when it was suggested Tests should be made more entertaining: 'If they want to see *park cricket*, let them go to the *park*.'

Pepper: An image that comes into play when batsmen have their **eye in** and are able to concentrate their fire: 'Trescothick *peppered* the covers with crisply timed strokes off the **back foot**'; 'Once Prior and Cook had *seen* the **shine** *off*, both began to *pepper* the short boundary on the Grand Stand side.' The metaphor is refocused when the verb turns passive: 'Van Jaarsveld's 114 came from 100 balls and was *peppered* with 14 fours and three sixes' – liberally sprinkled, in short. No doubt the outcome will have been salty as well in this further example: 'Waugh moved to short cover to *pepper* Lara with more *chat*.'

Percher: There is an exceptional usage from 1913 recorded in the *Oxford English Dictionary* in which *percher* seems to be synonymous with *bouncer*. But many club cricketers will instantly recognise it as a term for an absolute **dolly**: 'My goodness, Harbhajan's dropped a *percher*.'

Perfume ball: 'Sehwag's scintillating innings was cut short by a *perfume ball* that Malcolm Marshall would have been proud of.' A term used in the Caribbean to describe a nasty bouncer. The idea is it passes the batsman's nose close enough for him to *smell the leather*.

Periscope: When a batsman ducks under a short ball, he may be so busy taking evasive action that he can inadvertently leave his bat vertical in the air. The bat is invariably described as a *periscope* in these circumstances. Sometimes a failure to retract does no harm: '*Periscope up* from Zaheer there but he didn't get a *nick* on it.' Sometimes a fatal sequence of events is set in train: 'The ball *reared*, Dighe *went under* but left his bat sticking up *periscope-like*, the ball clipped the back of the upraised bat on its way through and Sangakkara did another passable imitation of a leaping trout going after a fly.' Better players of the *short stuff* navigate bouncers by *dropping the hands*.

Perish: Almost too existential a word for its regular purpose in cricket, even though in some instances it is meant to reflect an all-or-nothing approach: 'Shane Warne *perished* with a *heave across the line*.' On reflection, though, it is almost more startling to recall that, when a *chance* goes down, a batsman is *given a life*. We leave the last word on this profound topic to Dickie Bird: 'If I had to pick a man to *bat for my life* it would be Boycott, but he'd want to know how much it was worth before he took guard.'

Phone number: 'The Bulls' *middle order* read like a *local phone number* with Hayden's departure igniting a *collapse* of 4–2 in the space of 22 deliveries.' In other words, none of Queensland's *middle order* got out of single figures, and there were a few zeros involved.

Pick: When playing spinners, an alternative to *read*:
'There are three ways to *pick* a spinner – from the
hand, in the air or off the pitch.' Humble *park* cricketers confess to managing only the last, sometimes
when the *googly* has already turned past their *lavish*
drive.

Pick up: This phrase has three distinct meanings
which can be experienced within split seconds of each
other. A batsman may *pick up* the length of the ball
very quickly (or not *pick* it *up* at all if the *sightscreen*
attendant is not attending). He may be particularly
fond of his bat because of its great *pick-up* – in other
words, the weight distribution feels especially good in
the backlift. If he has sighted the ball well and is comfortable with the *willow*, he may then decide to take
the *aerial route*, *picking* the ball *up* over the infield.
Square leg is the usual direction for these *pick-up*
shots.

Pie thrower: 'Mike Kasprowicz gave new meaning to
the epithet *"pie thrower"* – coined by fellow
Australian Rodney Marsh – in a dreadful spell which
conceded 40 runs.' We cannot say with certainty
whether Marsh was the first person to use this image
in the context of *cafeteria bowling*, but a mocking
remark of his about the England attack quickly established the term on the county circuit in the mid-
1990s. Nor did we have the privilege of seeing Ian
Robinson bowl for Bangor University, but he perhaps
regretted allowing someone from the ranks to write
the team pen-pictures for the website: 'Unable to
swing the ball, our illustrious captain can only be
described as a *military medium*, *up and down* pie
chucker.'

Pinch-hitter: 'Kent's 183 looked *inadequate*, especially while the *pinch-hitter*, Hamblin, was *walloping*

the ball *to all corners* in his 24-ball *cameo.*' Since the
change in limited-over regulations which restricts the
number of fielders outside the *circle* in the first fifteen overs, teams have tended to promote big-hitters
like James Hamblin to open the innings and reporters
have imported the relevant term from baseball to
describe them. Even the most famous exponents of
the tactic are not guaranteed to load the bases:
'Kaluwitharana and Jayasuriya, Sri Lanka's celebrated *pinch-hitters*, both hit straight to third man in
the first four balls of the game.' Other borrowings
from baseball are rare, although there is the occasional reference to a *bunt* when a batsman tries to *dab*
the ball down looking for a single: 'In attempting to
retain the bowling, Speight *bunted* a catch off the
ubiquitous Dale.'

Pinch the strike: *Rotation* of the *strike*, especially in
one-day cricket, is an important part of the game.
Keeping or *farming the strike*, when trying to *shep-*
herd the tail, is an acknowledged skill. But *pinching*
the strike, especially when the pitch is *flat* and the
bowling attack is friendly, is not the done thing.
George Emmett clearly spent hours up the other end
admiring Wally Hammond's *batsmanship* when they
played together for Gloucestershire: 'Whatever else
you may say about Walter, he could count perfectly up
to six.'

Pitch liaison officer: Euphemistic term introduced
to English county cricket in 2000 for what used to be
known as an *inspector of pitches.* Journalists can forget
the new title when the ball *misbehaves* on the first
morning of a match and a *pitch liaison officer* is hur-
riedly summoned to the ground: 'The ECB's *pitch*
inspector arrived in time to watch Key and Symonds
crash 99 in just 16 overs.' Perhaps the name change
was designed to make the official who can impose

penalties for *unfit* pitches sound less like a policeman, although a visit from the *PLO* may alarm the
members even more.

Pitch smacking: While *gardening* is the polite
English term for running repairs to the wicket and
suggests leisurely pottering about, *pitch smacking* is
the more businesslike and *Bradmanesque* expression
– the kind of thing an Australian would naturally do,
like chewing on gum, *going hard* and winning a lot.

Plasticine: 'We seemed constantly to be batting
either on *dust* or *plasticine*. Of the two, believe me, we
preferred the *plasticine*.' This is Richie Benaud's
assessment of the pitches the Australians encountered in 1956, *prepared* especially for Laker and Lock.
The effect of rain on the uncovered, *wearing* wickets
meant that a lot of Australian-style *gardening* was
probably required.

Play and miss: What happens from the batsman's
perspective when the bowler *beats the bat*. Again,
the expression would never be used if the *miss* actually led to a wicket. Instead, the phrase, often seen in
a noun formation as correct as the shot described, is
used to convey the fact that *conditions* are difficult
for batting or that a player is hopelessly out of form:
'It took self-belief, but after a couple of *play-and-
misses* and edgy strokes, Laxman settled down to play
an innings of character.'

Play around: 'Youhana tends to *play around* his
front pad, coming down on the stroke from a wide
backlift.' This is a common problem of batting technique, to correct which Ed Smith recommends the
principle of *clearing the front leg*, especially as a way of
combating the ball *speared in* to the body *at the
death* in a one-dayer. The same kind of technical

problem may have been a factor in this next instance: 'First change Darren Thomas struck in his first over as Peter Bowler *played all around one.*' But the addition of *all* tends to suggest that the phrase should be seen as a more euphemistic version of *playing **across the line**,* just as *playing down the wrong line* sounds like a more elaborate way of *missing* altogether.

Play yourself in: Brian Lara is a traditionalist when it comes to Twenty20: 'It's good for people who want to watch a game after work, but I think the *art* of batting is to work out the pitch and *play yourself in.*' ***Having a look*** at the bowling is fundamental to ***building an innings*** and is a process which could take most of the day when Geoffrey Boycott was at the crease. At the other end of the spectrum, some opening batsmen have adopted a policy of ***flaying*** themselves in: 'Back in 1996, Jayasuriya's idea of *playing himself in* was to take a few swift steps down the wicket to loft the ball over cover or wide midwicket as his mood dictated.'

Plumb: Of a batsman, indisputably leg before: 'Yadav then trapped Nuwan Zoysa *plumb **in front*** of the wicket on the very next ball.' Of a pitch, unrelentingly true: 'No one, apart from batsmen perhaps, is looking for *plumb* pitches.' In both situations, *absolutely* can be added, even if *absolutely plumb* sounds tautologous.

Plunder: The likeliest idiom in the range applicable to heavy scoring: 'England enjoyed a morning session in which they *plundered* 177 at a fraction under six an over'; 'Naved-ul-Hasan joined Yardy in the afternoon sun to *pillage* the Middlesex attack'; 'Inzamam *rampaged* from 50 to 100 in just 46 balls.'

Poetry: Although it is batsmen who tend to be the *artists*, *poetry* – in the metaphorical sense at least – is usually the realm of fast bowlers with a *rhythmical* run-up: 'Harold Larwood, like Lindwall, had a glorious ***approach*** – like *lethal poetry.*'

Pole: Synonym for *stump*, more common in the singular – 'Got him, middle *pole*' – but possible in the plural, where any sudden rearrangement sounds for a moment like a medical operation: 'Boycott had his *poles* removed by Holding after a series of *leather-sniffing* bouncers.'

Popadom fingers: Nickname coined in the Essex dressing room for Nasser Hussain, given the frequency with which his digits were fractured. A phrase which also points to the importance of curry in the county pro's diet.

Post: There are two contexts in which this verb is used in cricket. Firstly, it means to put runs on the board: 'Adam Gilchrist's 73-ball hundred helped the home side *post* a *daunting* total of 328 for four.' Secondly, it means to put a fielder in a specific position, as Michael Atherton did to good effect in this instance: 'I *posted* Mark Ramprakash *on the hook* for Mark Waugh, who duly *obliged.*'

Pouch: We take this to be a native Australianism for *to catch* which has gone into the universal currency. Witness this example from the subcontinent: 'Yousuf Youhana completed the *slide* when a drive was brilliantly *pouched* by Zaheer Khan on his follow-through.' When Rod Marsh rugby-tackled a ***freaker*** who was holding up play, Richie Benaud – after a characteristically pregnant pause – remarked: 'That's the first one Rodney's *pouched* all day.'

Practice: Cricket is a game where preparation in the ***nets*** has not usually been ***optional*** and where drills on the outfield before play have become ever more sophisticated. Gone are the days when five minutes on the slip cradle and hitting up a couple of gentle *steeplers* constituted the old pro's warm-up. At the same time, the lexicon recognises moments *out in the middle* which seem more of a rehearsal than the real thing. If a game is *petering out* into a draw, there is the opportunity for the batsmen to clock up some *time in the middle*: 'The Maharashtra openers, Mansigh Nigde and Dheeraj Jadhav, *settled* for *batting practice* and *grinded out* 16.2 overs.' Meanwhile, if a player edges behind with an *open face*, it sometimes seems as if he has done it on purpose: 'McGrath struck first, removing his regular **bunny** Trescothick, who *gave* second slip *catching practice*.' Bowlers may cite as one more example of the atavistic prejudice against them the fact that there are not many references to 'bowling practice', even if it is considered important for them to get some *overs under their belt* early in a season or series.

Premeditated: 'Reetinder Singh Sodhi stepped out of his crease for a *premeditated* **slog** and missed the line of the ball completely as it turned a long way back to crash into his stumps.' If Sodhi had read the bowler's intentions correctly and smashed the ball for six, he would of course have been praised for *gambling* correctly or even *improvising* wonderfully.

Pressure: *Building the pressure* by bowling as many **dot balls** as possible is a mantra of the modern game. Often an end is kept particularly **tight**, until one batsman can cope no longer with his source of runs being cut off: 'India maintained the *pressure*, more so on Yasir, who was beginning to *twitch*.' Although it is the modern fashion to focus on *pressure* in sport more generally, alumni of the hard old schools are having none of it. Here is Brian Close reflecting on his selection for England as a teenager: 'It didn't create any *pressure*, there was no such thing as *bloody pressure* in those days. *Pressure* is a journalist's word.'

Primary: A *primary* is a *golden **duck***, as celebrated by the charitable *Primary Club*, whose members must have a *first-baller* on their CVs. References to *primary strokes* are more at home in swimming or tennis, but we have seen one in a 1947 *Times* report inspired by a ***tailender*** sticking to the *basics* of forward and backward defence: 'Doug Wright, who not only knows the *primary strokes*, but can play them, defended with ***studious*** serenity.'

Princely: 'What a *princely* entry! This boy has class' – John Arlott's commentary at the moment of David Gower stroking his first ball in Test cricket for four. No doubt the spirit of Ranji is felt to live on in the chosen epithet: 'Ramnaresh Sarwan and Kadeer Ali batted in *princely* fashion.' In their maturity the young bloods can then hope to lay claim to what Derek Birley calls the 'aureate adjectives', like ***imperious*** and ***majestic***.

Pristine: An occasional synonym for *flawless*, and with a ***classical*** edge to it: 'Martyn sticks to the *text-book* and composes *pristine* hundreds which, like the feats of the best wicketkeepers, pass almost unnoticed'; 'When the bowlers pitched too full, they would be treated to drives of *pristine* beauty.'

Probing: This word identifies the kind of controlled persistence required of a regular bowler, especially if the wicket ***offers*** no more than modest ***assistance***: 'Peter Kirtley kept *probing away* on a good length'; 'Anil Kumble's relentless *probing* dragged India back into the match.' The essential idea is to go on asking questions of the batsmen, as in this related example:

'Tahir *found* Michael Brown's outside *edge* with one of many *searching* leg-cutters.'

Procession: A traditional term for a rapid sequence of dismissals: 'The rest fell for single figures in a *sorry procession* before **lunch**.' In fact, it appears already in the historic account of the original **Ashes** Test by the English batsman who was left **high and dry**, namely Charles Studd: 'Then things began to change and a *procession* began.' W. G. Grace provides a further example, remembering a game where one side was 6 all out: 'Only nine overs were bowled, and it was a most *inglorious procession*.' In such circumstances, the duly ceremonious way for the batsman to depart would have to be by **trudging** off.

Prod: The risk in playing this routine defensive shot is of being too *tentative*: 'Youhana's *prod* at Kumble trickled onto the stumps via pad and boot.' *Prodding the pitch* by way of **gardening** is the likely prescription for settling the nerves.

Prop and cock: Unlike other combinations such as *tip and run* or *chip and chase*, this term does not describe improvised methods of keeping the scoreboard ticking over but a **tailender**'s haphazard attempts to **block**. The aim is usually to secure a draw or see the senior partner through to his *milestone*: 'Fraser *propped and cocked*, and after 5½ hours at the crease, Russell turned Alderman off his hips for the single that took him to three figures.'

Proper cricket: In a very primary sense, *proper cricket* begins when children first play with a hard cricket ball. This is an experience which puts some of them off for life, hence the proliferation of *Kwik*, *Kanga*, *Kiwi* and *Inter* cricket in schools. For graduates of traditional northern academies, *proper cricket* can start only when any hint of contrivance or nonchalance has been prohibited and there is due respect for the fully competitive nature of the contest. Neville Cardus, reporting on a typical **Roses** match, approved of the way every delivery was *treated on its merits*: 'The good ball was stubbornly opposed; runs, or efforts to get runs, were made whenever bad balls came along. This was *proper cricket*.' The distinction becomes sharper in the era of limited-overs games: 'Surrey had reached their apparently impregnable position by playing what was as close to *proper cricket* as you can get in this type of combat.' Indeed, *proper* now often means simply 'not one-day'.

Pudding: A *pudding* is a wet pitch. But we think that the following example is more about acclimatisation: 'Jayasuriya, with timing and footwork skew-whiff, has been batting as though pitches had been top-dressed with *tapioca* in the opening weeks of the season.'

Pugnacious: Falls somewhere in between *gritty* and *belligerent* when describing an individual innings: 'Stuart Matsikenyeri top-scored with 37 off 46 balls in a *pugnacious **knock**.*' When applied to a certain breed of batsman, it usually comes with some emphasis on their other character-building qualities: 'In the wicketkeepers' tradition, Rhodes is stocky yet athletic, and a *pugnacious* batsman'; 'Australia introduced a *pugnacious* Tasmanian, David Boon, who scored a courageous half-century on debut.'

Pulverise: Top-of-the-range hyperbole to describe the most devastating kind of batting performance: 'Pietersen arrived to play a *pulverising* innings of 80 off 50 balls.' The usage verges on tautology in this further example: 'Key and Strauss *pulverised* a *powder-puff* West Indian attack.' Not applicable, as far as we know, to what bowlers do.

Pummel: 'Hussey *pummelled* the Glamorgan attack to end 79 not out from just 58 balls.' This usage is indistinguishable from *hammer*, except that a *pummel* is the square-headed type used by stonemasons. Knowledge of the distinction probably doesn't travel far beyond the *cathedral grounds*.

Punch: This verb suggests strong forearms, together with good timing, mostly off the *back foot*: 'Matthew Walker *punched* the ball sweetly either side of the wicket.' The adjective, applied to a completed innings, as in 'Matt Walker's typically *punchy knock*', begins to connote character as well.

Punish: What good batsmen naturally do to bowling that is *wayward* or only verging on the *ordinary*: 'Jaques *punished* any hint of *width* on the off side'; 'Bicknell *punished* some *wasteful* new-ball bowling.' What marks out the great batsmen is a more than ordinary desire to *punish* all bowling, as we can sense from this observation on Bradman: 'In middle-age he has curbed one or two of his more *punitive* instincts.'

Purist: Probably little more than just an alibi these days for when the observer is moved to slip in a critical comment on technique: 'Richard Dawson is still bowling his off spin too quickly for the *purists*'; 'Pietersen tends to move in the crease a little too much for *purist* tastes.'

Purveyor: Mike Brearley puts the classic phrase *purveyor of leg spin*, along with *back-of-the-hand merchant*, in the category of 'orotund Edwardianese'. In a modern setting the quaintness of the term can sometimes be exploited to sow a few seeds of doubt about the wares on offer: 'With the *leggies* failing to come up to scratch, the gaze of the selectors has turned to *offies* who *purvey* a *doosra*'; 'Marginal losses of rhythm and confidence can turn a *holy terror* into a *purveyor* of **lollipops.'**

Puzzle: As a verb, almost too leisurely a word for the modern age, but it corresponds to what would now be called *asking questions* of the batsmen, as in this turn-of-the-century specimen: 'Darling several times on *perfect* wickets quite *puzzled* the Englishmen, keeping a fine length with a little **work** on the ball and being curiously deceptive in the *flight.'* A post-war example, from John Arlott, effectively glosses the term: 'Wardle *puzzled* – indeed frequently *baffled* – all the Australian batsmen.' Both words fall into the range that extends from *tease* to **bamboozle**.

Pyjama game: One of the ways in which supporters of the existing establishment belittled the *Packer circus* was to call its limited-overs concept the *pyjama game*. The phrase was suggested by the innovations of coloured clothing and day–night matches under floodlights (and probably also by the title of the Broadway musical by Adler and Ross). Originally, there must have been the intention to belittle the format as a namby-pamby affectation – Henry Blofeld, for example, has put it on the record that he has always slept naked, 'except at Eton where *pyjamas* were compulsory'. But the image (of *pyjamas*, not Blowers naked) is now used routinely and almost neutrally in reports on one-day performances: 'Flintoff was no less prolific in *pyjamas*'; 'With the *pyjamas* on, Michael Bevan was entirely without peer.' Some more sheepish types take longer to be comfortable with the necessary alterations in style: 'V. V. S. Laxman had a season which he spent making a nonsense of the claim that he was incapable of adjusting to the *pyjama stuff.'*

Q

Quack: One of the authors once walked to the wicket after a mini-*collapse* and was called 'the next little *quacker*' – at least he thinks that's what square leg said. The call of *ducks* is sometimes heard in press reporting, particularly if there are enough of them for the effect to be cacophonous: '*Quack, quack, quack, quack, quack* . . . and *quack*. South Australia equalled the domestic *first-class* record for a string of *ducks* as six batsmen failed to score in the Redbacks' first innings against NSW at the SCG yesterday.'

Quickie: This is not, at most cricket clubs anyway, a reference to something going on behind the pavilion but a generic term for a fast bowler. In the plural they tend to become *quicks*, when perhaps they sound just that bit faster.

R

Rabbit: Long-established term for a *confirmed **tailender***. Players who cannot **hold a bat** at all are occasionally described as *ferrets* or even *weasels*, on the grounds that they *go in* after the *rabbits*.

Race away: 'That will *race away* for four.' While the ball can travel like a *puck on ice* when the outfield is parched, this formula is used so often in commentary that it can mean little more than 'it was going hard enough to beat the fielder'.

Radar: Bowlers sometimes take a few *looseners*, or

even a few overs, to get their *radar* in *working order*:
'With Moody *finding his radar* after a difficult start,
the scoring rate again dropped.' On a very bad day, the
bowler's guidance system can prove to be not just
temperamental but completely switched off: 'Akmal
hit an *imperious lofted* off drive for six off the *hapless*
and *radar*-less Ajit Agarkar.'

Rag: In wet *conditions* when the outfield is sodden,
bowlers borrow a *rag* from the umpire in order to
keep the ball dry. Whereas, when the sun is beating
down and the ground is like *concrete*, a *rag* is what
the ball itself becomes: 'The ball was like an *old rag*
after 20 overs, and not one delivery *deviated* at all, all
day.' A bowler trying to induce *reverse* may deliberately scuff the surface of one side, but if the other cannot be kept smooth there will be nothing doing:
'Richards used one ball for 177 overs, by which time
it was as soft and unruly as a *rag doll*.'

Rain-affected: Cricket is not the only game to be
affected by rain, but it is the only game in which the
term *rain-affected* has become endemic. Play may be
curtailed in a *rain-affected match*, but a *rain-affected
wicket* can be positive for the bowlers, even though
the ball becomes *greasy*. Ellis Robinson, an off-spinner in the days of uncovered pitches, would later
recall the pleasure of listening to overnight rain: 'It
was the loveliest of sounds.' Some Yorkshiremen do
listen intently.

Rain dance: The recommended preparation for a
day's play when all hope of saving a game seems lost:
'A *rain dance* instead of *net practice* looks the best
chance of a shattered New Zealand batting line-up
saving the second cricket Test against Australia.' The
irony can be developed if the prayers are answered:
'Mahela's *rain dance* turned to a *jig of joy* as the

Islanders got out of jail.' Sometimes the bored spectators are the ones *praying for rain*: 'Let us not have
more *dead* Tests like this one, with 14 wickets falling
in four days and some of us doing the *rain dance* to be
spared the final day's play.'

Rank: In the classic combination *rank* applies to a
juicy long hop, but the adjective can also describe
other examples of *filth*: 'Giles succumbed to a *rank
full toss* from Dwayne Bravo and popped it straight to
Chanderpaul at mid-wicket.' And sometimes it is the
batsmen who are prone to excess: 'The Zimbabwean
top order collapsed, more because of *rank* bad *shot
selection* than good bowling.'

Rattle: Although stumps can be said to *rattle* when
they are hit, *rattling* usually indicates fast scoring:
'Sachin Tendulkar and Siva Vidyut were *rattling
along* at more than a run a ball'; 'Australia, the world's
best Test team, aim to *rattle up* a score of more than
300 in a day's play.' While such phrases pre-date
cricket, they accord well with the fact that score-
boards, particularly of a certain vintage, really do *rattle* when the runs are posted. There is a slight
adjustment to the formula if an easy target is reached
with the minimum of fuss: 'Richard Montgomerie
and Michael Yardy *rattled off* the requisite 35 runs for
victory.'

Read: *Reading the pitch* can be fundamental to the
outcome of the game and is therefore a ritual imbued
with a certain amount of formality – and sometimes
mystique – at all levels of cricket. In Test matches, the
familiar commentators don their best blazers to do
service as soil specialists, even if they are no longer
allowed to conduct the *car keys test*. In most amateur
matches, the players will go out to the middle, usually
before they have changed, to inspect the wicket and

attempt to *read* how it will play. Once the game has started, batsmen try to *read* the bowling, especially if there is a leg-spinner bowling **wrong 'uns**. They might also fail to *read* the **arm ball** of a finger-spinner or the *slower ball* of a wily seamer, in which case they will find themselves back in the pavilion reading the paper.

Rearguard action: 'Fraser played a vital part in England's fighting *rearguard action*.' On the Test scene a **losing draw** can go down in the annals. By contrast, the following report from the county circuit rates higher for its note of wistful irony than for its value as hard news: 'Word of the *rearguard action* spread, with an ice-cream van arriving at noon to tap an unpredicted market.'

Rearrange: A sardonic way of recording the **shattering** of a batsman's *timber* or *furniture*, as in this pointed example: 'Harmison gave the encounter a fitting last word by *rearranging* Glenn McGrath's stumps.' The usage is analogous to 'rearranging someone's features', as attested in underworld slang. It's **not cricket** exactly, but we seem to remember David Lloyd promising to *rearrange* Dermot Reeve's nose.

Rebel: The name given to members of any side organised outside the auspices of the relevant governing body. Used in particular of players who turned out for SAB *invitational* teams in the apartheid era: 'Foster became the fourth South African "*rebel*" to be rehabilitated after Gatting, Emburey and Jarvis.' In this case the reinstatement of the *rebels* led to a *rebel movement* within the MCC itself. For those of a right-wing disposition, the tag was objectionable because it castigated cricketers for seeking merely to earn their living by playing sport. For those of a left-wing temperament, it was equally grating because it dignified what they saw as disloyal and mercenary activity ('Gooch's *Dirty Dozen*') with an aura of principled resistance.

Recall: In the bar, cricketers are forever recollecting incidents amusing to themselves but rarely to other listeners. On the field, *recall* has a specific meaning when a fielder or captain calls a batsman back to the crease after he has been given out. If it is too late to bring back the **victim** of a *suspect* delivery, a bit of lateral thinking may be the order of the day: 'Although there was nothing the umpire Perry Burke could do to *recall* the departing Headley, he did *call* Lock's next **thunderbolt**.'

Red inker: Playing in his third Test match, Graham Thorpe eventually caved in to some **mental disintegration** thanks to Healy and Warne, who had continuously insinuated that he was looking to remain not out as wickets fell around him: 'Pride took over and I thought, "Sod you, I'll show you I'm not playing for a *red inker*."' Thorpe was stumped by yards. Although *red ink* or *red inker* are used as synonyms for **asterisk** in the trade, we must confess we have rarely seen a scorebook or scorecard where the not-outs have actually been filled in with a red pen.

Reduce: The operative verb when the bowlers engineer a **collapse**: 'Pakistan were *cruising* at 266–3 before Flintoff *grabbed* two wickets in three overs and Hoggard took two in five to *reduce* the hosts to 308–7 at tea.'

Regulation: Used adjectivally to record a straightforward catch, especially if it goes begging: 'Scott Styris dropped a *regulation* **chance** at second slip off Richardson.' The focus of the adjective needs a bit of unscrambling in this related example: 'Trescothick had made only 13 when Gilchrist fumbled a *textbook* *nick* to his left.' But the coaching manual is only of vestigial significance in these cases.

Repertoire: 'Strang has a wide *repertoire* – regular leg breaks, *googly*, top-spinner and *flipper* – and his control has improved considerably.' The term is a useful hold-all for the many intricacies of the spin-bowler's *art*. Meanwhile, the fast men have a different kind of repository: 'Tait has all the resources in his *armoury* to stick the ball up the noses of the England batsmen.'

Reprieve: A way of saying a batsman has had a *life*, in the context of his being dropped or otherwise let off: 'The *third umpire reprieved* Butt after endless replays proved inconclusive'; 'Gilchrist was bowled off a no-ball and next delivery marked his *reprieve* with a flicked four.' A whole team can be *reprieved* if their *rain dance* has the desired effect. Reporting on one of England's *Ashes* defeats in the 1950s, before the abolition of capital punishment, *The Times* cricket correspondent officially abandoned all hope: 'Not even the Home Secretary could have *reprieved* England.'

Respectability: A suitably abstract noun to register that a *decent* recovery has been made after an inauspicious start: 'Gloucestershire were *reduced* to one for three in the fifth over but achieved *respectability*'; 'A partnership of 87 between Ben Smith and Steven Davies *dragged* the innings towards *respectability*.' In the modern one-day game, where the field must be up in the opening overs, totals lent such an *air of respectability* are often treated with scant respect by the chasing side.

Response: Usually reported on when it is not forthcoming. Often it is the wicket which proves distinctly *unhelpful*: 'None of the spinners – Hirwani, Kumble or Shastri – could get a *response* from a pitch that was devoid of all *gremlins*.' Or a batsman may be guilty of **ballwatching**: 'Inzamam set off for a quick single to short-fine leg but the striker Razzaq did not *respond* to his call.' After the run-out of his captain, Razzaq may have had some responding to do later on his return to the pavilion.

Rest: 'Take a *rest* there, Bill.' One of the captain's ways of telling a bowler that his spell is at an end. Sometimes very euphemistic, so that the unspoken subtext is '. . . and the way you bowled today please continue to *take a rest* for the next twenty-five years.'

Reverse: *Reverse* is the adjective that goes with two of the most significant discoveries in the modern game, the ***reverse sweep*** and *reverse swing*. In the latter case especially, *reverse* is now universally understood and feared. Journalists and sub-editors seem as busy working on new coinages as the fielders are at **working** on the ball: 'Shreesanth got it to *go reverse*'; 'When Hoggard, out of the blue, *curved* a *reverser* in **late**, Dravid's *forward press* was beaten'; 'Jones is back in the *reverse-swing* of things.'

Reverse sweep: Also called a *back-handed sweep* in its early sightings, the *reverse sweep* is a valuable ***source of income*** in one-day cricket. However, a batsman's credit rating suddenly goes down if he gets out playing it: 'Grant Flower spoiled an innings of great **application** when he was bowled *reverse sweeping* at Monty Panesar.' Phil DeFreitas still can't forget one such high-profile dismissal in the 1987 World Cup Final: 'Gatt *reverse swept*, the twat. We were cruising.'

Rib-tickler: The term belongs nicely in this demotic piece of reporting: 'Hoggard's pitch-it-up *swingers* were the ideal foil to Harmison's ***bang-it-in*** rib-tick-

lers.' The batsmen who had to face Harmison may not
have found the experience particularly amusing. On
another day we might find the euphemism giving way
to a more neutral variant: 'Harmison concentrated on
maintaining a full length with just the occasional
admonitory "*rib-ball*"'. There is another mock-friendly
alternative, which has been in the language since the
sixteenth century but sounds as if it has come fresh
from the barbie or the braai: 'One delivery from Brett
Lee stands out from the match the other day. It was
bowled to Sehwag and it is what one calls a *rib-roaster*.'

Ridge: The archetypal *ridge* was in evidence at Lord's
in the 1950s and 1960s: 'Bailey would have strength-
ened the middle batting and his bowling might have
made all the difference on the "*ridge*" at Lord's.' This
had nothing to do with the equally renowned *slope*
there but was an uneven spot on the square which
produced variable bounce. Real or imagined *ridges*
can still give the **curators** grey hairs the world over:
'Sydney helped the seam bowlers and there was a
ridge at one end off which the ball alternately *flew* and
skidded through low.'

Ring: Until the mid-nineteenth century, there was no
official boundary line and therefore in important
games the play was enclosed by a *ring* of spectators.
This was a recipe for behaviour contrary to the **spirit
of the game**. The term survived as a synonym for
boundary – *Wisden*'s report on the all-conquering
1921 Australians describes Arthur Mailey as 'varying
very much in length and constantly asking to be hit to
the *ring*'. It is the advent of one-day cricket, especially
since a **circle** is physically marked on the pitch, which
has encouraged references to the inner *ring* of fielders
saving one: 'For a big guy, Symonds moves well, cutting off balls if he's *in the ring*.' To encourage his men
to keep it **tight**, a captain might refer to a *ring of steel*

(in homage to the City of London's security cordon) or a *ring of fire* (in homage to Johnny Cash).

Rip: Has become almost established as the technical term for the degree of spin a bowler can impart, in this case from the hand rather than off the pitch. For an off-spinner like Tim May, the terminology was not merely figurative, as he is reported by Michael Atherton to have given the ball 'such an almighty *rip* that a huge, bleeding gash was routinely opened on his spinning finger'. Among wrist-spinners, the term features especially in the ongoing career reviews of Shane Warne: 'He has made the statement many times over that he is not the *rip-it-as-hard-as-you-can* 23-year-old he used to be.' But nobody can deny that the great man remains a *little ripper*.

Rip out: One of a collection of phrases describing the effects of faster bowling. It can hurt: 'Immediately Daffy *ripped* one *into* my already stiff right thigh.' Or comprehensively defeat the batsman: 'Jones *ripped through* the flimsy defences of Pedro Collins.' Or knock a **pole** down: 'Martin-Jenkins *ripped out* Adshead's off stump.' Or knock the stuffing out of a batting line-up: 'Ormond *ripped out* Glamorgan's top **order.**' The last metaphor allows for a little sensitive amplification: 'England *ripped out* what little *heart* West Indies had left'; 'Ntini returned to *rip a hole* in the middle *order.*' Fortunately, the effect is not registered literally in the official scorebook.

Rock back: Describes the footwork associated particularly with batsmen who can spot the length early and who enjoy cracking the ball away from deep in the crease: 'Anwar *annihilates* any bowler *offering* **width** outside off stump, *rocking back* to cut anything fractionally off target.'

Roller: Like the *sightscreen*, this familiar piece of equipment can be referred to in figurative ways. The groundsman can be said to *start up* his *roller* when he sees a confirmed **rabbit** walking out at Number 11. The *effects* of the *roller* on the pitch are often remarked upon, even if the way a wicket *plays* in the first hour of an innings may not have much to do with which one the captain has *asked for*. Other possible effects can also be contemplated at moments of frustration: 'The game's administrators should be tied to a cricket pitch and *rearranged* with a *heavy roller.*' *Roller* also means a slow bowler who gives the ball a *gentle **twirl*** rather than a real **tweak** and so could not be described as the *biggest spinner* of the ball: 'If a *roller* like Allan Border could take 11 for 96 in a Test, it told us that **batsmanship** against spin had sunk to the depths.'

Roll the pitch up: Not an activity on the ground-staff's rota but what a cricketer suited by a particular surface would like to do: 'I bet Richard Hadlee wishes he could *roll this pitch up*, take it home with him and bowl on it every week.'

Roses: *Roses matches* between Yorkshire and Lancashire are always *fiercely contested*. This is true even of the second-eleven fixture, traditionally known as the *rosebud match*.

Rotation: As in arable farming, so in cricket, *rotation* is a fundamental principle, used in the management of both main departments of the game: 'We must focus more on *occupying the crease* and *rotating the strike* – the nuts and bolts of all batting'; 'The great West Indian fast-bowling juggernaut of four *rotated* pacemen would crush everything in its path.' However, the jury is still out on whether resting key players will refresh international sides: 'Steve Waugh believes Australia's current *rotation policy* doesn't make sense.'

Rough: A notable element in the ecology of the longer game, in which the secondary purpose of the fast men is to leave something for the left-arm spinner in particular to *exploit*: 'Giles *lured* the West Indian captain down the pitch and bowled him with a **beauty** that turned sharply *out of the rough.*' Often described as *rough **stuff***, perhaps subliminally encouraged by the rhyme with *scuff*. No doubt the analytical software is still in its rudimentary phase, but we admired Justin Langer's attempt at mensuration when playing for Middlesex: 'Tuffers was bowling into a *patch of rough* that resembled a family-pizza-sized dust pit.' Jack Fingleton preferred *roughage*.

Run in: 'He *ran in hard* in both the innings, **bent his back** and did a lot of hard work.' Rahul Dravid's praise for Shantakumaran Sreesanth is an example of how a captain always appreciates a fast bowler who can be relied upon to give everything, rather than just go through the motions. Someone in the England dressing room, to illustrate the point, once observed that 'even Gatt is harder to bat against when he really *runs in*'. Although he bowled *useful* medium pace in his younger days, Mike Gatting probably had more chance of registering on the Richter scale than in the wickets-taken column in the twilight of his career.

Run on the pitch: 'Tommy Greenhough apparently *ran straight down* the *track.*' Younger readers are advised that Greenhough was not a 100-metre runner but a Lancashire leg-spinner. Bowlers and batsmen obviously *run on the pitch* all the time, but this becomes worthy of note – and censure – only when they encroach upon the *danger area*. **Neutral umpires** in minor English league cricket are particularly vigilant about *running on the pitch*, even if there are only 80 overs to be bowled in the day, nobody is

wearing spikes and the covering of *grass* is so healthy
that the pitch would not *break up* this side of
Christmas.

S

Sandshoe crusher: Australian for *yorker*. *Instep
crusher* is a similar figure, which suddenly seemed less
figurative when the development of the very fast
boomerang into the *blockhole* highlighted the preference of modern batsmen for lightweight cricket shoes
as opposed to *diving boots*. See also **Waqared**.

Saving one: Or *on the one*. What the captain says to a
fielder when he wants him to *walk in* close enough to
stop the batsmen *stealing* a single, often resigned to
the fact that said fielder is too pedestrian or pig-
headed to obey the instruction.

Sawn off: 'A totally forgettable day. First, I ran out
poor Whitticase by most of the pitch, then I got "*sawn
off*" lbw by Shep.' A trade term for being on the wrong
end of a bad decision. Possibly the notion of being
trigger-happy has evolved into the image of a *sawn-off*
shotgun, as the umpire *fires out* the batsman.

Scalp: 'Gangling speedster Waqas Ahmed got the
prized scalp of in-form Faisal for 13.' A standard
expression for a valued wicket. **Decapitation strategy** takes things to the next level.

Scamper: 'Stewart, at 37, remained as youthful as a
butcher's pup. He stayed until four overs from the end
for a 144-ball 101, *scampering* enthusiastically between
the wickets.' *Scamper* is the requisite verb for keen run-

ning – especially for *singles* – unless you are *stealing* them instead.

Scientific: As the game of cricket evolved, *science* seems to have been the name given to what we would now call *technique*. As early as 1833, John Nyren drew a distinction between 'the *scientific* player and the *random* batsman'. These examples from Canterbury weeks in the early 1870s testify that the word signified *orthodox* batting in contrast to **slogging**: 'The **collapse** was a blow ably and *scientifically* countered immediately after by Mr I. D. Walker and Pooley, who by *steady* and A1 batting increased the score from 118 to 229'; 'Mr Yardley's 68 was a first class exhibition of *scientific defence* and brilliant hitting that included nine 4's, one a drive into the old hop plantation.' There was obviously not yet a **confectionery stall** at the St Lawrence Ground in 1871.

Scone: A verb denoting a direct hit on a batsman's head: 'Astle was *sconed* when on 32 by a short delivery from Jerome Taylor.' Sometimes a **lid** may be required in the **outer** as well as the *middle*: 'Steve Waugh will sign off at his beloved Sydney Cricket Ground, where his dad took him as a boy (and where he was once *sconed* by a meat pie while watching a *day/nighter* from the *Hill*).'

Scorch: Almost too dramatic a word to be more than an occasional variant for hitting the ball hard: 'Ramprakash *scorched* two drives through the covers to win his battle with Jones convincingly.' The verb can also suggest that a batsman is trying to set the scoreboard on fire: 'Matt Prior *scorched* to 37 from 18 balls.' But the quick bowler has his own form of heat *treatment* with which to retaliate in kind: 'One delivery yesterday that *scorched* the batting visor en route to the wicketkeeper underlined Hughes's hold over Graeme Hick.'

Score: 'I was in good form and felt good for a *score*.' In the cricketing context, a *score* never means twenty.

Scratch around: The idea of a *scratchy start* seems to have its origin in rowing, whereas *scratching around*, according to the *Oxford English Dictionary*, is more 'as a chicken does in searching for food'. No doubt both comparisons are lost on a batsman struggling for form or intent merely on survival: 'Graham Thorpe followed a *scratchy* seven in the first innings with five before he *played down the wrong line* to Robert Croft'; 'Thorpe, again looking thoroughly *out of sorts*, *scratched around* for 24 balls and nine runs.' The formula is so well-worn that cricketers can attempt to breathe new life into it: 'Never mind *chicken tonight*, it's more like bloody chicken this afternoon the way I'm *scratching around*.' Or reach into their collection for a different cultural reference: 'Rudolph had looked *scratchier* than an old 45.'

Scuttle: When a ball *scuttles through*, it **hurries** on and keeps low. There is a metaphor available in the case of the faster bowler: 'Kirtley produced a *torpedo* that *scuttled through* and bowled McKenzie.' But although the verb suggests pace off the pitch, it is more usually confined to the slower bowler's sphere of operations: 'Warne bowled Strauss with a *scuttler* on a fourth-day pitch.' Batsmen can also *scuttle through* for a quick single.

Scythe: A less controlled or more **agricultural** version of the cut shot: 'Kirkpatrick *scythed* the first ball away for four square on the off side.' But not every batsman is quite sure what implement he will end up playing with: 'Dhoni walked out with a *scythe* but he didn't just blindly *lash out.*' Old Father Time, who presides over those who preside at Lord's, has no such uncertainty.

Seam-up: Top-line bowlers can be praised for the exemplary way in which they keep the *seam upright* and get the ball to move about: 'Corey Collymore was outstanding. He *hit the seam* and made the batsmen play and really troubled them.' But *seam-up* has emerged as a fairly pejorative term with which to categorise the auxiliary brigade of *bits-and-pieces* players who can get away with *trundling* in on *green* English wickets.

Searing: The fashionable adjective for recording very fast bowling: 'Sami, whose bouncers to the body at *searing* pace had troubled every batsman, made the vital *incision* soon after *lunch.*' The terminology adjusted to the local lifestyle when the same bowler got *operating* in Perth: 'Australia were being *charred* like shrimps on the barbie at 78 for five.'

Second fiddle: The standard expression for the junior role in a partnership, which may sometimes mean that an attacking player will choose to curb his natural instincts: 'For a time Pietersen seemed content to play *second fiddle* to Nic Pothas.' Neville Cardus, after the first day of a Test in which Bradman went past 300, referred to the Don's main partner Woodfull as '*Kreisler's accompanist*' – still a kind of back-handed compliment. For a partnership metaphor from a different musical genre, see *jugalbandi*.

Second season syndrome: 'Cullen's first challenge will be to negotiate the dreaded *second season syndrome.*' This condition afflicts players and teams in a variety of sports, but it is most pronounced in cricket, as Dan Cullen will have discovered, because of the

time the opposition get to *work* new players *out*:
'Several of his five-wicket **hauls** in his debut summer
were the product of batsmen attacking him because of
his lack of experience. Now they are wiser.' A very
unlucky cricketer becomes a ***one-cap wonder*** while
suffering from *second season syndrome*.

See off: This is what opening batsmen are required to
do to the *new ball*, not necessarily by hitting it everywhere but by staying in: 'England looked content to
see off the new ball threat of Aussie quick Cathryn
Fitzpatrick.' In a tight situation or one-day game, the
batsmen may also decide to *see off* the spell of a particular bowler: 'The experienced duo of Atapattu and
Sangakkara *saw off* debutant paceman Butler, who
bowled his full *quota* in one spell of one for 25, and
shifted gears thereafter.'

Semblance of control: 'While Peter Martin's
outswing kept a *semblance of control* from one end, the
first six overs from the pavilion end cost 76 runs all
told.' If the batting side is *running riot*, any bowler
who is getting off comparatively lightly but not threatening a serious counter-attack can be said to retain a
semblance of control. If the fielding side get off to a bad
start, their captain may have to ***throw the ball*** much
earlier than planned to a bowler experienced enough
to staunch the run rate: 'Titmus frequently had to
come on after fifty minutes to *restore* some *semblance
of order*, even on a pitch **helpful** to the seamers.'

Send-off: There is a graduated scale of assessment
applicable to this kind of event. Example one is inno-
cent of suspicion: 'Flintoff *sent* Malik *on his way*, the
batsman hitting straight to Ian Bell in the covers.'
Example two does not reach the critical level on the
scale, but some directions to the pavilion appear to
have been offered: 'Habib was not happy about the

send-off he received from Shafayat.' Example three warrants an official penalty: 'Simon Jones was fined for giving Ramnaresh Sarwan a *send-off.*' Example four goes off the scale, in the sense that it enters the literature instead, in this case via Martin Johnson: 'Merv Hughes *sent* Atherton *on his way* with a verbal broadside that did not, through binoculars, appear to contain the words: "Bad luck, old boy."'

Set: This time-honoured expression for when a batsman has his *eye in* does not imply that he will be incapable of using his feet for the rest of the innings.

Settled: Before a nervous starter can get *set*, he has to get *settled*: 'Lehmann was never *settled* and got out to a shot that he would not enjoy seeing on replay.' In nineteenth-century journalese, the verb was used in the sense of *settling* a batsman's *account*, usually by catching him out: 'Carpenter's *left-hand* catch at point that *settled* Jupp was a rare bit'; 'Mr Absolom, by a splendid *left-hand* catch from his own bowling, summarily *settled* Mycroft.' *Accounted for* is the modern equivalent.

Shape: Provides a useful way of referring to *lateral movement*: 'The Somerset top **order** simply could not cope with the ball *shaping back in* to the right-hander.' The word can also contribute to a fuller aesthetic appreciation of first-rate bowling: 'Chaminda Vaas bowled Iain Sutcliffe with a **beauty** that *started life* on middle-and-off before *shaping away* to *clip* off stump.'

Sharp: A hundred years ago, if the captain asked his square leg to be *sharper*, he may have been trying to move him *finer*. Today there would be no doubt that he wants him to wake up, walk in and make sure he is **saving one**. The opposite of *sharp* in this context is *asleep*, though Raymond Robertson-Glasgow found a

more literary and euphemistic alternative: 'It should
have been caught at mid-on but I do not know what
happened with mid-on. He was what you might call
basking in vigilant content.'

Shatter: 'Cairns took 4–26 in a seven-over spell, *shattering the stumps* of former internationals Craig
Cumming and Gareth Hopkins.' This does not,
ninety-nine times out of a hundred, mean that the
stumps have actually been snapped into pieces, only
that the wicket has been *broken* in the sense of being
rearranged. Sometimes such a scene is an intimation
of the *shattered* dreams of the losing side: 'Maninder's
shattered stumps sealed an improbable victory for
Australia.'

Shed: Australian for *pavilion*; Yorkshire for *indoor
cricket school*.

Shell-shocked: The trade description for batsmen
whose nerve has been broken by the *short **stuff***: 'If
word gets around that "X is *shell-shocked*" or "Y
doesn't *fancy* it", as soon as they come in the fast
bowler will be summoned.' Describing England's
sojourn in New Zealand, after a winter's bombard-
ment by Lillee and Thomson, Simon Rae pictures 'the
batsmen coming out of their *bunkers*, blinking in the
benign sunlight of Eden Park, Auckland, before running stylishly amok'. On a tour to the West Indies,
when the **battery** of Roberts, Holding, Garner and
Croft was taking aim, Javed Miandad felt it was a matter of dodging bullets rather than taking cover: 'You
can see why we felt we were facing a *firing squad.*'

Shepherd: 'Samaraweera, the final recognised batsman, made a poor 36 not out, neither *shepherding* the
tail nor playing shots.' It is, in fairness, harder to *shepherd **rabbits*** than it is sheep.

Shine: A kind of secondary contest goes on between the batsmen who want to *knock* the *shine off* the ball and the bowlers who want to *keep* the *shine on* (one side of the ball at least). Occasionally it is the bowlers, not the batsmen, who try to take the *lacquer* off the new ball so that the *tweakers* can grip it: 'Solkar and Abid Ali bowled *gentle* medium pace to *see the shine off* the ball before the spin quartet took over.'

Shirtfront: It is of course assumed, when describing a bland pitch with this term, that the shirt has been carefully pressed and starched so that its surface is smooth and white. These days you can't be too sure what's going to come out in the wash: 'On a *shirtfront* but against a testosterone-propelled pace attack, Tendulkar hit a vivid and memorable stream of shots.'

Shot selection: It is difficult to know whether the phrase originated in golf, basketball, snooker or even film-directing, but it is now very common for cricketers and their advisers to think of *shot selection* as one of the key tenets of good *batsmanship*: 'Buchanan said Australia's batsmen paid the price for *poor shot selection* after they slumped to 258 all out'; 'The most striking ingredient of Warne's 122-ball innings was his *judicious shot selection*, notwithstanding the one that cost him his big moment.'

Shoulder arms: Derived from rifle drill, although in cricket's version the batsman does not actually have to rest the bat on his shoulder to be described as *shouldering arms*. In match reporting, the information is usually provided in embarrassing circumstances when the *full face* should have been *presented*: 'Hollioake was bowled, *shouldering arms*, the ultimate indignity.' In our second example, Yousuf has been *done* by the old *three-card trick*: 'Balaji *suckered* him into *leaving* with a couple of good outswingers, then

brought one back into him from outside off as
Youhana *shouldered arms*.' Quite distinct from ***opening the shoulders***.

Shovel: This term seems to have acquired a certain
technical standing in Allan Donald's appreciation of
Andrew Strauss: 'He plays that *shovel pull* to balls not
that short really well.' But generally it suggests a batsman more careless of technique, even if it's possible
he can tell one side of the wicket from the other: 'The
Pakistan leg-spinner *shovelled* and ***smeared*** his way
to a half-century.' In John Arlott's day, it only served
to denote a class player getting tired and not keeping
the ball down: 'May *shovelled* Johnson to Lindwall at
long leg: by then, though, he had made 101.'

Shuffle: Usually regarded as a doubtful habit in a
batsman who, although he may be *productive* to leg,
may also be a prime ***candidate*** for lbw: 'Shafayat is
compact and ***wristy*** but has a tendency to *shuffle* into
his shots, which was his *undoing* yesterday.' Acute
cases of *shuffling across* can lead to the batsman
falling over. There is also a figurative usage which
corresponds to ***rotation***: 'Inzamam *shuffled* his bowling pack beautifully.'

Shut up shop: Early in an innings, to use a metaphor
common in football, the batsmen might *set out their
stall*, whether by playing very ***watchfully*** or launch-
ing an all-out attack. Later on, if things have not gone
entirely to plan, they may decide to *put up the shutters*
and close for business: 'The Bellerive wicket proved
to have the better of all the bowlers and little could be
done to ***dislodge*** the Tasmanian ***batters*** who had
well and truly *shut up shop*.'

Shy: It seems that when a *shy* at the stumps registers
a *direct hit*, this is the exception rather than the rule:

'Cairns was then gifted five runs when Strauss *shied* at the stumps at the bowler's end as the batsmen ran a quick single and the ball shot through to the boundary.' As an adjective, *shy* is an understated way of saying 'frightened': 'In 1952 there was a suspicion that the Indian batsmen were a *touch shy* of the *quick stuff*.'

Side-on: In discussions of ***classical*** technique the traditional view is that cricket should be a *side-on* game. The *two-eyed* stance and the *chest-on* action are therefore not to be seen in the ***MCC Coaching Manual***. The late Fred Trueman was a proud exponent of the *side-on* game, although he failed to see the funny side when a *Test Match Special* correspondent asked him whether wicketkeepers should also stand *side-on*.

Sighter: The batsman's equivalent of the ***loosener***, when he is assessing the pace of the pitch or the length of a new bowler: 'Symonds allowed himself a couple of *sighters* from Smith and then ***bludgeoned*** his third ball high over the ***sightscreen*** for six.'

Sightscreen: In the same way that professional snooker players used to fuss about chalking the cue of a half butt before playing a screw shot, professional batsmen can get obsessed about the positioning of the *sightscreen* before taking guard. Occasional players at some less well-appointed clubs tend to be more philosophical about there being no tip on the cue and no *screen* at either end. However, the *sightscreen*, known as a *sightboard* in Australasia, not only serves a vital practical function for batsmen in the middle but offers some metaphorical possibilities for scribes in the press box. If the bowlers are getting exceptional ***carry***, they can observe that the keeper is nearly *all the way back* to the *sightscreen*. If the bowlers are forcing the batsmen to play back, they can scale up the hyperbole: 'Sydney a few years ago was like greased lightning, and Miller, Lindwall and Walker were likely to pin opposing batsmen to the *sightboard*.' When, on the other hand, an old **workhorse** is labouring to the crease, Martin Johnson finds the effect more *It's a Knockout* than knockout: 'Fraser's **approach** to the wicket currently resembles someone who has caught his braces in the *sightscreen*.' And then there's the old joke about a fast bowler's run-up being so long that he can *shake hands* with the *sightscreen attendant*. Rodney Marsh even got the attendant in on the act, noting wryly that, before Packer, the man pushing the *screen* probably earned more than the cricketers using it.

Silky: This term is tailored to give the feel of smooth stroke-making: 'Usman Afzaal sent a typical *silky* cover drive to the fence'; 'Robert Key went on to show some *silky* shots in his 67.' The early glow of hindsight can also lend the adjective a **classical** quality: 'An innings of *silky elegance* from Vaughan lingered in the memory.'

Silly: In the end means more or less what it says of players prepared to field very close to the wicket. Now tends to qualify *point*, *mid-off* and *mid-on* only, although Richie Benaud has used it to indicate the position at **Boot Hill**: 'I *crowded* Cowdrey with a fielder at *silly leg* in the Lord's Test in 1956.'

Sitter: Although the cliché of the *sitter* is well-established in football, it does appear that cricket was responsible for bringing the neologism into ball sports in the late nineteenth century. It was presumably developed from the idea of a 'sitting duck', but the point with the *sitter* is that it is just waiting to be *missed*. In modern reporting, the term is preceded by *absolute*, unless the correspondent feels like articulating the bowler's frustration more painfully: 'Nafees then *inexplicably* dropped an *inexcusable sitter* off Tharanga at second slip.'

Skiddy: Describes bowlers – often below average height – who get the ball to *hurry* through off the pitch. Here is the very tall Bruce Reid talking about one of the players he coached at Hampshire, James Bruce: "He is a *skiddy* bowler who *hits the deck* hard, a bowler who rushes batsmen a bit. He bowls the odd one that *goes through* and is always *there or there-abouts*.' In this context, *goes through* means 'through to the wicketkeeper' (*hitting* the gloves *hard*) rather than 'through the *top*'. *Skiddy* can also be used of an individual delivery which exhibits the opposite of *tennis-ball bounce*: 'Malcolm Marshall's *skiddy* bouncer was enough to make the toughest of batsmen a touch *shy*.'

Skittle: 'Lancashire were *skittled out* for only 49.' Cricket has moved on from *skittling* the wickets *down* to *skittling* the whole side *out*. More like ten pins than nine pins, in the end.

Skyer: A catch in the category of a *steepler* as opposed to a *dolly*, and often very difficult to judge: 'Mohammad Kaif ran on all sides of a *skyer* which, as any minister from West Bengal worth his salt will tell you, ol' Dada would have *pouched* with *effortless* gazelle-like strides.' In this example *Dada* is not a Bengali version of Geoffrey Boycott's *granny* but the deposed Indian captain Sourav Ganguly.

Slant: Denotes the natural *angle* of delivery *across* a batsman. A little rule of thumb is that this word tends to be used for a right-arm bowler bowling to a left-hander, or vice versa: 'Mullally removed Guy Welton with a clever piece of swing bowling in the 11th over when, after continually *slanting* the ball across the right-hander, he *slipped in* a big inswinger.'

Slap: 'I came in and *slapped* a few around.' Jon Lewis's account of a quick-fire 47 is intended to be self-deprecating, even while flirting with connotations of corporal punishment or domestic violence. Although the verb can be used to indicate a ***loose*** shot which results in a catch, it normally signifies rough *treatment*: 'In one-day cricket especially, if you don't do something with the ball, you'll get *slapped*, ***lashed*.*' It also comes out whenever the zinc cream is applied or if the ICC *slap* a player with a fine or ban.

Slash: Closely related to the ***flash***, this shot tends to go in the air through or over the slip cordon: 'Powell played a ludicrous *slash* at Simon Jones and was caught at third man.' In South Africa, the term *slash-and-burn* can sometimes be applied to limited-overs cricket rather than land clearance. Other belittling monikers for the one-day format include *beer-and-skittles* and *slap-and-tickle*.

Sledging: Australian legend has it that Grahame Corling was nicknamed 'Percy *Sledge*' by his teammates for using language 'as subtle as a *sledgehammer*' in the earshot of a waitress. The term was then deployed for enquiries about a batsman's ancestral heritage rather than a lady's immediate availability. *Sledging*, even if it takes the *biscuit* sometimes, is now accepted as *part and parcel* of the modern game. Compare ***mental disintegration***.

Slipper: It may sound counter-intuitive, but this is the word for a fielder who is a *safe **pair of hands*** in the ***cordon***: 'Dravid is usually an outstanding *slipper* and he should have had that.'

Slog: Belongs by tradition to the unaesthetic category of words and shots. A reverend gentleman once came to the moral rescue of Gilbert Jessop by pronouncing him to be a 'mighty *hitter*' as opposed to a 'blind *slogger*'. The term has achieved a degree of recognition in the modern *slog-sweep*, although some local administrators may have doubts about the merits of this stroke: 'A *slog-swept* six over mid-wicket scored a *direct hit* on the Worcestershire committee room.' But the *slog* is now ready to receive full accreditation in the sphere of Twenty20, which has already sanctioned the previously pejorative term *slogfest*.

Slow and low: Rhyming description of what would not be considered a good *cricket wicket*, unless you are Geoffrey Boycott **booking in** for *bed-and-breakfast*: 'The pitches, tired and *slow and low* after a long South African season, have not helped interest in the tournament.' In **first-class** cricket, *slow and low* pitches tend to cause **bore draws**.

Smart piece of work: Can be used for any piece of fielding, but reserved particularly for moments when the keeper *whips off* the bails dextrously. However *smart*, this exercise sometimes amounts to what Cardus once called a 'rhetorical attempt' at a stumping: 'That was a very *smart piece of work* from Steve Rhodes, but I think we'll find Maynard's back foot was well behind the line.'

Smear: This word comes in handy for commentators who cannot conjugate **smite** and also because it can, unusually, describe a shot regardless of which part of the ground it is aimed at – or out of: 'Keegan *smeared* his first ball over *point* for four'; 'Sreesanth strikes back with a *smear* for four through *extra cover*'; 'Afridi *smeared* his second ball *straight* **down the ground**'; 'Hall *smeared* the very next delivery into the hands of Clarke at *mid-on*'; 'Marillier tried a *smear* over *mid-wicket*'; 'Mashrafe Mortaza aimed yet another wild *smear* in the direction of the *square-leg* umpire'; 'Botham tried to *smear* Trevor Hohns halfway across Europe.' Although there is a tendency for a *smear* to go to the leg side, the major qualifying factor is that it is an ugly shot. Perhaps there is a hint of the **agricultural** by association with sheep-smearing, or perhaps the fact it is attested as Australian slang for 'to thrash' or 'to murder' is relevant. Either way, a *smear* will not be appearing in the **MCC Coaching Manual** unless one of the **members** spills his sherry.

Smell the leather: Either a piece of friendly advice if you want the batsman to defend with textbook **watchfulness** or a piece of **sledging** if you are not giving him many *in his own* **half**.

Smite: A biblical word for striking of biblical proportions: 'The Fijian Uluiviti was a big-hitting batsman who once *smote* a 35-minute century in a minor game.' Although sometimes it becomes routine journalese for 'scored': 'Botham hit 49 and Marks *smote* 44.'

Smoko: 'Had a fifth bowler or an all-rounder been chosen, Warne could have been given a "*smoko*" without unduly weakening the attack.' Australian for a tea break, extended to cover a bowler taking his sweater and a **rest** from the attack. Particularly apposite in the case of the great leg-spinner.

Smother: While batsmen are taught to *cover* movement in the air, the more **classically** trained amongst them also *step out* to *smother the spin*. The ancient precepts will not necessarily prepare them for a modern phenomenon like the **helicopter wrist**: 'Matthew Sinclair was *gone* for a **duck** when he looked to go forward and *smother the spin* of Muralitharan, but he lost his balance and was stumped.'

Snaffle: The verb to be reached for when the ***chance***
is not quite ***regulation***: 'Dravid, the lone slip, flung
himself to his wrong side and *snaffled* the catch as the
ball was going past him.'

Snicko: It seems that the name of every technologi-
cal innovation brought into television coverage of
cricket has to be abbreviated. Perhaps this is to make
the device seem more familiar to the viewers.
Perhaps it reflects the Australian predilection for
shortening words (in 1932, the *Sydney Sun* was
describing Jack Fingleton as 'a brilliant field from
any *possy*'). In any event, what Channel 4 called the
snickometer, recalling other gadgets conjured up by
free-to-air broadcasting like the *swingometer* and the
clapometer, was abbreviated by Channel 9 to *snicko*.
By the same logic, the *speedometer* is *speedo*, *Hawk-
Eye* can become *Hawk*, and *super slow motion* is cut
down to ***super slo mo***.

Snorter: 'Harmison produced what the old guys
would have called a "*snorter*" that whipped through
Astle's guard at 92 miles an hour.' Reporting on a one-
dayer at Bristol in 2004, Ted Corbett seems to think
this is an archaic term. But we keep hearing it on the
field, especially from lippy keepers after a ***perfume
ball***. Probably a contraction of *rip-snorter* (first dictionary citation 1840), it conflates the ideas of something dangerous and something high-grade – no doubt
Ed Giddins and Dermot Reeve would concur.

Soft hands: The required technique for combating
extra bounce, whether from the quicks or the spinners: 'By taking a big stride, and playing with *soft
hands*, Vaughan has coped admirably with the big-
turning off breaks.' Also, a useful way of *dropping* the
ball *down* for a quick run: 'For me, the key to picking
up singles is playing the ball with *soft hands*.'

Sorry, bat: What a bowler invariably says, usually with an apologetic arm raised, when he has just bowled a *beamer*. One day he might mean it.

Source of income: This usage derives from the idea of a *productive* stroke: 'Jeff Crowe's *sole source of income* seemed to be from the square cut, which he played from wide of the leg stump if need be.' Good running can also create a surplus: 'Our speed between the wickets can mean up to 50 runs a day as *sheer profit*.' Batsmen who concentrate on their productivity become known as *prolific* scorers.

Southpaw: A staple in Indian-English prose for the players whom Alec Bedser described as *batting on the wrong side*. Hence, Sourav Ganguly is 'the *dashing southpaw* of Kolkata', Dinesh Mongia is 'the sizzling *southpaw* from Punjab' and Kumar Sangakkara is 'the classy Sri Lankan *southpaw*'. Despite the left-hander's traditional weakness against the ball *angled* across him or pitched into the *rough*, he is often as difficult to bowl to as *southpaws* are to box.

Souvenir stump: 'It was Warne who led the Australians into the Lord's Pavilion with a *souvenir stump* in one hand, the match ball in his pocket and the outstanding analysis of 6 for 82.' *Souvenir stumps* are probably more auctionable than *commemorative medallions*, which may be why umpires Bird and Shepherd used to bring out old ones after tea in one-day finals. This next quotation provides evidence of Australian self-confidence and of the way in which cricket is one of the few walks of life where *souvenir* can be used as a verb: 'Despite the morning's threat of West Indian resistance, the anticipation of victory soon became so embedded that Darren Lehmann *souvenired* the stumps in celebration an innings early.'

Spank: Another in that group of words which the English always seem to have used for corporal punishment or punishing cricket strokes: 'A delightful little bit of cricket was enjoyed by the spectators in witnessing Mr G. F. Grace make three 4's from one over of his big brother's; all three hits were *spanking* drives.' In the Wanderers ODI when South Africa chased down a world-record total, one of the Australian bowlers was left feeling particularly sore: 'Mick Lewis was *spanked* for a record 113 runs.'

Spar: How this word gets into cricket is not easy to explain, since *spar* can mean 'the cross-bar of a gate', 'to strike with a spear' and, in boxing, according to Samuel Johnson's genial definition, 'to fight with prelusive strokes'. It comes out, however, as akin to *fend* or *fence*, and the effect is typically the same: 'Robert Key was beaten early by a fine ball from Heath Streak, *sparring* to second slip.' Nyren's *Young Cricketer's Tutor* has a recommendation that we would find incongruous nowadays: 'The position of the wicket-keeper in his standing should be that of a man preparing to *spar*.' But this was obviously the prelusive attitude 1833-style.

Spear: This is a suitably *hostile* instrument in the hands of the fast bowlers: 'Tendulkar drove and cut with élan until Donald *speared* him on the front boot with a yorker'; 'Shoaib then *speared* one into Kumble's rib cage.' The price for such hostility is that some deliveries are *speared harmlessly* down the leg side, often resulting in four byes or wides. But the tendency for *spears* to be directed from off to leg is most pronounced with those off-spinners who *push it through*, when what is supposedly an attacking weapon is used to enforce a defensive tactic: 'Hemmings used to *spear* it at middle and leg while the seamers took a breather.'

Spearhead: The opening bowlers are said, in a routine expression, to *spearhead the attack*. But the practised observer will occasionally pick out something novel as the game unfolds: 'Simon Jones acted almost as *spearhead* at *second change*'; 'Mohammad Sami, the hitherto *blunt spearhead*, quickly sent back Gautam Gambhir and Virender Sehwag.'

Spell: Most likely unit of reference for assessing a bowler's performance, like *innings* for one batsman, *stand* for two batsmen, *session* for a team. Some confusion can be caused by the fact that, in Australian racing parlance, a *spell* is a break from training. Therefore, when Ponting gives McGrath a *spell*, he is more likely to be taking him off than putting him on. This second example reporting on the selection of a Test squad may clarify: 'Amongst the pacemen, Jason Gillespie has been *spelled* and Michael Kasprowicz has been put out to *pasture*.'

Spin twins: Archetypally, the ***calypso** twins*, Sonny Ramadhin and Alf Valentine, although any two slow bowlers who *bowl **in tandem*** for any length of time are likely to qualify for the title: 'Then there were the two spinners from Trinidad called Inshan Ali and Jumadeen. Pick up the *Express* newspaper and all you read about was "the *spin twins*".' The categorisation can also be used to comment ironically on the bowlers' ages: 'The *new spin twins* Pat Pocock and Phil Edmonds had harried India to defeat in the second Test at Delhi.'

Spirit of cricket: This concept is now enshrined in a preamble to the Laws of the game, even if it can still sometimes come into potential conflict with those Laws. The modern Australian side aims to protect the integrity of the game with almost Methodist zeal: 'Our own players have set very high standards for themselves through the *Spirit of Cricket pledge*, and as an organisation we have set ourselves a target of having zero breaches.' Quite so, and Ricky Ponting was just having a quiet word with the *sightscreen* attendant as he walked back to the Trent Bridge pavilion in 2005.

Spit: Verb used exclusively for balls which turn *viciously* out of the *rough*: 'Warne's first delivery *spat* out of the *footholes*, struck Trescothick's bat and carried to Ponting at *silly point*.' Reading the papers after a match-winning innings for Glamorgan on a *crumbler* at Colchester, Javed Miandad came upon this development of the theme: 'A sports journalist later wrote that the wicket had deteriorated so much that the balls were coming off its surface like *fat flying off* from a *frying pan*.'

Splice: 'The ball hit the *splice* of the bat and seemed to be looping over Douglas Hondo, at short fine leg, but the fielder took a brilliant one-handed catch.' The bottom of the bat handle becomes worthy of note when a bowler *extracts* extra bounce to hit it. In cricket, therefore – unless someone has been *Freddied* or seated next to David Boon on a long flight – *spliced* is going to mean *dollied up*: 'The ball *spat* at him from a very similar spot, to be tamely *spliced* to gully.' *Sitting on the splice* indicates *stonewalling*.

Spoon: If a batsman *spoons* a shot it is always mistimed and it often *offers* a *dolly* to a waiting fielder: 'Steve Adshead *spooned* a *loose* drive to cover'; 'Dravid's dismal run continued, as he *spooned* a harmless short ball *straight down* Johnson's *throat*.'

Sporting pitch: 'When Chatfield came out to bat in the 1985 Dunedin Test New Zealand still needed another 50 runs to beat Pakistan on a *sporting pitch*.'

A pitch which is described as *sporting* can simply be a good *cricket wicket* which has something in it for the *quicks* early in the match and then encourages the spinners as the game develops. More often than not, though, a *sporting pitch* equates to a *result wicket*, on which the batsmen never feel *in*. And sometimes, as was the case at Dunedin, it is a euphemism for a *dangerous track*: 'Lance Cairns had already been carried off on a stretcher, his skull fractured by a bouncer from Wasim Akram.' For once, the vocabulary is not being chosen from the batsman's perspective.

Spray: In cricket, a reference to *spraying it around* is much less likely to suggest that the man of the match has opened his champagne than that a bowler's **radar** is sadly awry: 'Fidel Edwards tended to bowl too short and was also guilty of *spraying it around*'; 'Where India's bowlers had *sprayed* it all over *like a water cannon*, Australia's bowlers generally bowled keeping their fields in mind.' Perhaps the image arose because bowling **both sides of the wicket** is considered an unforgivable extravagance. When batsmen *spray* the ball around, they are cut more slack in that they are either trying to dominate the bowling or having some fun in a lost cause: 'Brett Dorey claimed a wicket on début when he ended Shaun Pollock's *late spray* of four sixes in a 31-ball 46.' Meanwhile, when a batsman or fielder gets hit, apart perhaps from when he gets **boxed**, the ubiquitous *magic spray* is cricket's equivalent of the 'magic sponge'.

Squared up: An expression to support the theory that playing **side-on** is the best method for *getting behind* the ball. If a batsman dealing with movement away from the bat presents his chest to the bowler, he is liable to present a catch to the waiting **cordon**: 'Jonathan Hughes was *squared up* and taken in the slips off Amjad Khan.' Without any attendant detail, being *squared up* is as likely to indicate an lbw, as in this second example: 'Chris Bassano was *squared up* by Ashley Noffke.' Finally, there are instances where the **victim** is comprehensively turned **inside out**: 'Cameron Borgas was *squared up* and bowled by another good one in Bird's next over.'

Stand and deliver: 'Dravid posted his 11th ODI career hundred with a *stand and deliver* pull shot to the mid-wicket *fence* off paceman Dilhara Fernando.' Batsmen who *stand and deliver* tend to take on the bowling by **opening the shoulders**. But while fortune can favour the brave, the expression is often used to underline the fact that a batsman should have moved his feet rather than trusting entirely to his *eye*: 'Chris Gayle must be asking himself time and again why he attempted that atrocious, *stand-and-deliver*, heavy-footed swing against Steve Harmison.'

Stay at home: While this phrase might be used of a player who declines to tour, it is much more likely to describe a batsman who prefers to play spin bowling whilst remaining **creasebound**. Traditionalists consider such technique against the turning ball to be safety-first at best and self-defeating at worst: 'Compton was a magnificent player *down the wicket*, but I don't suppose he was stumped on average more often than the batsman who *stayed at home* and occasionally dragged his toe from behind the line in forward defence.'

Steepling: The traditional adjective for what might be thought of as a cricketing version of an 'up and under', when the ball is a disconcertingly long time coming down: 'Things might have been different if Steve Kirby had not *spilt* a *steepling* hook by Bicknell on four.' The adjective can also be applied when a bowler **extracts** enough lift to be a nasty proposition:

'More human catapult than *classical* fast bowler, Malinga discomfited every batsman with occasional *steepling bounce* and *genuine pace*.'

Stickability: The *Oxford English Dictionary*'s first citation for this word is from 1888: '*Stickability* ... is the most important ability a farmer can possess.' In cricket, *stickability* is also an important ability, but not normally associated with an *agricultural* approach to batting: 'It may not please the *purists*, but Chanderpaul's determination and *stickability* have made him into a highly effective performer.' And yet we might almost detect a hint of something *agricultural* in this further example: 'Hussey would have given the batting line-up an extra *dollop* of *stickability*.'

Stick of rhubarb: Boycottism for the equipment required against the kind of bowling attack he would have loved to play against at *both ends*: 'This is rubbish bowling is this, Michael. My mum could play this with a *stick of rhubarb*.'

Sticky wicket: Has gone into the English language for metaphorical purposes, even if covered pitches mean the phenomenon has gone out of the collective English memory. The anecdotal tradition preserves relics from the era of *natural wickets*, such as this exchange between Wilfred Rhodes and Emmott Robinson as they inspected a sodden Headingley pitch drying out quickly under the afternoon sun: 'Rhodes pressed the turf with a forefinger and said, "It'll be *sticky* at four o'clock, Emmott." Whereat Emmott bent down and also pressed the turf with a forefinger. "No, Wilfred," he said, "half-past."'

Stifle: The authorised term for when a bowler cuts short his appeal, usually because he has caught the

sound of a ***nick*** off the bat. But this is only at one end
of the spectrum: 'England must have had about 30
lbw appeals, ranging from *stifled* to *screaming*.'
Stentorian was heard regularly in the Homeric period
of cricket reporting, and can emerge even now in an
epic Test match: 'Clarke survives a *stentorian appeal*
for lbw from Flintoff as England keep the ***pressure***
on.'

Stingy: 'Good bowling, Gussy, keep it *stingy, stingy*.'
Bajan vernacular for ***economical*** bowling.

Stock: A *stock bowler* is a ***change bowler*** as distinct
from a ***strike bowler***, although the distinction may not
be categorical: 'Because of injuries Ormond was both
strike and *stock bowler* again yesterday'; 'Throughout
the tour Bill Johnston was the mainstay of the attack
in his dual role of *shock* and *stock* bowler.' Meanwhile,
the *strike bowler* will want to have a *stock ball* to provide the main thrust of his attack: 'Gough put more
work into improving his *stock ball* and was rewarded
when it earned more than half his 20 Test wickets in
the series.'

Stonewall: Several cricketing terms, like being
bowled a ***googly*** and playing a ***straight bat***, have
been adopted in military and political circles.
Stonewall is a term that appears to have come the
other way. Thomas Jackson, the Confederate leader,
was given the nickname by General Barnard E. Bee at
the first battle of Bull Run in 1861. It was not entirely
clear at the time whether Bee was criticising Jackson
for his lethargy or praising him for his steadfastness.
General Bee could not clarify the matter as he was
killed very shortly afterwards, but history has decided
on the second interpretation. In cricket, where the
first recorded usage dates from 1867, the context
decides whether *stonewalling* – playing with an

utterly ***dead bat*** to keep out all comers – is a good or a bad thing: '***Nightwatchman*** Hoggard *stonewalled* effectively for 37 balls before Franklin found his ***edge***'; 'Mark Richardson put the crowd to sleep with some excruciating *stonewalling*.'

Straight: Although ***variation*** is essential to their craft, most bowlers will want to be sure that they have the ability to bowl *straight* on the '***You miss, I hit***' principle. This applies less to those bowlers whose ***stock*** ball is meant to spin: 'I'm afraid to say I didn't see Geoff Miller turn one *off the straight* all day.' However sure of his top-spinner, Richie Benaud was not amused when somebody in the 1958–59 England touring team was overheard in the ***nets*** referring to *a Benaud* as a delivery which did not deviate at all: 'All I wanted to do was show them that Benaud was no "*straight*" spinner, and to upset the specified MCC plan that by merely pushing forward they would stop me taking wickets.' Australia deservedly won that series 4–0, although less magnanimous MCC ***members*** still mutter about the way Ian Meckiff's arm ***straightened***.

Straight bat: The ***classical*** way to play is *with a straight bat*, so that the expression has gone into the English language to mean giving nothing away, either by being very guarded or very strict. Surprisingly, the first *Oxford English Dictionary* citation for what is a very common figurative usage dates from as late as 1973. Mumbai economist Dr Ajit Ranade is a big enough cricket fan to put some colour back into it: 'Cricketer Sanjay Manjrekar's batting style was influenced by years of *gulli* cricket, which forces you to play your shots only between mid-on and mid-off. Chidambaram's Budget reminded me of this *straight bat* approach, defined by compulsions of the coalition dharma and the need for fiscal *rectitude*.' Perhaps when Finance Minister Chidambaram injects more liquidity into the Indian economy he will launch a *flurry* of *straight sixes*.

Straight down his throat: 'Big top *edge* – in the air – there's a man out there – Allan Border – getting under it – *straight down his throat*.' A figure for a catch when the fielder barely has to move from his original position. Not to be taken literally, unless you are Billy Birmingham deliberately misunderstanding for comic effect, in which case Merv Hughes comes to the rescue and unblocks Border's windpipe. In Birmingham's *12th Man* sketches, Bill Lawry contracts Tourette's syndrome whenever a Victorian breathes, Tony Greig gets excited about the bowlers running in 'hord and forst', and Richie Benaud generally tries to keep control. Although Birmingham and Tom Gleisner, in his Warwick Todd persona, more than flirt with political incorrectness, their work provides a welcome antidote to the modern-day cult of the *baggy green*.

Straighten: Two things *straighten* in cricket: *balls* (often *wicket balls*) and *arms* (often in a *suspect* fashion): 'Lee got one to *straighten* and Smith was *palpably* lbw struck on the back pad'; 'The ICC had mooted a limit of 15 degrees of permissible *straightening* for bowlers of all types; Harbhajan's *doosra* was believed to have been measured at 22.' Kerry O'Keeffe is sceptical about the laboratory tests on bowlers' *actions* carried out for the ICC by Australian experts: 'Boy George would be considered *straight* at the University of Western Australia.' O'Keeffe will probably not be receiving an invitation to be guest speaker at that university's School for Social and Cultural Studies.

Strangle: Appeals can be *strangled*, but the verb is more commonly used when a batsman gets an unlucky *tickle* on a poor delivery *slanting* well past his pads:

'Clarke, after one *glorious* off drive, was *strangled* down the leg side off what would have been a wide.' We have heard a reference to *strangulation* in Jim Maxwell's commentary, drawing out the pain further.

Streaky: The adjective for runs scored more by luck than judgement, especially edges which fly through the slips: 'The *streaky* four to third man off Rudra Pratap that got Farhat *off the mark* was no indication of the *carnage* to follow.' A usage which seems to conflate the ideas of the ball going like streaked lightning and the batsman being on a winning streak. Nothing to do with *freakers* though nor, any longer, with Kevin Pietersen's hair.

Street fighter: 'There is something of the *street-fighter* mentality in Javed's cricket.' A soubriquet which always seemed to attach itself to the combative Javed Miandad, recognising also perhaps that many Pakistani and Indian cricketers begin their *love affair* with the game by playing *tape-ball* in the street. Peter Roebuck once compared the way Miandad *negotiated* the turning ball with the way a rickshaw driver negotiates the streets of Karachi. Javed generously chose to take this as an unqualified compliment: 'I appreciated Roebuck's comment for what it was, an honest appraisal of how the dynamics of my urban background had formed my cricket.'

Strife: An Australianism beloved of Bill Lawry and his old sparring partner Tony Greig: 'Another wicket for Lawson and England in *real strife* now.' The English equivalent is *desperate trouble*. You won't hear references to both *trouble* and *strife* in cricket unless Phil Tufnell is talking about his marital history.

Strike bowler: 'My aim is to be Australia's *strike bowler*. I've made no secret of that.' Brett Lee also makes no secret of the fact that he considers *strike man* to be synonymous with what, in the latest argot, would be called the **go-to bowler**: 'I want to be the number one bowler for Australia.' However, captains with equally grand aspirations can try to base success on the old adage that fast bowlers *hunt in pairs*: 'Ronnie Irani said today Essex could become a huge force in county cricket again – if they can sign *another strike bowler.*'

Striker: 'Bosman is a **clean** *striker of the ball* and after taking a few overs to set his sights, he then launched into the Lions' bowling.' In cricket reporting, *of the ball* seems to be tacked on to *striker*, perhaps to avoid confusion between big-hitting batsmen and free-scoring frontmen. It should be noted that the Bosman in this example is not Jean-Marc but Loots.

Strokeplay: The *quality* and *array* of a batsman's *strokeplay* are likely indicators of how attractive he is to watch. The aesthetic factor is certainly in evidence in the following example: 'Flintoff's *rugged strokeplay* contrasted with Law's more *dreamy* cover drives and **effortless** *whips* through mid-wicket.' Here the word *dreamy* in particular has an air of almost wilful nostalgia for the *classic* age.

Studious: Means **watchful**, but often with the implication of *slow*. Also seems to apply automatically to university graduates or batsmen wearing spectacles, before they master contact lenses. Peter Roebuck qualified on all counts.

Stuff: Used to be a synonym for **filth**, particularly from a spinner, but now prevalent in the two phrases *short stuff* and **rough** *stuff*: 'Harmison came *charging in* and let a tirade of *short stuff* go at both batsmen';

'Evan Gray will be aiming for the *rough stuff* outside
Gower's off stump.'

Stygian gloom: 'The middle half of this game, and
the end, was played out in *gloom* so *Stygian* that
Dickie Bird would have been reaching for the
smelling-salts and a handy flashlight.' A topos for
reporting on *bad light* at Headingley and in Hades.

Submarine: More common in rugby for an illegal
tackle on a player in mid-air, this term is reserved in
cricket not for **beamers** but for *grubbers* which
bounce so low they appear to go under the surface:
'Soweto's only turf pitch played very low and
Atherton was almost *"submarined"* by the day's first
delivery.' Sometimes the figure can switch to the
weapons on board rather than the vessel itself:
'Statham often *skids* through low and this particular
morning on a *broken* wicket he was bowling *torpe-
does.*' Compare **scuttle**.

Succumb: The dictionary is uncompromising in its
pursuit of the definition: 'to yield to the attacks of a
disease, etc . . . and hence to die'. But the word flourishes in cricket reporting not so much because it is
redolent of doom, but because it can accommodate
such various reasons for a player losing his wicket:
'Hassan Adnan *succumbed* to a ball that *stopped on*
him'; 'From Anurag Singh onwards batsmen *succumbed* to overambition.' Compare **perish** and
undone.

Super: As a general rule, anything called *super* in
cricket is quite the opposite. The *supersub* was a short-
lived ICC invention which merely increased the
advantage of winning the toss. The *Super Six* sounded
like a creation of Enid Blyton or an indoor hockey
tournament, but was a league format with one eye on

revenue which enervated the World Cups of 1999 and 2003. The 2005 *Super Test*, centrepiece of the *ICC Johnnie Walker Super Series*, was a mismatch between Australia and a highly paid, highly unmotivated *World XI*. In their previous incarnation, *Super Tests* were part of Packer's *World Series Cricket* and, while the standards of play and levels of interest steadily improved, they were not exactly the same draw as the baseball World Series on which the circus's razzmatazz was modelled. Only when Richie Benaud talks about a *super **delivery*** or says *super shot that* is the trade description really reliable.

Super slo mo: The modern cricket ***analyst*** can now set up his own access to the new technology: 'Hollioake missed the ball, then watched Frost take it in *super slow mo*, giving him all the time he needed to regain his ground.' India is in no sense averse to gadgetry, but it also has its folklore to revert to for an even more suggestive analogy: 'Sehwag edged Shabbir and Taufeeq Umar at slip made an effort so full of torpor that it recalled the image of the eternal *crocodile* resting with its mouth open.'

Swagger: Some batsmen are thought to reveal their greatness even in the way they stride to the crease. In the 1930s, Bradman's *swagger* when he came out of the pavilion ***first drop*** was thought to show a touch of class and arrogance. In modern times, the word has been associated particularly with West Indian batsmen: 'Richards, like Sobers before him, is one of those few players whose purposeful *swagger* to the wicket was worth the price of admission.' It is even possible for especially ***swashbuckling*** batsmen to *swagger*, albeit momentarily, when leaving the crease: 'Mahendra Singh Dhoni, never mind that Team India was *tottering*, ***danced*** down the wicket with *rock star swagger* to hit it over mid-wicket.'

Swashbuckling: An adjective applicable to **bats-manship** of the **dashing** kind. It sounds as if it belongs to the age of Errol Flynn rather than that of Andrew Flintoff, but it is used almost as a matter of course for any meaningful innings by crowd-pleasers like Shahid Afridi and Adam Gilchrist. Shane Warne also seems to qualify for the term, whether he is batting for Hampshire – 'A *swashbuckling* innings from the skipper on the first day at Southgate' – or St Kilda: 'Warne's *swashbuckling* innings, his second ton for the Saints, was scored off just 91 balls.' Emmott Robinson, representing Yorkshire, had no time for what Cardus referred to as the *'flashing bat* school' – 'He dismissed it with one good word: "*Swash-buckle*" he called it.'

Swat: 'Short balls were *swatted* away to the leg-side **fence**.' The term is possibly meant to suggest the *rolling* of the wrists recommended for controlling the hook shot. John Arlott proposed such a distinction, but without asserting the usage as being quite so technical: 'As always, Tennyson hooked – sometimes varying that stroke with one reminiscent of a man *swatting* a fly.'

Sweeper: Recently imported from football, although the cricketing equivalent usually has a lot more ground to cover patrolling the boundaries each side of the wicket. *Stopper*, a now obsolete term for a fielder (especially behind the keeper), is an expression which seems to have gone the other way.

Sweet spot: 'Lara **danced** down the wicket to Azhar Mahmood to hit him superbly through cover, right off the *sweet spot*.' Although it may be more important to know where the *sweet spot* is if you are trying to hit a home run in baseball, it is also an important part of cricket-bat production. Indeed, the manufacturers are forever making claims about a *sweet spot* which is *extended*, *longer*, *bigger* or *lower*. The *sweet spot* is not necessarily quite the same thing as the **meat** of the bat, in that the emphasis is on perfect and **effortless** timing, with no vibration through the handle. But an observation by Steve Waugh suggests the bat-makers' advertising is indeed justified: 'Years ago the bats we used had a *sweet spot* of a couple of inches. Now the *sweet spot* is the entire bat.'

Swipe: Such shots are *massive* in intention and *ugly* in execution: 'Morkel tried another *big swipe* off the next delivery, but a *thin edge* was taken by keeper McCullum.' The **premeditated** *swipe* can actually be so long premeditated that it becomes a topic of discussion, as Peter Roebuck intimates: '"Big Bird" Garner said today that he was "done *swipin*'". We shall see.'

Swish: This might be listed, somewhere between **waft** and **slash**, among the gamut of incautious shots played outside the off stump, and most notably by **tailenders** *having a swish*. At the same time, though, *swish* seems to have become almost the technical term for any gestural or gratuitous use of the **willow**: 'Stuart Law *swished* his bat angrily at the tameness of the dismissal'; 'Ben Hutton was given a level-one reprimand for *swishing* his bat at the stumps after being bowled.'

T

Tadi-master: Mumbai slang for a batsman who completely dominates the bowling: 'Sehwag is an accomplished *tadi-master*, who is so dreaded that bowlers, while running in, say silent prayers.'

Tailender: The English fondness for the underdog helps to account for the prevailing mythology here: 'Chris Tremlett hit two massive *tailender's* sixes'; 'Then came a *lusty* stand of 73 between Nottinghamshire's last-wicket pair, hitting out for pleasure in the manner of *tailenders* of yore.' Modern international cricket requires the lower **order** to make a more sober contribution: 'Daren Powell showed great **application** to support Lara.'

Take: As an idiom, this usually means to *take the strike*: 'Gatting *took* Qadir for several overs to *protect* first Ian Greig and then Derek Pringle, both of whom had previously been utterly **bamboozled** by the leg-spinner.' More occasionally, a batsman may deliberately let himself be hit rather than risk *popping up* a **chance**: 'Boycott *took* several Pascoe **rib-ticklers** on the body.'

Taken for a ride: There is no connotation of being deceived or hoodwinked when it is a bowler getting the treatment: 'Do not forget Harold Larwood was *taken for a ride* by the Australian batsmen more than once.' The phrase functions here, in effect, as a straight synonym for **carted**.

Take on: A batsman can *take on* the bowling by venturing to play his **big shots**, and especially the hook: 'Aravinda *took* Imran *on* and hit him for two arresting sixes.' But the more common usage occurs when he *takes on* a fielder, especially for a second run: 'Vaughan's **knock** ended when he *took on* A. B. de Villiers' throw from third man and lost.' Clever club cricketers with a good enough *arm* will give you an easy two the first time you *take* them *on*, then *rifle* the ball over the stumps from sixty yards the second – and last – time you try it.

Target killings: A phrase used by Pakistan selector
Wasim Bari to describe decisions against his two best
batsmen, Inzamam and Yousuf, in a one-day final
played against the *baggy greens* in Amsterdam.
Perhaps the metaphor suggested itself to Bari at an
emotional moment when the common complaint
about *trigger-happy* umpires reminded him of the
Australians' *decapitation strategy*.

Taxi: If a *walking wicket* comes to the crease, the
requisite piece of *sledging* is to pretend to hail a hack-
ney carriage in order to convey the batsman back to
the pavilion. The same kind of gag can serve to
lighten the tone of complaints about slow over-rates:
'Griffith, timed at seven minutes for an eight-ball
over, was advised in Melbourne to *take a taxi*, so long
was he in getting back to his far-distant mark.'

Tennis-ball bounce: 'The Oval has a bit of a *featherbed* wicket with *tennis-ball bounce* rather than the
rough, abrasive ones at Edgbaston and Old Trafford.'
Some people may disagree with Matthew Hayden's
reading of English pitches, but what he is suggesting
is that the bounce at the Oval is *spongy* rather than
skiddy. The former is a less daunting proposition for
the batsman and less likely to rough up the ball for
Irish purposes. However, *tennis-ball bounce* may
sometimes suggest genuinely uncomfortable lift:
'Alfonso Thomas troubled the top *order* on a pitch
where there was some *tennis-ball bounce* at times.'

Terminator: The title bestowed on Michael Bevan
for his prowess as a *finisher*. Bevan's work was usually not quite as spectacular as it might sound, in that
he usually *chased* down targets in a methodical manner: 'If Michael Bevan was the *grafting*, dependable
"*Terminator*", Australia's new middle-*order* hero
Symonds has become the *dominator*.' Perhaps in the

end it is more fitting to apply the word to a wicket-taking bowler: 'Some call McGrath a machine, others name him the *Terminator*.' Meanwhile, the special portmanteau word invented for Harbhajan Singh is heaven sent for headline writers: '*Turbanator* derails *Rawalpindi* **Express**'; '*Turbanator* on ICC's suspect list.' Monty Panesar is auditioning for the role of *Turbanator II* and already has the sub-editors hard at it: '*Sikh* and destroy.'

There or thereabouts: 'Zaheer Khan used his head, bowled within himself, and focused on just keeping it *there or thereabouts*, cramping the left-hander for room for **strokeplay**.' The expression seems to be a more traditional version of *in the right* **areas**, since we can trace it back to Wilfred Rhodes: 'I can keep 'em *there or thereabouts*.' Long seen in racing columns to predict that a horse will *not be far away*, the phrase also appears in pre-season cricket previews: 'Sussex are still going to be *there or thereabouts* and you can't write off sides like Surrey, Warwickshire or Kent either.' This tipster named almost half the field before the 2005 County Championship and still didn't find the winner.

Thin: A reduction of *thin* **edge** to form a verb, as in 'Stephen Peters *thinned* a lifting ball behind.' But the practised summariser will tend to revert to a more traditional formulation: 'Ed Smith was adjudged caught by Prior off what must have been the *thinnest of edges*.'

Third umpire: When *referrals* were still an innovation, the official making the decisions was more likely to be the *video umpire*, but the terminology has now settled down. *Third umpires* are sometimes felt to be conservative or incompetent. The point can be made ironically, as in this piece of internet commentary:

'Harmison's yorker *flattens* middle and off. Even the *third umpire* would have given that one out.' Or a little less subtly, as in Navjot Singh Sidhu's observation that 'Eddie Nichols is a man who cannot find his own buttocks with his two hands.'

Thrash: This term usually features towards the end of a team's innings when the *lower **order*** sets about *having a thrash* or *making hay*: 'Some *merry* late *thrashing* from Ismail Dawood and Tim Bresnan brought 52 from the last five overs.' Since Twenty20 cricket is all about *making merry*, *thrash* will presumably become the compendium term which encompasses all the others: 'They have *crashed, bashed, smashed* and ***slashed*** and the spectators have gone giddy with delight.' Some of the giddiness at these evening games may also be attributable to the spectators themselves being a bit *smashed*.

Three-card trick: The classic *three-card tricks* in cricket are two outswingers followed by an inswinger and two short-pitched deliveries followed by a ball pitched up to invite the drive. But the term can also be used when the batsman is trumped by other ***variations***, as when Shoaib *suckered* his ***victim*** with two ***lollipops*** followed by a faster bouncer: 'Akhtar tries the *three-card trick* with the next ball and Pietersen *obliges*, trying to pull another short one that was on to him quicker.'

Through the gate: 'Please shut the gate,' says the Country Code, while the coaching manual says: 'Keep bat and pad together.' The two enjoinders ought to reinforce each other as a reminder of the best technique. As long as you don't leave your best technique in the ***shed***: 'Robert Key was bowled *through the gate* by Ervine's first ball.'

Through the shot: Just as golfers are given swing tips, so batsmen are advised to get properly *through the ball*. Being *through the shot*, on the other hand, occurs when the bowler **holds one back** or the batsman **succumbs** to overeagerness: 'Warne bowled a slower leg break from wide of the crease and Pietersen was *through the shot* early.' The outcome is usually a **spooned**-up catch or else *rattled timber*.

Throwdown: 'Before play began I had a woeful *"throwdown"* **net** with Phil Neale.' The England manager was not having a judo session with Ashley Giles but trying to help him get his timing right by chucking down a few easy balls from ten yards or so.

Throw the ball: The formula, not for the action of a **chucker**, but for that of a captain making a bowling change, especially if he is running out of options or summoning one last great effort from his **spearhead**: 'At one minute to six, Worrell *threw the ball* to his lion-hearted fast bowler, Wes Hall, and prayed for a miracle.'

Throw the bat: A regular way of describing attempts, successful or otherwise, to play **big shots**: 'Vaughan *threw the bat* at a wide ball from Harvey and was caught by Hancock'; 'The final **blaze** came from Tinashe Panyangara, who *threw the bat* with glorious abandon.' The **willow** does not normally come out of the batsman's hands in these circumstances, but it can do on his return to the pavilion, *bat thrower* being a generic term for players who have tantrums after their dismissal: 'I am not a *bat thrower* normally, but this afternoon it flew across the dressing room accompanied by a foul oath.' Examples of literal *bat-throwing* on the field of play include a bizarre method of avoiding *edges* to balls aimed into the **rough** stuff (patented by D. A. Reeve) and a fit of pique from the user of an aluminium bat (patented by D. K. Lillee). The custodians of the Laws reacted promptly in both cases.

Thunderbolt: Can be applied to a fast bowler in person, but used more often with reference to a delivery sent down more quickly than expected: 'Lee was fast and furious, bowling the most *rapid* measured ball of the summer – a 156.2 km/hr *thunderbolt*.' Sometimes the surprise factor can result from the bowler's ***action*** as much as the extra pace: 'Tony Lock's *thunderbolts* were the subject of much discussion.'

Tickle: A faint *deflection*, almost invariably to leg, and fatal unless indicated otherwise: 'Murray Goodwin *tickled* the second ball of the day down the leg side.' The usage was appreciated, inevitably, by Brian Johnston, who notoriously observed: 'There's Neil Harvey round the *corner*, legs open wide, waiting for a *tickle*.' Jack Fingleton's response is also recorded, and was possibly just as premeditated: 'He's waiting for a catch as well.' This brand of humour has been filed for posterity by a *Test Match Special* listener from Sheffield under the motto 'Aggers – Johnners – Leggers over'.

Tight: A word which neatly lines up the activity of bowling with its statistical implications. In the most directly cricketing sense it functions as the opposite of ***loose***: 'Spinner Lakpa Lama didn't allow any batsmen to better him with his *tight **line and length*** throughout the tournament.' Add in the bowler's analysis, and it becomes virtually a synonym for ***economical***: 'Graeme Welch produced a *tight* opening spell of 9–4–9–2.' At the end of a one-dayer, in which wickets are not necessarily of the essence, the economic imperative opens up the metaphor: 'Muralitharan's *tight* hold on the *purse strings* took the game.'

Titmus, F. J.: 'Ladies and gentlemen, a correction to your scorecards: for "*F. J. Titmus*" read "*Titmus, F. J.*"' This announcement, communicated over the tannoy at Lord's in 1950, provides a sublimely ridiculous example of how the distinction between gentlemen and players was jealously guarded at **Headquarters** to the bitter end. In early scorecards professionals were referred to by surnames only as befitted the lower ranks, but they eventually graduated to having their initials placed after their names. Surrey captain Percy Fender, who is documented as playing a version of what we would now call the **reverse sweep** in 1921, was ahead of his time also in choosing to lead professionals and amateurs onto the field through the same gate. This was not immediately appreciated by the authorities at the *Home of Cricket*: 'We do not want that sort of thing at Lord's, Fender.'

Toe-ender: A ball hit off the bottom of the bat: 'Harmison is rather unlucky to see a Chanderpaul *toe-ender* fly along the ground through the slips for four.' If the shot is particularly **streaky**, the batsman may be offered *chalk* by the ever-helpful fielders, while if it **dollies** *up* a catch it qualifies as a **knob-ender**.

Tonk: This is not regarded as a *first-class* verb suitable for reporting on **first-class** cricket. Alan Ross recognised this when covering an *up-country* match during an English tour of Australia: 'Our spinners have been *tonked* about yet again by uncouth **country** batsmen.' Perhaps this match marked the first appearance of that upstanding Australian Warwick Todd, a character always prepared to *go the tonk*.

Top: *Going over the top* is not quite so perilous in whites as in khaki, but **taking on** spinners in this way does have its dangers: 'Moin *went over the top*, a four looked a foregone conclusion, but Campbell reached overhead and plucked the ball down with no apparent effort.' When balls *go through the top* (of the playing surface), it is usually a safe bet that the pitch will **break up** badly by the last innings: 'Having won the toss and elected to bowl I think the fourth or fifth ball *went through the top*, so I thought, "Oh dear, we've made the wrong decision here."'

Torrid: 'Thorpe had a *torrid time* in the Test and that's what our bowlers are there for – to test the best batsmen out.' *Torrid* is a slightly more nuanced word for a *fiery* burst of fast bowling which borders on the *intimidatory*. After the winding up of the **fast bowlers' union**, some of the most frightening *quicks* could sometimes get a taste of their own medicine: 'Sure enough, Marshall received some *torrid short-pitched* **stuff** from Wasim Akram and edged one to Saleem Yousuf.'

Tosser: A reference to a *useless* or *hopeless tosser* will usually get a snigger in the back of the box, as well as informing listeners that the coin keeps coming down the wrong way for a particular captain. Recent England skippers have had so little experience of *calling right* that emergency measures have been considered: 'Vaughan has not ruled out the use of a substitute "*tosser*".'

Touch-up: If we leave aside his insensitive use of the word *grovel*, Tony Greig's vocabulary is often teasingly euphemistic. For example, the act of *roughing up* a **tailender** with some *short* **stuff** is made to sound a fairly harmless proposition after the event: 'McGrath's fallen **victim** to a *little touch-up*.'

Trampoline: Traditionally the *trampoline* is a metaphor for a bouncy pitch: 'Ambrose took seven wickets for one run in 32 balls on a *trampoline* of a pitch at Perth.' The more facetious school of modern journalists can bounce the word around for other purposes. As an ex-bowler, Mike Selvey does not find the spectacle of state-of-the-art one-day cricket appealing: 'Boundaries are minuscule, pitches *pristine*, bats *trampoline* the ball so that the *value* of a shot carries inflation like the Zimbabwean dollar.' Martin Johnson provides us with another antonym for ***flypaper*** *gloves* in this equally colourful passage on poor Geraint Jones: 'He has a pair of wicketkeeping gloves that appear to have been hewn from a *trampoline*, and his attempt to catch Jason Gillespie by sticking out an arm was less like watching a professional athlete as one of those old Morris Minors with a semaphore trafficator.'

Trap: The *leg trap* is the most traditional place for the fielding side to *snare* a batsman, although the rule restricting fielders behind square and the covering of wickets has made it almost obsolete as a technical term. In the modern game two men ***posted*** out in the ***deep*** for the top-edged hook have become the stereotypical *trap*. If the batsman insists on bringing them into play, the reporter may in turn insist on adding some colour to the trope, as when the Australian captain fell ***victim*** to a ***three-card trick*** in a domestic game: 'As soon as Ponting hit the ball he knew he was out, Brant barely moving to *swallow* the catch like a *Venus fly trap*.'

Trapezist: This image seems to have been in vogue to describe athletic cricketers in the 1950s and 1960s: 'Jackie McGlew is a notable example of a cricketing *trapezist*, although in his enthusiasm he did once bust up a shoulder making one of his flying dives'; 'Evans, with a leap like a dying *trapezist*, caught the ball a yard or more down the leg side.' The virtual disappearance of the *trapezist* from the cricket lexicon probably has more to do with the dramatic improvement of fielding standards than the decline in popularity of circus artistes. But John Woodcock did have a go at describing Rodney Marsh in similar vein: 'For much of the time he resembled a *performing dolphin* – or a goalkeeper at practice.'

Trimmer: Not a word we have ever seen used of Mike Gatting, even after pre-season training. Instead, the idea conveyed is of a delivery which is a *bail-trimmer*: 'Gillespie promptly greeted Tillakaratne Dilshan with a *trimmer* delivered at high pace that cut away from the bat and took the off bail.' A more archaic variant is *bailer*: 'One run later Studd was bowled with a *bailer* without scoring.'

Trudge: A batsman walks, or occasionally even *swaggers*, out to bat, but he is expected to *trudge* back to the pavilion, since his heart is heavier than before. The manner of this performance is sometimes more worthy of attention than the innings just played: 'Junior Murray batted for about five minutes, four and a half of which were consumed by his *pallbearer's retreat* to the pavilion after missing a straight ball.' Meanwhile, Matthew Hoggard's credentials as a **workhorse** are endorsed by his 'tradesman's *trudge* back to his mark'.

Trundle: This was once a proper synonym for *bowl* in the underarm era. It survived the change to round-arm and then over-arm bowling, as evidenced by this example from the 1883 *Wisden*: 'Spofforth occupied a place in the eleven, but "the **Demon**" was the least effective of all the *trundlers* in the match.' Over time, the term became reserved for bowlers who could not be said to **run in**. The following remark from Richie Benaud dates from 1962: 'If I am having a bad spell against a slow left-hander, I try to get a couple of fellows who *trundle up* that sort of **stuff** to bowl at me in the **nets** for an hour.' It is more typical by now to find the noun form *trundler* applied to a bowler who comes in at less than **military medium** and serves up **dobbers** or else a *floaty* kind of spin.

Tuck: Batsmen are comfortable *tucking* the ball *away* off their **legs**, but they can also find themselves uncomfortably *tucked up* just before playing a shot. There is also a third usage which makes them feel more than comfortable: 'Solanki and Hick *tucked into* some *inviting* bowling.' Here we are entering the **cafeteria** zone.

Tug: 'Popplewell then *tugged* hugely over the tents at deep mid-wicket.' Perhaps we should clarify that Peter Roebuck is praising Nigel Popplewell's *prodigious length* here in the sense that the batsman has *slogged* a cross-batted six. But *tug* can refer to any shot where the ball is **worked** from off to leg, especially if this is against the spin: 'Vaughan's ugly attempt, while off-balance, to *tug* Warne through the on side was a careless, inattentive piece of cricket.'

Tumble: *Tumbling* often goes with *catch*, and records may *tumble* if the wicket is a **landing strip** or a **gluepot**, but the standard usage applies to a **flurry** of wickets falling or even to a full-scale **collapse**: 'As wickets *tumbled* around him, Tendulkar made a century of rare brilliance'; 'Kenny Benjamin took 5 for 65 as India *tumbled* to 114 all out at Mohali.'

Turf: A now obsolete term for the playing surface, particularly when it was difficult or dangerous: 'If only McCarthy had tried to hit the stumps England could scarcely have survived on such *treacherous turf*'; 'Alfred Mynn, The Lion of Kent, bowled with a terrifying *hum* on *murderous turf*.'

Turn square: When the amount of spin available to the slow bowlers is prodigious enough to meet with their full satisfaction, the ball is said to *turn square* or to *turn at right angles*. It is reported that the **ball of the century** from Shane Warne which spun *the width of Mike Gatting* covered a lateral distance of 31.2 inches before breaking the wicket. Gatt would have been much happier if it had literally *turned square* (or turned into a square meal).

Tweak: Despite the occasional tongue-in-cheek reference to *tweakers*, the verb tends to be used admiringly of what spin bowlers do: 'He wrapped his huge index-finger round the ball and *tweaked* the off break savagely.' This was Tom Goddard, closely observed by John Arlott. By comparison, *twirl* hardly suggests that your *spinning finger* would ever get sore.

Twirl: Equivalent to *spin*, but often used in a fairly insouciant way, as one or two fancier variations would suggest: 'Gayle's *twirly stuff* has reaped him 12 wickets in five outings'; 'Hopefully Warwickshire's own *twirly-man*, Collins Obuya, was an interested spectator.'

Two-man's-land: A Ken Barringtonism for the **area** a bowler should be targeting in order to make the batsman unsure whether he is coming forward or going back. If the phrase ever caught on, it would be equivalent to the **corridor of uncertainty** with respect to length rather than line. Obviously Barrington conflated the idea of being **in two minds** with that of being in *no-man's-land*, but this location in cricket is where a batsman finds himself if he is going to be run out by yards, and where **village green** wicketkeepers stand on slow wickets – neither *up* nor *back*.

Two-sweater day: 'Apart from a couple of **Mexican waves** that went around the ground in mid-afternoon –

and spectators had to find some way of keeping warm on a windy, *two-sweater* day – the full house watched the play intently.' Cricket people, even if they are not *out in the middle*, measure temperature by the number of layers it is advisable to wear. Certain grounds around the world have a reputation for coming up with seven-sweater days: Fenners and The Parks in April, the Basin Reserve and the Bellerive Oval in October, the Racecourse Ground and Grace Road in July.

Two-toned: Richie Benaud produced this expression to describe the typically English combination of help-ful *cloud cover* and a seaming wicket: 'At Nottingham I had my first experience of "*two-toned*" English *con-ditions*, with the ball doing things both through the air and off the pitch.' Writing for *Cricinfo* in India, Paul Coupar felt that Matthew Hoggard had disproved the 'threadbare cricketing cliché' that he could not find the *edge* of the bat 'unless operating on *green pitches* under *gun-metal* skies'. But this piece of writ-ing helps us with the *two-toned* colour scheme.

Typical: More than anything else in cricket, it is the pitches on which the game is played that are typecast, especially by reporters keen to show off their local knowledge: 'It is a *typical Karachi wicket* which should have good bounce in the beginning and help spinners later in the game'; 'It's a *typical North-ampton pitch* and however hard Mallender *hammers* them into it, they'll always keep low.'

U

Unchanged: Bowlers like to have a quick shower and to put on a fresh shirt during the intervals in play (or in Test cricket while a sub like Gary Pratt comes on to field for an over or two). But *unchanged* is simply a handy way of indicating a bowler *operating* from the same end without a break: 'Bandara kept Sussex *on the **back foot*** as he bowled *unchanged* for 20 overs for just 58 runs.' Here *on the back foot* is figurative rather than cricket-specific, so that there is no suggestion that Bandara was bowling short.

Underclub: Borrowed from golf for what happens when a batsman ***holes out*** right on the boundary and would have had six with another few yards' *carry*: 'Solanki *underclubbed* to long-off, hitting against the spin.' The error is usually due to poor ***shot selection*** rather than having brought out a lighter bat by mistake.

Underpitching: The opposite of *overpitching*, but not normally described as such unless the intentions are *intimidatory*: 'Thomson was given an official warning by umpire Bailhache for *underpitching*.' In fact, the word is seen more often in the instructions to home-brewing kits than in cricket reports.

Undone: 'I had not thought death had *undone* so many,' wrote T. S. Eliot in 'The Waste Land'. This verb with a literary feel is useful for recording the manner of a dismissal precisely because the manner is made instrumental in the record: 'Van Jaarsveld was *undone* by Mushtaq Ahmed's ***googly***'; 'Hemp was *undone* by Tremlett's extra bounce.' Live commentary, by contrast, would go for something more demotic like 'that's ***done*** him' or 'it *did* him in the *flight*'.

Unerring: Applicable to a bowler's line or length and to a fielder's throw. When it comes to batting, the term points to a combination of strength and precision: 'Solanki produced a six hit *unerringly* over long-off'; 'Whenever anything *loose* came his way, Pothas *dispatched* it *unerringly*.'

Unfit: In cricket, used of pitches much more than players: 'In 1999, after a visit by ECB *ground inspector* Harry Brind, requested by the Portsmouth grounds-man, the field was ruled as *unfit* for *first-class* cricket.' Because of the way the relevant Laws are phrased, the word can also be applied to the condition of the ball or *conditions* overhead: 'Once we consider the light *unfit for play* we *offer* it to the batsmen.'

Unfurl: 'Tom New, as his confidence grew, began to *unfurl* some *fluent* strokes'; 'Michael Vaughan only *unfurled* his more *expansive* strokes as he approached his century.' A likely verb when a batsman gets into full flow or the *members* with brollies spot some dark clouds over the pavilion.

Unison: What the fielding side *goes up in* when the *shout* is especially confident or desperate: 'Bucknor stayed immobile as Balaji and those behind the stumps *went up in unison* once the ball whizzed past the outer *edge* of Inzamam's bat.' No technology has yet been devised to distinguish whether a *concerted appeal* is spontaneous or orchestrated, but there may be a clue if third man and square leg have their arms raised for an lbw.

Unlikely: Useful in narrative since it predicts or cor-roborates a particular outcome as more than likely: 'Jim Troughton set off for an *unlikely* single to mid-wicket'; 'Gloucestershire were *bundled out* for 232 in pursuit of an *unlikely* 411 to win.' In both cases the subject in question was always going to *struggle to get home*.

Unlucky: 'Nasser Hussain dropped a sharp *chance* off Waugh late in the day with Gough *again the* *unlucky bowler.'* It is a convention of cricket reporting that anybody who has had a catch *spilt* off his bowling is *unlucky* (even if he sent down a **rank** *long hop*). We can also infer that Gough had seen at least one other *chance* **grassed** earlier in the day. If he had been smashed around the **park**, he would probably have been described as *unfortunate* or *hapless*, while if he had repeatedly **beaten the bat**, he would have bowled well *without much luck*.

Unplayable: Every bowler's ideal ball, one which does not necessarily defeat a batsman so comprehensively that he misses it altogether but which he cannot defend with any control: 'Hooper received an *unplayable* delivery that he edged over the slips.' In this case Hooper was *good enough* to *get a touch*.

Up and down: With reference to a pitch, this phrase indicates *variable bounce*: 'The wicket was a bit *up and down* and it's one you never feel *in on.'* With reference to a bowler, it suggests an inability to turn anything *off the* **straight**: 'Cecil Parkin, the cleverest spin bowler of our time, was reduced by Australian **turf** into a more or less *up-and-down* bowler.'

Uphill game: Not a reference to the slope at Headingley, but what was once an extremely common phrase to describe the efforts of a team battling hard to overturn a large first-innings deficit, whether successful or not. This example relates to the second Test at Sydney in 1891–92, where the Australians won by 72 runs after trailing by 162: 'It can safely be said that the records of **first-class** cricket furnish few instances of a finer *uphill game.'*

Upper cut: A cricket shot rather than a punch, even when Dennis Lillee and Javed Miandad were squaring up to each other. In the following example you

might be left wondering but for the explanation supplied between the dashes: 'Tendulkar unleashed his
upper cut – the **lofted** shot over the slip **cordon** – again
and again.'

Uppish: Suggests more an involuntary kind of stroke
which travels at *catchable height* than when a batsman
hits the ball *on the up*: 'Boucher played an *uppish* shot
through backward point'; 'Atapattu cut *uppishly* off the
back foot only to see the ball fly to Nicky Boje at gully.'

Uproot: Used to describe the effect of a ball which
knocks one stump out of the ground without making
a conspicuous mess of all three: 'Harmison beat James
Pipe for pace, *uprooting* his off stump.' As usual, there
is room for a little creative variation: 'Lee *excavated*
Andrew Strauss's off stump with an inswinging
yorker.' *Pluck out* is more standard, and our findings
suggest it may be the preferred term whenever the
middle stump is removed. But *uproot* remains apposite in the context of falling *timber*.

Urn: Traditionally *little* or *sacred* and, thanks to the
rhyme, something the captains of England and
Australia are expected to *return* with. A much safer
place to put the **Ashes** than a **wheelie bin**.

V

V: The *arc* of the pitch between mid-off and mid-on in
which **classical** batsmen play their shots, especially
early in an innings when they are showing the
maker's name. Maybe this is why the Slazenger bat
logo is a *V*. In these days of **wagon wheels** and **one-
day shots** we have learned that the *V* is not necessar-

ily the most *productive **area***. Indeed, one notable
player has a heretical view on where the *arc* is supposed to be: 'Sehwag plays in the *V* alright, the *V*
between cover point and third man.'

Variation: Abdul Qadir seems to think his craft is not
especially mysterious: 'Spin bowling is four things.
One, *line and length*. Two, *variation*. Three, using
the crease. Four, using fielders. That is spin bowling.'
Just as teams in general should profit from a *varied
attack*, so spinners whose ***repertoire*** allows them to
sow *seeds of doubt* in the batsman's mind are likely to
prosper. But Mike Selvey records Fred Titmus looking
to keep it even simpler than Qadir: '*Variation*? I get
enough from trying to bowl six balls an over in the
same place.'

Vera Duckworth: The *Duckworth-Lewis system* was
invented by two professional statisticians to revise the
ask for the side batting second in *rain-affected* one-
dayers. The county-circuit slang was presumably
coined by a player whose wife tapes *Coronation Street*
for him when he is travelling to away games: 'I don't
think *Vera Duckworth* would have helped us much the
way we went about chasing the target.' Sometimes
Vera's intervention does seem to resemble that of
Lady Luck, even though there is a consensus that it is
the most equitable way possible of recalculating the
runs required. Students of the game who have got past
the stage of realising that *D/L* is not an abbreviation
for 'driving licence' or 'de luxe' may wish to begin
their further reading with Duckworth, F. C. & Lewis,
A. J.: 'A fair method of resetting the target in interrupted one-day cricket matches', *Journal of the
Operational Research Society* (Mar 1998), Volume 49,
No. 3, pp 220–27. We can attest that the two gentlemen are professionals, like ***Titmus, F. J.***, because
their initials come after their names.

Vicious: We naturally expect this word to attach to the *bouncer*, as in: 'Lee bowled four consecutive *bouncers* of escalating *viciousness*.' By tradition, however, it is more characteristically applied to sharp turn, especially on a *spiteful* wicket. Arthur Mailey, author of *10 for 66 and All That*, was proud to assert his claim in this regard: 'I never met a bowler who could spin the ball more *viciously* than I.'

Victim: This identification of a dismissed batsman reflects the way the battle between bat and ball is so often portrayed, with the bowler hunting down his prey, whether a *prize* **scalp** or a frightened **rabbit**. The word is useful, though, when making a breakdown of a bowler's analysis according to the manner in which the various batsmen have **perished**: 'Five of Kumble's *victims* were bowled, beaten either by his **zip** off the pitch or else frustrated into playing **across the line** by his accuracy'; 'Mark and Steve Waugh and Adam Gilchrist were among Shoaib's *victims*, all of them beaten by sheer pace and **reverse** *swing*.' Tim Rice was thinking of hostility expressed in a different way when he once joked that Ian Botham had claimed five successive *victims*, all of them in economy class.

Vigil: 'Jacques Rudolph's *vigil* continued as South Africa maintained their bid to frustrate Australia on the final day of the first Test in Perth.' **Occupation of the crease** by a **nightwatchman** is rarely extended enough to qualify as a *vigil*, but the term is still appropriate for a batsman playing a very long innings over two days in an effort to secure a draw. When Geoffrey Boycott applied himself successfully to a *vigil*, he would be the only person still fully awake when stumps were finally drawn.

Village green: No doubt there is some recess of the English mind in which the *village green* stands proudly for the idyllic origins of the game. But in the everyday terms of cricket reporting the concept now has no higher status than pond life. Already in 1902, when reviewing Victor Trumper's confident progress through the land, *Wisden* commented as follows: 'All bowling *came alike* to him and on many occasions he *reduced* our best bowlers for the time being to the level of the *village green*.' In 1989, Michael Atherton went through his own personal experience of decline and fall when asked to **tweak** his **occasional** *leggies* against Australia. He served up some utter *filth* to Dean Jones: 'In that over I took the *village green* to the Test arena and the embarrassment stayed with me for a long time after that.'

Visibly disappointed: 'Inzamam was *visibly disappointed* when given out leg before to Anil Kumble.' This is the modern code for saying that a batsman has made it clear he does not think he was out. He has to be careful to ensure that his *disappointment* is *visible* enough to make the point, but not so demonstrative or audible as to incur the wrath of the match officials. Chris Broad is the English cricketer most famous for showing on-field dissent. In the space of eight months in 1987–88, he *stood his ground* for over a minute in Lahore refusing to accept the umpire's caught-behind decision, took a petulant *swish* at his stumps in Sydney after being dismissed for 139, and mouthed obscenities picked up by the cameras when very *visibly disappointed* by a leg-before decision given to Marshall at Lord's. Mr Broad is now a *Test match referee*.

Voop: The local word for a *slog* in Trinidad and Tobago: 'Having smashed Harmison for three consecutive fours, if Gayle had had the wisdom of Haynes he would not have essayed such a wild *voop*.'

W

Waft: 'Jon Batty *wafted* to be caught behind'; 'An unconvincing Sean Ervine *wafted* to second slip.' Such shots tend to be *aimless* and **airy**, they are often played with *minimal footwork*, and the results are typically as indicated. You would almost think there was an award on offer for getting out in this way: 'It was a feeble stroke, the *waft* of *wafts*, one hand coming off the handle.'

Wag: What the *tail* does when it scores some runs: 'Australia's *tail wagged* ferociously to bring them right back into the first Test.' Bowlers are not said to 'dock the tail' when they send the last few batsmen back to the pavilion in summary fashion.

Wagon wheel: 'Sehwag's *wagon wheel* shows just how efficient he was in **creaming** boundaries on the off side – 37 of his 46 fours came in that region.' In earlier times the diagrammatic representation of scoring shots played in an innings was called a *stroke sheet*. The new name was probably not suggested by the brand of marshmallow biscuit, however velvety the shot-making, but simply by the appearance of strokes as *spokes*: 'Laxman's "*wagon wheel*" resembled the Ashok Chakra in the middle of India's flag, with as many *spokes* as there were places on the field.'

Walk: 'It seems that to *walk* – when a batsman departs the crease when he knows he's out rather than await an umpire's decision – is just **not cricket**. At least, it's not in the modern game.' The old joke is that Australians and South Africans only *walk* when the car breaks down; certain English gentlemen were suspected of always *walking* except when it really mattered.

Walking wicket: 'Ponting's lowest point came in India in 2001, where he was a *walking wicket* against spinner Harbhajan Singh.' When you are a *walking wicket*, you are as good as out even when you are on your way in.

Waqared: A tabloid portmanteau of *Waqar* and *knackered*, used to caption photos of *detonated* stumps or batsmen hobbling back to the ***hutch*** after being defeated by Younis's infamous ***sandshoe crusher***: 'Taibu had reached 28 when he was *Waqared* in classic style, lbw to a ***vicious*** *reverse-swinger.*' *Wasimed* did not quite catch on in the same way because it does not sound so painful or so idiomatic, but Akram's yorker was nearly as *lethal*.

Wasted on thee: One of the anecdotes in cricket which seems too good to be wasted, and is therefore repeated in pavilions and press articles every season, involves a bowler first dismissing a ***jazz-hat*** with an *unplayable **jaffa*** and then dismissing the batsman's lofty assessment of the delivery by saying, 'Aye, 'twere *wasted on thee.*' The role of the crusty northern professional in the story can be taken by Emmott Robinson, Wilfred Rhodes, Harold Larwood or Fred Trueman. Add a *bloody* or two to taste.

Watchful: Indicates that a batsman is in defensive mode, trying to *watch* the ball – obvious though that might seem – and making sure he is not distracted by any extraneous influences: 'Flower was even more *watchful*. He is too long in the tooth to take any notice of the stares and ***glares*** of Johann Louw.'

Wayward: A regular term to describe ***loose*** bowling or bowlers ***spraying*** *it about*. This sort of thing typically invites the batsmen to help themselves or to ***tuck*** in, as well as encouraging other idiomatic variations: 'Sarwan *feasted* on Mohammad Akram's *way-ward fare* with shots *all round the wicket.*'

Wear: If a pitch is *wearing*, it is showing signs of **breaking up** and should be conducive to spin. If a batsman *wears a couple*, he could well be playing at the Racecourse Ground in high summer. However, the reference is less likely to be to a **two-sweater day** than to balls taken on the body, especially if the **maker's name** might be visible afterwards: 'Atherton was forced to *wear a few* during Donald's ferocious opening spell.'

Weight of runs: 'The Bears buried their opponents under *sheer weight of runs.*' While *bowling out teams twice* is fundamental in the *first-class* game, the success of some teams (like Warwickshire's in the 2004 County Championship) is built on posting massive first-innings totals to apply the necessary **pressure**. An irresistible number of *tons* is also the recommendation for individual batsmen striving for international recognition: 'Rudolph *forced his way* into the South African squad in November 2001 by *sheer weight of runs* in domestic cricket.' If a batsman has successfully *nudged* the selectors in this way, the suspicion sometimes lingers that he is not actually Test-class.

Wheel away: 'Shaun Udal *wheeled away* in celebration after dismissing opener Salman Butt.' Some bowlers now observe the same ritual on taking a wicket as strikers do after scoring a goal. But the more enduring image in cricket is of bowlers engaged in patient, and often unrewarded, toil: 'Tom Cartwright *wheeled away* from the Nursery end all afternoon without success'; 'Jason Brown *wheeled away* from the Abington Avenue end without much **assistance** from the pitch.' Both examples seem almost like still photographs holding the game in a time frame before the celebration rituals came into vogue.

Wheelie bin: The image applied to Ashley Giles, in print by David Hopps and then on air by Henry Blofeld, on account of his perceived immobility. The left-armer took there to be an inference of *can't bat, can't bowl, can't field*: '*Test Match Special* is all *chocolate cakes* and *jolly japes*, but I didn't enjoy being called a *wheelie bin*, and nor did my family.' Giles might have achieved the almost poetic transformation from *wheelie bin* to *King of Spin* but for a celebrated misprint.

Wheels: 'Good *wheels*, son, good *wheels*.' Modern vernacular for *pace*, heard from the slip **cordon** when their **quickie** has *hit* the keeper's *gloves hard*. Often, in club cricket, a way of glossing over the fact that the delivery has been called a wide.

Whingeing Pom: A concept at the heart of the Australian philosophy of playing cricket. The notion of the 'whingeing Aussie' exists only as an ironic reflection upon the English weather.

Whip: This is a more forceful and *wristier* version of **working** the ball to leg: 'Key *whipped* Fidel Edwards through mid-wicket and reached his hundred with a four.' The wristiness is also likely to be a characteristic of any bowler with a *whippy* action.

Whistle down the mine: In all cricket-playing counties that had a coal industry, except perhaps Kent, the time-honoured method of finding a paceman: 'Harold Larwood was the epitome of the Nottinghamshire "*whistle down a mine shaft* for the next fast bowler" tradition.'

Whitecoat: Trade term for the *umpire* which invites comparisons to various medical professions, especially opticians and psychiatrists. But the classic exchange involves Dennis Lillee and Dickie Bird. After a decision which left him particularly aggrieved, Lillee enquired whether the umpire's eyesight was failing. Bird is supposed to have replied: 'It's your eyesight that's going, I'm the ice-cream seller.'

Wicked: Typically describes a *lifter* or a *shooter*, or any delivery indicating *spite* or *devil* in the pitch. Used also, by extension, for any other circumstance that your correspondent would not have relished: 'James Adams edged a **beauty** that swung *wickedly late*'; 'Michael Brown did well to chase down a *wickedly* high, swirling catch.'

Wicket: The primary meaning is the target of two sets of three stumps and two bails pitched twenty-two yards apart – hence a batsman is caught *at the wicket* if the keeper is *standing up*. The word also evolved to refer to the twenty-two yards itself. Most importantly, it stands for the fundamental event in a cricket match, which typically has to happen ten if not twenty times in a game for a team to win. In the burgeoning genre of internet commentary, it is the only word which definitely qualifies for both upper case and an exclamation mark.

Wicketless: A manufactured adjective which saves a bit of time when reporting on a day's play: 'All told Caddick sent down 28 innocuous and *wicketless* overs.' If a bowler has had a prolonged barren spell, he can be designated a special category: 'Harbhajan Singh today came perilously close to being reclassified in player bios as *right-arm wicketless*.' This is perhaps marginally better than being described as *left-arm optimistic*, a rather cruel adaptation of the usual nomenclature once applied to the Australian *left-arm orthodox* bowler Murray Bennett.

Wicket to wicket: It may be the obvious aim of the game to bowl *wicket to wicket*, but this routine phrase designates those bowlers who get really *close to the stumps* and sustain *nagging* accuracy: 'Astle bowled admirably, maintaining a *wicket-to-wicket* line and finishing with figures of 13–4–17–1.' A *wicket-to-wicket* bowler will characteristically have lots of shouts for lbw and a few warnings for *running on the pitch*. The observation is normally made of the quicker men but can be applied to the spinners, as in this sage piece of advice from Gooch on the perils of sweeping Kumble: 'He's too quick and he bowls *wicket to wicket* which brings lbw into play.'

Width: In the longer forms of the game, *width* is probably worse than a *wide*. The latter may be illegal, and will cost one run, but – leaving aside the bonus of a possible stumping – the batsman will not be able to *free his arms* and *dispatch* the ball for four. Whereas *width* is well on the way to being *filth*: '*In his pomp* Robin Smith used to *smash* the ball through point at the first sign of *any width*.'

Wiles: 'Warwickshire's bewitched and bemused batsmen *succumbed* to Mushtaq's *wiles*.' It is a topos of cricket reporting that batsmen are *tempted* and often *seduced* by the *wiles* of spinners. Seamers are allowed to be *wily* but they are not, apparently, allowed to have *wiles*. The slow bowler's methods of ensnarement usually involve *variation* or *flight*, although in this further example sheer persistence also seems to play a part: 'Warne bowled almost no *flippers* and not many *wrong 'uns*, but depended on craft, *wile* and *guile*. He took wickets by skill, by force of personality, by subterfuge.'

Willow: Probably as old as the game as a synonym for *bat*. And no doubt the alliteration in *willow-wielder* has helped this expression to continue to outlive the sword-fighting era: 'Post his tennis elbow affliction the **master** *willow-wielder* has seen his career graph dip sharply in the one-day format.' Meanwhile, although it can be difficult to remember whether **leather** should always precede *willow* when it comes to an appreciation of the sound, Geoff Lawson was happy to trust his own ear: 'There's nothing like the sound of *flesh on leather* to get a cricket match going.' Order is restored in the phrase '*willow* on *door*', sometimes used to record the *bat-thrower's* return whence he came.

Winkle: 'At some cost, Ashley Mallett *winkled* out the tail.' The idiom derives from *prising* a *winkle* out of its shell, and the exercise typically requires the expenditure of effort. Indeed, the less figurative verb tends to enhance the suggestion of difficulty, as in 'Alex Gidman could not be *prised out.*' A **mopping-up** operation, by contrast, is usually something of a formality.

Winks: Insider slang for the enthusiasts who follow England on tour without wishing to be conscripted into the **Barmy Army**. Matthew Engel provides the gloss: 'The tourists used to be known to the players and travelling hacks as "*Winks*" (short for Wankers Incorporated) on the grounds that some of them were a bit, well, boring. In these sensitive days, this is partially being superseded by "*Hillmans*" (Hillman Hunters, punters).'

Wisden: The cricketer's *Bible*, consulted whenever there is a matter of law or record in dispute or when you want to spend a few hours surfing through its pages without remembering what you were looking for in the first place. One anecdote has Clement Attlee, on a visit to President Truman, bowling

American reporters a *googly* when asked whether he had been reading the latest political briefings on the plane over: 'No, I've been reading *Wisden*.'

Withering: As definitive as any adjective to describe *fierce* hitting: 'Afridi *thrashed* a tired attack with strokes of *withering* power.' Like *blistering*, it anticipates the supposed effect on the fielder's hands and the probable effect on the bowler's morale.

Wizard: Only bowlers who can give it a *tweak* seem to be allowed into the magic circle: 'The "*Wizard* of *Fizz*" is a legend amongst champion leg-spin bowlers.'

Wobble: A nice idiom for getting movement through the air: 'Mo Sheikh *wobbled* the new ball to good effect.' The noun will carry a clearer suggestion that no great pace is involved, as when 'Ponting took a punt on his *wobblers*.' Here, as well as alluding to the Australian captain's nickname, the reporter hints that the *baggy greens*' grip on the game was becoming shaky. But the result in this instance was a lapse of concentration by Michael Vaughan: 'His opposite number's *occasional trundlers* did for him.'

Wood: The advisability of *getting* some *wood* on the ball depends very much on whether you would otherwise have been *plumb* lbw or whether you are instead bringing the *bat-pad* men *into play*: 'Dharmani *lunged* forward to *smother* the spin on a Ramesh Powar delivery but *got some wood* on his forward defensive shot and was gleefully snapped up at *silly* point.' *Having the wood on* is an Australian idiom for – 'Aggers, do stop it' – holding the Indian sign over somebody, often applied when bowlers consider a player to be their *bunny*: 'It seemed Shane Warne and Glenn McGrath *had the wood on* Dravid.'

Work: 'Neil Fairbrother is a past master at *working the ball into the gaps*.' Fairbrother's style points to the influence of one-day cricket, as does Steve Waugh's wider analysis: 'Batsmen have expanded their options by moving around the crease, *working* the **angles** and *going aerial* more often.' *Working the ball around* has become the operative phrase with regard to batting, although there is a definite tendency to favour the leg side. As for bowlers, they used to *get work on* the ball in order to **tweak** it, but the practice of *ball-tampering* has rather taken over: 'There are teams who "*work*" *on* the ball in a rampant manner.'

Workhorse: 'Walsh was a real *workhorse*. He has rendered great service to West Indian cricket for 16 years.' This is the type of bowler that the captain knows he can always call on to bowl *into the wind* or when all **semblance of control** has otherwise been lost. It helps the imagery if such bowlers are slightly shambling in appearance and not, to be brutally honest, of **express** pace. Angus Fraser knew the score: 'I look like I do on the field because what I do is *knackering*.' As for the imagery, Fraser was once described by Mike Selvey as 'Eeyore without the *joie de vivre*'. He has now retired to join Selvey in the press box, and there always comes the moment when a grand servant must be put out to grass: 'Rafiq has given his best and one must know it is time the *old workhorse* grazed on greener pastures back home.' Spinners are not authorised to be *workhorses* – they can only *get through* a lot of work.

Wrecker: A word which could conceivably be used of a batsman *smashing* an attack to pieces but which lends itself more readily to a bowler who *demolishes* the opposition: 'Harvinder Singh was the *wrecker-in-chief* for the visitors with a five-wicket **haul** at the Kota Maidan.'

Wrist position: While further enquiries might be called for if *wrist position* was being coached at the Wankhede Stadium, it is fundamental to a mastery of swing. Sometimes the uninitiated can be forgiven for wondering which is the most important component in the swing bowler's bag of tricks: 'It doesn't matter if the ball is white or red, if the pitch is brown or green, or if the atmosphere is heavy with moisture or dry as a bone, there seems to be some magic of arm action, seam position, *wrist position* and pure bowling alchemy that makes the ball swing when bowled by Pathan.'

Wristy: Applied with unerring regularity by Empire and Commonwealth journalists to subcontinental batsmen. From Ranji onwards the categorical observation is that they *get the ball away* through *wristwork* rather than brute force. The spiritual home of *wristy* players appears to be Hyderabad: 'Jaisimha could thump the ball when the mood overtook him, but he had *wrists of steel* that he employed to stylish effect. Azharuddin's *wristy* batting style had considerable impact on Laxman's by his own admission.' The adjective would be purely tautological, however, if applied to a *wrist*-spinner.

Wrong 'un: Probably originating in horse racing, this term meant something you couldn't trust long before it was adopted by Australians to mean *googly*.

X

X-shaped: Lawrence Booth's coinage for the mode of appeal adopted by Richard Hadlee, arms and legs out-stretched in supplication. It has been known for the deep-throated entreaties of other bowlers to qualify for an *X certificate*.

Y

Yahoo: A *slog* which is always *big* or *wild*, like the creatures in *Gulliver's Travels* for whom Swift invented the name. Perhaps readers of the *Guardian*'s internet commentary are expected to appreciate the lack of cultivation in such shots: 'Meanwhile, Langer *fresh-airs* a *big yahoo* at Giles, and the ball sneaks between Geraint Jones's legs for four'; 'Dhoni, meanwhile, is getting *religiously forward* after the *wild yahoo* of the previous over.'

Yakka: Australian slang for manual labour appropriated by Simon Hughes in his award-winning autobiography *A Lot of Hard Yakka*. The titles of other books in the genre – Peter Roebuck's *It Never Rains*, Jonathan Agnew's *8 Days a Week* and Mark Ramprakash's *Four More Weeks* – provide supporting evidence that **brighter cricket** is not always possible on the English county circuit.

Yard of pace: 'On his day, Heath Streak is a very *useful* seamer, but his injury problems have meant that he has lost a *yard of pace*'; 'Rikki Clarke has added a *yard of pace* to his previously *pedestrian **seam-up**.*' An expression added to the repertoire of the cricket journalist from games like football and rugby. Although racehorses still run over *furlongs*, nobody calls the *twenty-two yards* of the cricket pitch a 'chain'.

Yeoman: Some West Country professionals like Harold Gimblett were from real *yeoman stock*, but

members of the cricketing *yeomanry* tend to be
sturdy fast bowlers, especially when they put in
heavy stints of work on tour. In India in 2001, for
example, Andrew Flintoff and Matthew Hoggard
were described as 'two Test rookies pressed into *yeoman service* with the new ball against a stellar batting
line-up'. We have also seen references, in tributes to
grand servants of the game who plodded their weary
way through season after season, to 'the pink-faced,
heavy-limbed *yeoman* of Essex' (Christopher Martin-
Jenkins on Graham Gooch) and 'the foot-slogging
yeoman' (John Etheridge on Angus Fraser). But the
most bizarre invocation of the *yeoman* spirit we have
encountered comes in this description of Abdul
Qadir's ***facial hair***: 'The eyes narrow ominously
and the fringe of dark beard hints at brigandage and
plunder, not at all like the straightforward *yeoman*-
growth of Gatting.'

Yes–no interlude: 'Dave Thewlis ***perished*** run out,
after a *yes–no interlude* with Carseldine.' This description of an almighty *mix-up* in the running between
the wickets is not seen so much now as memories of
the quiz show *Take Your Pick* recede. In its one minute
Yes–No interlude, contestants were forbidden from
using either word; in cricket's version, there will tend
to be at least one *Yes* and one *No*, followed by other
monosyllables on the way back to the pavilion. The
likely order of calling means that a *needless* run-out
can also be described as a '*Yes No Wait Sorry*' situation
– indeed there is a travelling cricket team (and race-
horse-owning syndicate) in England which is known
as the *Yes-No-Wait-Sorries*.

Yips: More common in golf and darts, but this nervous affliction can affect bowlers also, either because
they cannot get their run-up right or because they have
problems letting go of the ball properly: 'Last seen

spraying it *around* in the **nets** in Harare, where he was attempting to recover from the *yips*, Nicholson has fought back impressively.' Keith Medlycott is the most often-cited example of an English player whose career was ruined by the *yips*, although after early retirement he has gone on to be a successful coach and is now the ICC *Umpires' High Performance Manager*.

Yorker: The technical term for a ball which meets a batsman on a *blockhole* length, often with fatal results if he cannot **dig** it *out* or **jam down** on it. A *yorker* can always be a *death ball*, but is the main weapon in the armoury of a **death bowler** because it is difficult to get away: 'A good *yorker* is almost completely *six-proof* in a game where batsmen no longer settle for four.' There is also an occasional usage with the reflexive verb when a batsman **dances** down the track and turns a full toss into a *yorker*: 'Poor David Steele **chasséd** down the wicket to Hemmings and *yorked* himself.' The word is often put forward as a characteristic example of cricket's unique vocabulary. Its etymology is discussed almost as frequently, the possibilities including the suggestion that the ball was invented in Yorkshire, the fact that *york* was slang for 'deceive', or that the first *yorkers* were bowled with a **jerky** action. Yorkshiremen prefer the first of these attributions.

You miss, I hit: 'More than Wasim Akram or Imran Khan, Waqar championed the simplest but deadliest cricket philosophy: *You miss, I hit.*' The virtues of bowling straight are never to be underestimated – although it helps to be bowling straight at 90 miles per hour. If a commentator is lost for something to say after a batsman has been **clean** bowled, especially if the television pictures are still showing the **rearranged** timber, he will often say nothing more than these four simple words.

Z

Zat: The shortest abbreviation for the sound of an appeal, where spelling is always a conundrum as we are somewhere between a noise and a word. The politest enquiry will tend to be pronounced and recorded as *'How's that?'* but *Howzat* is the most common formulation, while *Owzat* is the brand name of a rudimentary playground game with two hexagonal dice guaranteed to produce realistic scores like 82 for 7 off 6 overs. Alternative forms include *Howzaat*, *Howizzee* and, as recorded in *The Compleet Molesworth*, *OWSATSIR OW WASIT EHOUT*.

Zing: For the young turks of Indian-English cricket writing this word lends a touch of Bollywood and a little extra life, as if this were needed, to their prose. First Siddhartha Vaidyanathan: 'Nafis was one of the five batsmen who were *undone* by Pathan's swerve and *zing*.' Next Dileep Premachandran: 'Following the World Cup dream-turned-nightmare, Pollock's bowling *lost* its *zing*.' Then Prem Panicker: 'Dhoni showed the *zing* he can add to this batting line-up.' Finally, Rahul Bhattacharya: 'Laxman arrived but was soon unseated, lbw, by a *zinger* from Sami.'

Zip: In the trade *zip* can signify not very many runs, as in 'we were seven down for *zip*', or absolutely no wickets: 'The Titans raced to 80 for *zip*.' But *zip* is also a quality which can *hurry* batsmen along. For a spinner, it can be synonymous with *rip*: 'Kaneria found his *zip*, his big leg break, his accuracy.' For pacemen who *hit the deck*, *zip* can be a slightly sharper equivalent to *nip*: 'The pitch *offered* zip to the quicker bowlers.' Finally, *zip out* can work in the same way as *rip out*, or if anything a bit more rapidly: 'Fine swing bowling by Wells *zipped out* the top **order.**'

Zone: A state of being referred to by sports psychologists and reported on, most notably in cricket, by Michael Atherton from Johannesburg: 'For the only time in my career, I was *in the zone.*' Ed Smith, arriving *out in the middle* for his first Test innings, found Nasser Hussain 'very much *in the zone*', or, as he spelt it out, 'unbelievably focused'. All batsmen should therefore aspire to be *in the zone*, so long as it is the 'almost trance-like state' described by Atherton and not the *red zone* which means *Hawk-Eye* is giving an lbw decision.

Zooter: The *mystery ball* in Shane Warne's **repertoire**, or imagination, which looks like an orthodox *leggie* but comes more out of the palm of the hand and goes straight on. *Zoot* can mean *flash* or *stoned* in American slang – both of which the bowler may have been called in his time – but his specific reason for naming the **variation** in this way is unknown. Perhaps we should leave the last word on this subject, if not on all subjects, to Geoffrey Boycott: '*Shooter* and *zooter*, my foot.'